THE EXPERIENCE OF ANCIENT EGYPT

THE EXPERIENCE
OF ANCIENT EGYPT

Rosalie David

London and New York

First published 2000
by Routledge
11 New Fetter Lane, London EC4P 4EE

Simultaneously published in the USA and Canada
by Routledge
29 West 35th Street, New York, NY 10001

Routledge is an imprint of the Taylor & Francis Group

© 2000 Rosalie David

Typeset in Garamond by
The Florence Group, Stoodleigh, Devon

Printed and bound in Great Britain by
Biddles Ltd, Guildford and King's Lynn

British Library Cataloguing in Publication Data
A catalogue record for this book is available from the British Library

Library of Congress Cataloging in Publication Data
David, A. Rosalie (Ann Rosalie)
The experience of ancient Egypt / Rosalie David.
p.   cm.
Includes bibliographical references and index.
1. Egyptology—History.   2. Egypt—Civilization—to 332 B.C.
I. Title.
PJ1071.D38   1999
932'.0072—dc21   99–30521
CIP

ISBN 0–415–03263–6

*This book is dedicated to the memory of
Jean Conlan, a member of the Certificate in Egyptology course,
University of Manchester, 1992–5*

CONTENTS

———— .◆. ————

ILLUSTRATIONS

—— •◆• ——

MAPS

——— •◆• ———

ACKNOWLEDGEMENTS

———— •◆• ————

I am very grateful to Routledge, and particularly to Ms Vicky Peters, for the advice and support provided throughout the production of this book.

I should also like to thank the Manchester Museum, the School of Archaeology, Classics and Oriental Studies at the University of Liverpool, and the Director and University Librarian at the John Rylands University Library of Manchester for their kind permission to reproduce the photographs. I am especially grateful to Miss Patricia Winker of the University of Liverpool, and Dr Dorothy Clayton and Miss Anne Young of the John Rylands University Library of Manchester for all their help in obtaining the photographs.

The following people have contributed greatly to the completion of the book, and I should also like to express my gratitude to them: Mr G. Thompson for producing the photographs from the collection of the Manchester Museum; Mr A. Allen and Mr J. Sharples for the maps and line drawings; and Mrs Audrey Johnston for all her help in typing the manuscript.

I am particularly grateful to my husband who, as always, has provided invaluable practical help and advice.

Rosalie David
Manchester

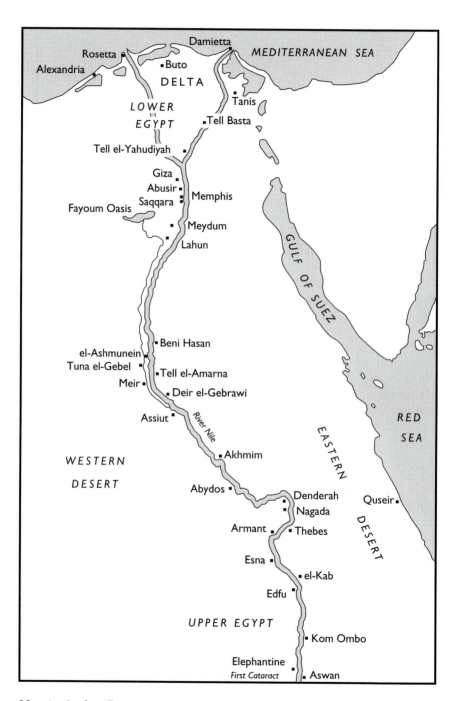

Map 1 Ancient Egypt

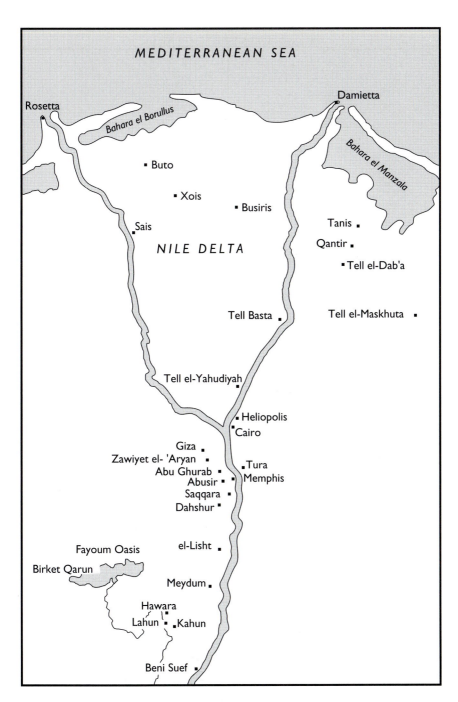

Map 2   Lower Egypt

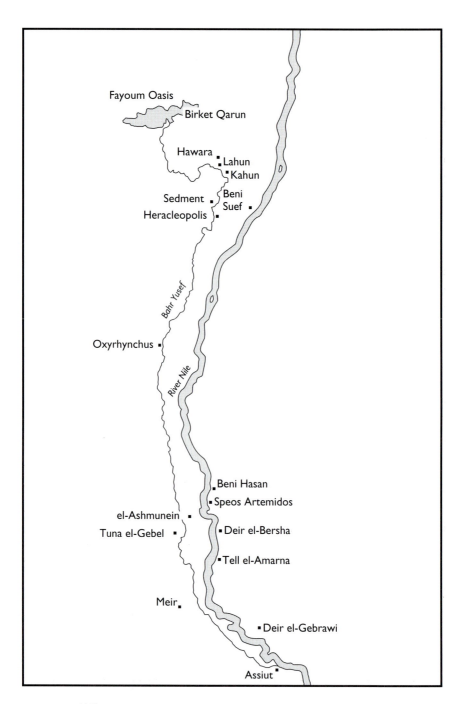

Map 3 Middle Egypt

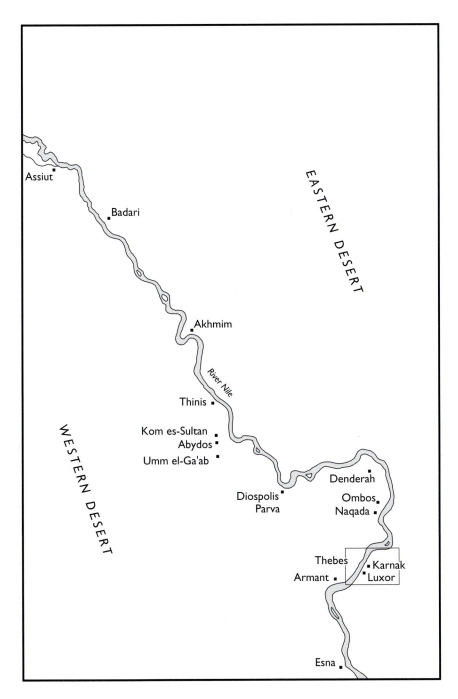

Map 4 Upper Egypt (north)

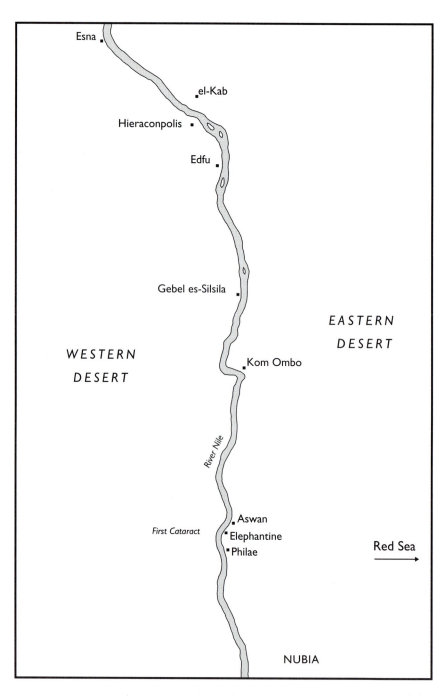

Map 5 Upper Egypt (south)

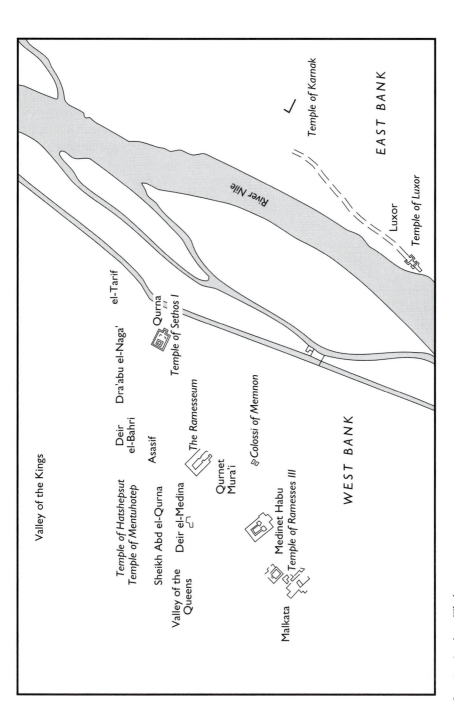

Map 6 Ancient Thebes

INTRODUCTION

———— •◆• ————

Archaeology is sometimes presented as a discipline that is capable of discovering and revealing the past in terms of clear and well-defined facts.
However, there is a great variation in the quality and quantity of the evidence
that different cultures have bequeathed to modern scholarship. Some, such
as Egypt, have left great monuments, a wealth of artifacts, and a rich literary
legacy, while other cultures have often only provided fragmentary evidence.
Nevertheless, it is a widely held view that the archaeologist can deliver the
absolute truth about the past, based on clear-cut evidence and indisputable
facts. There is a demand for definitive statements from archaeologists
who set out to provide a current description or explanation of an ancient
civilisation or culture.

However, the reality is very different. Evidence always requires interpretation, but since it is often partial or contradictory, the experts can often
only draw imprecise conclusions. This book sets out to consider the ways
in which the interpretation of the evidence can alter over a period of time.
In some cases, this change in focus comes about because new facts are
discovered, but it can also result from the different and sometimes controversial ideas and attitudes that, over the years, have been presented by
archaeologists and scholars. It is a fact that evidence can be interpreted in
a variety of ways and that these different opinions can often be equally
convincing; also, the various explanations often reflect the current beliefs
and attitudes of the society in which the archaeologist or historian lives
and works. Thus, nineteenth-century Egyptologists, or early Christian
travellers who visited Egypt, often viewed the monuments and customs of
the ancient Egyptians in biblical terms, whereas more recent interpretations
have generally attempted to consider and judge the Egyptians within the
context of the beliefs and customs of their own civilisation.

This book will attempt to assess how and why our views of ancient
Egypt have changed over the centuries, and to show that archaeology, and
the interpretation of the evidence it produces, are dynamic and ongoing
processes. The study of ancient Egypt provides an excellent example for
this approach, since it has both a long history as an academic discipline
and a current, active archaeological profile. It is a discipline that has gradually moved from 'treasure hunting', biblical associations, and a Classical
interpretation of the civilisation to a more science-based approach in terms
of both excavation and post-excavation studies. The first objective of early

Egyptologists was to understand the language but, in recent years, there has been a perceptible broadening of this attitude to include studies in related fields, such as pottery analysis, carbon-dating techniques and the study of diseases and diet. Increasingly, this approach has required the inclusion and assistance of specialists in other fields. However, there are still some reservations and difficulties about the use of new scientific methods in Egyptology, particularly where these techniques produce results that are at variance with the historical or inscriptional evidence.

A survey of the history of Egyptology indicates how and why the subject has developed along particular lines, and it also demonstrates how the attitudes, working methods and opinions of generations of Egyptologists have helped to shape the structure of the subject. Essentially, current Egyptology, and our interpretation of ancient Egyptian civilisation, are the result of chance discoveries and of the personal contributions of many scholars. The ways in which we view ancient Egypt have usually been coloured by our own beliefs and environment over the past few centuries, from the early travellers who visited the sites down to the modern researchers who have access to sophisticated techniques of examination. Even the evidence supplied by excavation in Egypt has provided us with an essentially 'one-sided' view of the civilisation. The ancient Egyptians built their religious monuments in stone so they would endure 'for eternity', but constructed their domestic dwellings from mud-brick, and so far, excavation of the better preserved religious monuments has far exceeded work on the settlement sites. This, in turn, has produced a narrowly focussed and imbalanced picture of the society.

Again, there is a geographical imbalance of evidence, since sites in the south of Egypt have survived better than those in the Delta, because environmental factors in the north have not provided the same dry, warm conditions which have so effectively preserved monuments, tomb contents, and mummified remains at the southern sites. Also, in recent years, major resources have been devoted to international rescue operations in Nubia, where the building of two dams at Aswan and the subsequent flooding of whole areas have necessitated immediate action. Therefore, external circumstances have largely dictated the pattern of excavation in Egypt, and in the past, there has been no overall cohesive plan or approach. Now, however, increased attention is being given to settlement sites and to a more scientific, multidisciplinary study of the excavated material. It is also significant that archaeology in Egypt has always been affected and influenced by the political background of the country. Napoleon's expedition to Egypt, the rule of Mohammed Ali and his more liberal attitude to foreigners, and the role played by modern Egypt as an important focus for European power struggles have provided the background for, and sometimes directly influenced, the course and development of Egyptology.

However, despite the incompleteness of the archaeological evidence, and the fact that much of our knowledge is limited to particular periods of

Egyptian history, Egypt still provides one of the best opportunities to study the development of an early culture. Because the civilisation continued for some 5,000 years, and because of favourable climatic and environmental conditions, a wealth of information has survived in a relatively good state of preservation.

First, there are the monuments – pyramids, temples and tombs – which have endured. Many remained visible above ground in post-pharaonic periods, ensuring that the existence of the ancient Egyptian civilisation was not entirely forgotten. These buildings were continually visited by Classical, medieval, Renaissance and later travellers and writers, although they frequently misinterpreted their meaning and purpose. Over the past two hundred years, however, excavation has revealed many monuments and sites which were previously hidden from view, and the clearance of sand and debris from tombs and temples has enabled the architecture, art and inscriptions to be appreciated and studied. Second, in addition to the standing monuments, archaeologists have discovered a wealth of material in the tombs and settlement sites, which provides Egyptologists with evidence about funerary beliefs and customs, and everyday existence. Third, our knowledge of Egyptian civilisation is greatly enhanced because, in addition to these buildings and artifacts, we also have access to an extensive religious and secular literature. For this reason, it is possible to obtain a more profound understanding of Egypt than of many other early cultures where no evidence of literary activity survives or where the script has not been deciphered and cannot be read. Once Champollion had deciphered Egyptian hieroglyphs, and he and his successors began to translate the texts correctly, ancient Egypt ceased to be a complete mystery or a source of amusement and ridicule. From the literature, it now even became possible to identify Egypt as the source of many beliefs and attitudes which lay behind western civilisation.

Translation of Egyptian texts has enabled the modern world to appreciate Egypt's rich legacy and to identify the concepts which were later transmitted through Hebrew and Greek sources. At best, archaeology can only provide a limited view of a society, but the ability to read the literature opens up a world of thought and belief which can sometimes even contradict the archaeological evidence.

Two examples in Egyptology effectively demonstrate the importance of written sources in being able to provide an accurate interpretation of the ancient evidence. First, the early travellers often reached ludicrous conclusions about the significance and meaning of monuments such as the pyramids, and early scholars arrived at some equally puzzling conclusions about the symbolic significance of hieroglyphs. However, the decipherment of hieroglyphs, and Egyptologists' consequent ability to read the texts helped them not only to identify the monuments correctly, but also to understand the grammar and syntax of the language. Second, no texts have survived from the earliest (predynastic) cultures, and although archaeology has provided some evidence to enable a partial interpretation of these cultures to be made, many of the beliefs and customs of these early communities can only be surmised from later historical evidence.

Material from the predynastic and early dynastic periods has helped Egyptologists to understand and interpret the concept of kingship in ancient Egypt, while evidence from the monuments and literary sources of later periods has provided information for several studies on the role of kingship. These have considered the importance of the kingship as an institution which survived in Egypt for some 3,000 years, and have also examined aspects of the structure of the state. Again, some detailed research has been undertaken on the economy, and on Egypt's relations with her neighbours, which varied over the centuries and involved a combination of warfare, trade and diplomacy.

In this book, the experience of Egyptology is approached in two ways. In the first part, it describes the current interpretation of various aspects of the subject, and discusses some of the main opinions. This summary includes recent archaeological and literary evidence about the historical framework and chronology, funerary beliefs and customs, the religious practices of the living, and the daily lives of the people. It also explores the scope and limitations of literature as a means of understanding the civilisation.

In the second part, a survey of the history of Egyptology is given, to show how the current interpretation of the subject has evolved and developed. There have been various contributions to the development of the subject, including the early Classical accounts, the descriptions provided by the medieval and Renaissance travellers, and the decipherment of hieroglyphs which enabled scholars to read the texts and accurately identify the monuments for the first time. The history of archaeology is also traced, from the earliest excavations, which were a treasure-hunting exercise, through to key events such as the establishment of a national museum and an Antiquities Service in Egypt. The impact of the increasing awareness, first seen in the nineteenth century, of the need to use scientific disciplines and new techniques is also considered, as well as the importance of other contributions such as epigraphy, and biomedical studies on human remains.

Egyptology can provide many instances of how and why a discipline has changed over the centuries, from interpretation of the Giza pyramids and Great Sphinx, to theories associated with more recently excavated sites such as the cities of Tanis and Amarna. It is evident that, in the twenty-first century, there will continue to be a revision of opinions on many aspects of the subject, not only because of new archaeological discoveries and updated translations of texts, but also because Egyptologists themselves will undoubtedly continue to produce dynamic and changing perspectives on their subject.

PART 1

A PORTRAIT OF
ANCIENT EGYPT

CHAPTER I

THE HISTORICAL OUTLINE
OF ANCIENT EGYPT

—— •◆• ——

The basis of the modern chronology of ancient Egypt rests on several literary sources, the most important of which are the writings of Manetho. He was an Egyptian priest (305–285 BC) who lived during the reigns of Ptolemy I and Ptolemy II and was employed at the Temple of Sebennytos in the Delta. He had knowledge of Egyptian hieroglyphs and Greek and, as a priest, access to original source material including ancient records and king lists. He would also have been able to draw on his own personal experience of religious beliefs and practices, and the rituals and festivals. He is credited with eight works; his most important, the *Aegyptiaca* (*History of Egypt*), was written in the reign of Ptolemy II.

In this book, he compiled a chronicle of the Egyptian kings from 3100 BC down to 343 BC. Written in Greek, this was based on the original lists and registers which the priests retained in the temples. He began his history with the commencement of Dynasty 1 in *c.* 3100 BC, and the accession of Menes, the first king to rule a united Egypt. He divided the history into thirty dynasties but a later chronographer added a thirty-first dynasty which included three Persian kings who ruled Egypt as part of their empire. Currently, this whole period is known as the 'Dynastic', 'Pharaonic' or 'Historic Period', and Egyptologists retain Manetho's division of Egyptian history into this sequence of dynasties. However, there is no clear understanding of the exact definition of what a 'dynasty' meant in Manetho's terms: sometimes, a dynasty included rulers who were related to each other by family links, or sometimes the dynasty changed if there were no direct successors or another family group seized the throne. However, in other instances, one family seems to span more than one dynasty, with no indication that the changeover had occurred because there was any violence or conflict.

Manetho's account provides estimates of the lengths of reigns, and he also includes popular stories about the rulers, obviously drawing on informal information that came to his attention, as well as the official records. If this history had survived intact, it would constitute the best extant chronological source for ancient Egypt, since it was clearly based on the author's first-hand experience of the ancient records. However, no complete version of Manetho's work has yet been found, and it is only preserved in edited extracts in the writings of the Jewish historian, Flavius Josephus (*c.* 70 AD), whose work was still being used in the

Renaissance as a basic source for studying ancient Egypt; and in an abridged form in the works of the Christian chronographers, Sextus Julius Africanus (*c.* 220 AD), Eusebius (*c.* 320 AD) and George the Monk, known as Syncellus (*c.* 800 AD).

The two versions provided by Eusebius and Africanus do not always give the same lengths for kings' reigns, and Manetho's own chronology of the reigns, and the years he gives for each reign, are not always confirmed by other sources. Sometimes, instead of providing details of individual reigns, only the total number of rulers is given, and the names of some kings appear in distorted forms which do not correspond to the writing of the names given in other inscriptions. Again, there is no corroborative evidence from other sources for some of the anecdotes.

In some instances, it has been possible to use information from excavations and other historical texts to confirm or refute Manetho's statements. Perhaps the most obvious example concerns the Predynastic Period, the era prior to *c.* 3100 BC, when Manetho listed the gods and demi-gods as the rulers of Egypt before human kings came to power. However, the excavations of Flinders Petrie (see pp. 135–6) and others have shown that predynastic cultures (*c.* 5000–3100 BC) did actually exist, and that, at first, local chieftains and then the kings of the two kingdoms in the north and south ruled the country during this period when the foundation was laid for the social, religious, artistic and technological developments which later influenced the Dynastic Period.

Jean François Champollion's decipherment of Egyptian hieroglyphs in the early nineteenth century was crucial to our modern understanding of the chronology of Egypt (see Chapter VIII). His work was based first on deciphering the names of various Egyptian rulers, and subsequently, on using Manetho's list of kings to clarify the position of each of these kings within the chronological sequence; then, he was able to confirm that his identification of the ruler was correct. Despite its limitations and problems, Manetho's chronology remains the basis of the current, accepted sequence of rulers and dynasties. However, it was Champollion's initial discovery and subsequent work which revolutionised the study of Egyptian history by enabling scholars to read the ancient texts. This provided Egyptologists with access to knowledge about Egyptian chronology and the order of reigns which was preserved in several inscriptions known as the 'king lists'. Two of these lists – the Turin Canon of Kings and the Palermo Stone – were respectively inscribed on a papyrus and a stela, while the others – the Table of Abydos, the Table of Karnak, and the Table of Saqqara – occurred on temple or tomb walls.

The Turin Canon is a list of kings written in hieratic on a papyrus which dates to the reign of Ramesses II (1290–1224 BC). It is now housed in the Egyptian Museum in Turin, Italy. It contains some information which is also found in Manetho, giving the name of Menes as the first king of Egypt,

Figure 1 The stela of Sebek-khu, a very important historical record, discovered at Abydos by Garstang in 1901. Sebek-khu, a soldier, fought for King Senusret III, and the inscription provides the earliest extant record (*c.* 1850 BC) of an Egyptian pharaoh waging war in Asia.

and listing the gods and demi-gods as the rulers of the Predynastic Period. It supplies the complete years of each king's reign and any additional months and days, but since only fragments of the papyrus have survived, only 80–90 of the total of royal names are preserved.

The Palermo Stone is a slab of diorite, and the main fragment is housed at Palermo; other, incomplete fragments which probably came from the same stone are in the Cairo Museum. Originally, the stone would have been an upright, free-standing piece (a 'stela') which was probably set up in a temple. It was inscribed on both sides with horizontal registers, each divided vertically into compartments filled with hieroglyphic texts. These inscriptions provide a continuous, year-by-year record of the events of the reigns of the first five dynasties, from Menes down to Dynasty 5. They record the outstanding event of each year, including military victories, construction of temples, festivals and mining expeditions.

Some of the king lists were inscribed on the interior walls of the temples, so that the previous kings of Egypt (whose spirits were believed to be present in their names on the list) could receive spiritual sustenance from the rituals and offerings made in the temples. In return, it was thought that they would approve and accept the ruling king as the legitimate overlord of Egypt. In the Abydos List, inscribed on a wall in the Gallery of the Lists in the Temple of Sethos I (1309–1291 BC) at Abydos, figures of King Sethos and his son Ramesses II are shown in the accompanying scene, making offerings to seventy-six previous rulers who are represented by their names which are enclosed in cartouches.

The Karnak List occurs on one of the walls in the Temple of Karnak at Thebes. It dates to the reign of Tuthmosis III (1490–1436 BC), and originally included the names of sixty-one kings, but when it was discovered in 1825 AD, only forty-eight names were still legible. The list gives the names of some kings not mentioned in other lists, but it does not provide an accurate sequence of their names. Finally, the Table of Saqqara, found at Saqqara on a wall in the tomb of Tjuneroy, an overseer of works, included the names of fifty-seven previous rulers whom Ramesses II had selected to receive worship, but only fifty of these are now visible because the wall has been damaged.

Therefore, although the king lists are a very important chronological source, there are limitations in using them as accurate historical records. Essentially, they were placed in the temples or tombs to play a part in the rituals and offerings, and were never intended to be historical records. It was not therefore necessary for them to be complete; for, while evidently they included only the names of rulers from Menes down to the king in whose reign the list was prepared, they also excluded rulers whom later generations did not regard as 'legitimate' or acceptable to the gods. No lists have yet been discovered which are of a later date than the reign of Ramesses II, and even the extant tables are damaged or incomplete.

Further problems are encountered in attempting to establish an accurate chronology, because the ancient Egyptians did not date their inscriptions using the same kind of consecutive system that we follow today, such as 1900 BC or 1300 AD. Instead, from Dynasty 11 onwards, events were dated in terms of the regnal years of each ruler, for example, ' In Year Five of King Amenhotep III'. Since we do not have complete details about the consecutive order of the reigns, nor the full length of each reign, there is difficulty in trying to determine the real date (in our terms of reckoning) of a monument or an event.

Therefore, even the evidence provided by Manetho's history, the various king lists, and the many other extant inscriptions, which give the names and dates of kings, is insufficient to establish an accurate chronology of ancient Egypt. This is because none of these sources provides a complete sequence of kings or gives full details of the lengths of their reigns. Also, historical inscriptions have not survived from every period, and for some reigns the surviving evidence is very scanty. It is not even possible to compile an accurate consecutive list of rulers, as there were co-regencies (when a king and his designate successor ruled together for a time) and there were times when kings or even dynasties ruled in different areas of the country simultaneously, but each dated their key events and monuments to the regnal years of the different rulers.

Therefore, in order to establish a basis for an absolute chronology, it has been necessary for Egyptologists to seek other evidence. For the later periods in particular, historians have been able to use comparative archaeological and inscriptional evidence from other Near Eastern civilisations, from the Bible, and from the writings of the Greek author Herodotus. It has also been possible to rely on astronomy to fix particular dates, particularly those associated with the heliacal rising of the dog-star Sirius (the Greek Sothis).

The appearance of Sirius was an important event to the Egyptians because they believed that the star's rising caused the inundation of the Nile. However, inscriptions which record this event, and place it in a particular year of a king's reign and on a particular day of the Egyptian movable calendar, are rare. Only four are known from the New Kingdom and one from the Middle Kingdom, but even these few examples help historians to make calculations which correct the errors that have arisen from the fact that the Egyptian calendar did not have a leap year.

Thus, the chronology of ancient Egypt poses its own problems, but it is equally difficult for the Egyptologist to construct an accurate historical framework, although various scholars have addressed this matter. A German historian, E. Meyer (1855–1930), concentrated on placing Egypt within the context of ancient Near Eastern history, and led the way in constructing a chronology for Egypt that would agree with evidence from the surrounding countries. Together with Gaston Maspero and Breasted, he made the most significant contribution of his generation to interpreting Egyptian history. J. H. Breasted (1865–1935), the American Egyptologist who founded the Oriental Institute in Chicago, also made considerable strides in the field of historical research. He collected a corpus of historical inscriptions which came to form the basis of the five volumes of his *Ancient Records of Egypt* (1906–7), which provided researchers with translations of the most significant extant historical records. In addition, in 1905, Breasted published *A History of Egypt,* which remains one of the most important general histories of Egypt.

Another authoritative writer of this period, H. R. Hall (1873–1930), wrote a book entitled *Ancient History of the Near East* (1913) which set Egyptian history in its wider context. Other more recent histories have included Sir Alan Gardiner's *Egypt of the Pharaohs* (1961), which provides a detailed and scholarly introduction to the subject and considers some of the major problems encountered in constructing a history of Egypt. There is also J. A. Wilson's *The Burden of Egypt* (1951), a scholarly but readable history. Wilson (1899–1976) was an American Egyptologist who became director of the Oriental Institute at Chicago; among his other important works were his translations of Egyptian historical texts, which were included in *Ancient Near Eastern Texts Relating to the Old Testament* (ed. J. B. Pritchard, 1950 and 1955).

As well as these general histories, some scholars have produced works that concentrate on particular aspects of the subject. Notable among these are W. F. Edgerton's studies on *The Thutmosid Succession* (1933) and *Historical Records of Ramesses III* (1936); and W. C. Hayes's *The Scepter of Egypt* (1953 and 1959), which describes the history of Egypt until the end of the New Kingdom, through the collections of the Metropolitan Museum of Art, New York. His highly acclaimed study, *Most Ancient Egypt* (1965), which is an account of a part of the Predynastic Period, was only the introductory chapter of a planned history of Egypt which was never completed because of his death, but it signifies Hayes's importance as a historian. Other specialist studies include the works of R. A. Parker (1905–1993) on the astronomy and chronology of ancient Egypt, particularly *The Calendars of Ancient Egypt* (1950); and, in more recent times, K. A. Kitchen's scholarly study of the later dynasties, entitled *The Third Intermediate Period (1100–650 BC)* (1973), and his compilation of late New Kingdom inscriptions, *Ramesside Inscriptions* (1968–)

Nevertheless, although several serious studies have been produced which deal either with the general history and chronology, or with particular historical problems or aspects, it must be emphasised that the sources for Egyptian history – a period extending over 5,000 years – are relatively scanty. Also, within this material, the evidence for some periods is more extensive than for others; in particular, the sources for the First, Second and Third Intermediate Periods are, at best, limited and are sometimes non-existent.

The unevenness of the evidence is partly due to the chance of discovery and excavation, but it is also the result of the pattern of digging and recording that has been followed in the past. In future, any revised reconstruction of the history will need to incorporate evidence acquired from newly excavated or re-worked sites, from the discovery of fresh material or the re-interpretation of previously known facts, and from any updated and revised translations of inscriptions.

CHAPTER II

FUNERARY BELIEFS AND CUSTOMS

——— •◆• ———

Since the ancient Egyptians had a fervent belief in continued existence after death, and equipped their graves and tombs with goods for individual use in the afterlife, there is an abundance of material, from the monuments, artifacts, and literature, for the study of funerary beliefs and customs.

The burial sites are scattered throughout Egypt; there are graves, tombs and pyramids, which are arranged in large cemeteries (necropolis; pl. necropolises). The earliest graves date to the Predynastic Period, and provide most of the extant evidence for the earliest cultures. Around 3400 BC, a new type of burial place was introduced for the leaders of these communities; instead of the shallow pit-graves at the desert's edge, they were now buried in mud-brick tombs, which incorporated a superstructure above ground where the tomb goods were stored, and a substructure below ground for the burial. This type of tomb (which Egyptologists now call a 'mastaba') continued in use for the upper classes during the Old Kingdom although, by then, the pyramid had been introduced for a king's burial. In the Middle Kingdom, rock-cut tombs were excavated into the cliffs along the riverbanks, and became popular for the wealthy local governors; although pyramids were briefly reintroduced in the Middle Kingdom, they were discontinued in the New Kingdom. Instead, rock-cut tombs in the Valley of the Kings and Valley of the Queens at Thebes provided the new location for royal burials of this period. Therefore, throughout Egyptian history, mastabas or rock-cut tombs accommodated the burials of wealthy nobles and officials, and sometimes members of the royal family, whereas the vast majority of the population continued to be buried in simple graves on the edge of the desert.

It was customary for great cemeteries to grow up around the royal burial places which were themselves located near the ancient capitals. Thus, the Giza and Saqqara necropolises (which served the city of Memphis) and the West Bank tombs which accommodated the population of the southern capital, Thebes, are particularly important, although excavation at burial sites throughout Egypt has continued to add to our knowledge of funerary customs. Also, the work undertaken by Petrie, Emery and others on the predynastic and early dynastic tombs has provided much information about the early development of religion and funerary architecture.

Perhaps the Giza pyramid area provides one of the best examples of how interpretation of the archaeological evidence can vary over time. Even in antiquity, the pyramids were visited as a tourist attraction. Herodotus was there in the fifth century BC, and he refers to the graffiti scrawled on the outer casings of the pyramids which had probably been left there by tourists, while, during the Roman Period, the pyramids became popular with tourists and writers such as Pliny the Elder. Today, it is difficult to imagine that the purpose of these monuments was ever disputed (although no intact burial has ever been found inside a pyramid), but for centuries, travellers and scholars pondered their true significance. Pliny believed that they were royal burial places but that they had been constructed with the aim of providing employment for a peasant workforce which otherwise might have become rebellious (an idea revived in recent times). Julius Honorius (pre-fifth century AD) referred to a legend which claimed that they were granaries built by Joseph, and this theory was generally accepted by Renaissance scholars, although a French traveller, Jean Palerne (1557–1592), refuted this idea, stating that the Pharaohs had built them as tombs. However, another Frenchman, the Duc de Persigny (1808–1872), tried to prove that the pyramids were constructed as screens against the desert sand in an attempt to prevent the Nile from silting.

Arab writers attempted to show that the pyramids were built as places where people could seek protection against natural disasters, and there were also accounts (almost certainly fanciful) of the magnificent treasure they had seen inside. Other early authors suggested that the pyramids were observatories or even sundials that marked the changes of the sun at the solstices. In the nineteenth century, some researchers claimed that the pyramids were repositories of arcane wisdom, and that they had mystical significance for the modern world. The most distinguished of these was Charles Piazzi Smyth (1819–1900), Astronomer Royal of Scotland, who surveyed the Great Pyramid in 1865, and published two books in which he developed the idea that the measurements of the Great Pyramid enshrined God's plan for the universe, and that this knowledge would be revealed if the measurements could be properly understood. Even today, Smyth's ideas continue to influence the beliefs of pyramidologists, and they initially inspired Flinders Petrie's own interest in Egyptology.

The Giza necropolis has been more systematically excavated than any other site in Egypt, and the Great Pyramid has been surveyed and measured more times than any other Egyptian monument. The first survey to reach a reasonable standard of accuracy was produced by John Greaves in 1646, and Nicholas Shaw's survey of the pyramids in 1721 was also a useful study. Many early travellers visited the site and produced sketches, plans and measurements, and early excavations also added new information. G. B. Caviglia (1770–1845) was employed by Salt and others to excavate the Great Sphinx and explore the pyramids and nearby necropolis. He worked for a time with Colonel Vyse (1784–1853), who also employed J. Perring (1813–1869), a British civil engineer. They undertook a major survey of the pyramids which remained the most important account throughout the nineteenth century, until it was superseded by Petrie's work there in the 1880s. Petrie's first studies in Egypt centred around this survey of the Great Pyramid, and this remained the definitive work until the Survey Department of the Egyptian Government produced new, more accurate measurements in 1925.

The explorations of these early archaeologists revealed the construction and arrangement of the internal chambers of the Great Pyramid. In 1818, the nearby Pyramid of Chephren was entered by Giovanni Battista Belzoni (the first European to gain access to the interior), and he discovered the king's sarcophagus, and uncovered the adjoining Mortuary Temple. The nearby Valley Temple, discovered by Auguste Mariette in 1853, is the best preserved monument of Dynasty 4, and subsequent excavation of the whole Chephren complex in 1909–10 has helped to reveal its architectural layout and features which later became the pattern for all pyramid complexes. Associated with the Chephren pyramid is the Great Sphinx which was first excavated and restored by King Tuthmosis IV (*c.* 1420 BC), and then, in modern times, by Caviglia (1817). It has been cleared and restored on several occasions; there are still controversial theories about its date and purpose, although it remains the traditionally accepted opinion that the Sphinx was contemporary with the Chephren complex and formed part of its overall religious function.

The third major pyramid at Giza, which belonged to Mycerinus, was also investigated by Vyse who used gunpowder to gain access to the interior in 1837–8. The complex was subsequently thoroughly excavated by G. A. Reisner for the Harvard–Boston expedition. He uncovered the Mortuary and Valley Temples, and, in the latter, found the slate triads and other royal statues which have provided some of the finest examples of early royal sculpture.

The Giza pyramids formed the central feature of a whole necropolis area. Members of the royal family, priests and officials were buried in fields of tombs situated around the pyramids, and these non-royal (private) burial places have been extensively excavated by early explorers and later expeditions. They provide a unique opportunity to study funerary architecture and, from their fine wall reliefs and sculptured statues, they supply information about funerary ceremonies and everyday life.

An exciting and relatively recent discovery at Giza has been the royal boat found in 1954 by Kamal el-Mallakh, in a stone boat-pit on the south side of the Great Pyramid. This contained the previously undisturbed burial of a cedarwood, flat-bottomed boat which had been dismantled into over a thousand pieces. Arranged in thirteen layers, it had been placed inside the pit, in the period immediately after the reign of Cheops, the owner of the Great Pyramid. The boat has been meticulously reassembled and restored by Ahmed Youssef, and is now displayed in its own museum adjacent to the site of its discovery. Its exact function remains uncertain: there has been speculation as to whether the boat was in regular use in the king's lifetime, or sailed only once to bring the king's body to the pyramid for burial, or it may have been intended for royal voyages in the celestial ocean during the king's afterlife. This boat-pit is one of five known to exist in the vicinity of this complex: three, cleared earlier by Reisner, were found to be empty, but in the fifth, sealed pit, the use of scientific probes has revealed that it contains the remains of another boat which awaits excavation.

Despite the extensive excavations that have been undertaken on the Giza plateau, there are many discoveries still to be made and many questions remain unanswered. The method of constructing the pyramids, the possible existence of further chambers hidden within the pyramids, theories about the Great Sphinx, the excavation and recording of the private tombs, and the recent discoveries relating to the pyramid workmen's cemetery are only some of the important themes that will continue to be explored in coming years.

At the other great northern necropolis, Saqqara, early archaeologists also excavated and explored the pyramids and tombs. The discovery of the Pyramid Texts, inscribed on the walls of some of these pyramids, has provided the most significant body of early funerary literature. The excavation of the Step Pyramid, the world's earliest known, complete, major stone building (*c.* 2630 BC), and its surrounding complex has supplied information about the earliest architectural and religious developments associated with this unique monument. An important discovery was made within the enclosure by Z. Goneim (1911–1959), excavating for the Egyptian Antiquities Service. He discovered the unfinished pyramid of King Sekhemkhet of Dynasty 3, and when he began excavating the site in 1952–6, he uncovered underground galleries, jewellery and an empty sarcophagus. Many detailed reports have been produced about the excavation of pyramid sites, but the definitive general study of the history of pyramid development remains the account by I. E. S. Edwards, entitled *The Pyramids of Egypt* (1985).

In the south of Egypt, the necropolis on the West Bank, opposite the modern town of Luxor, was used for the later royal and non-royal burials of the New Kingdom (Dynasties 17–20). Apart from Giza, this was the site most visited by early travellers, and it then became the focus of intense archaeological activity throughout the nineteenth and twentieth centuries. The architecture of the tombs and the scenes on the interior walls provide much evidence about funerary customs, religious beliefs, and everyday life during the New Kingdom.

Early travellers such as Claude Sicard (1677–1726) and F. L. Nordern (1708–1742) visited the area and correctly identified it with the ancient city and necropolis of Thebes; they also recognised that the rock-cut caves in the mountainside were private tombs (although another visitor, James Bruce (1730–1794), thought that they were dwelling-places when he visited Thebes in 1769). Next, the great epigraphic expeditions arrived in Egypt, and made detailed plans and sketches of the tombs and wall-scenes, while individuals, such as John Gardner Wilkinson, Robert Hay and James Burton, worked independently, copying tomb scenes and inscriptions which provided new evidence for interpreting the civilisation of Egypt. After Mohammed Ali opened up Egypt to foreign interests in the mid-nineteenth century, Thebes became the focus for foreign excavators whose main aim was to acquire treasure for their wealthy patrons. G. B. Belzoni and Bernardino Drovetti virtually monopolised the excavation possibilities at Thebes during this period and, generally, such treasure-hunting activities destroyed valuable and irretrievable evidence. Later, serious archaeologists such as Alexander Rhind, the Theodore M. Davis expeditions, and Howard Carter introduced scientific methodology into their work at Thebes, and there were some spectacular discoveries, culminating in Carter's excavation of the tomb and treasure of Tutankhamun. This brought an unparalleled and unprecedented opportunity to examine a virtually intact royal burial of the New Kingdom, and until Pierre Montet's discovery of the royal burials at Tanis in the 1930s and 1940s, this remained the only extensive royal treasure to be found in Egypt.

From the beginning of the twentieth century, new attitudes about the archaeological sites developed, which included serious attempts to conserve and protect the monuments: the local families who lived in the tombs were moved to other accommodation, and the tombs were cleared and numbered. Also, projects were initiated to record the architectural features and artwork of the tombs, in facsimiles, photographs and drawings. In 1927, the first volume appeared of the series compiled by Bertha Porter and Rosalind Moss, entitled *Topographical Bibliography of Ancient Egyptian Hieroglyphic Texts, Reliefs and Paintings*. This was devoted to the Theban necropolis, and included a description of the wall scenes and inscriptions in all the known tombs, which were listed in numerical order and identified on a map. Subsequently, special studies undertaken by various scholars have dealt with particular aspects of religion and funerary customs, but there is still no comprehensive account of all the known tombs and their decoration, with an interpretation of the significance of these scenes.

After Champollion deciphered Egyptian hieroglyphs in 1822, when he and Ippolito Rosellini led their joint expedition to Egypt, they spent a couple of months at Thebes in 1829, recording scenes in the tombs to augment their supply of hieroglyphic inscriptions. This venture was a key event because, for the first time, scholars could read and translate the hieroglyphic texts they found at Thebes, and could identify the ownership of the tombs and interpret their religious significance.

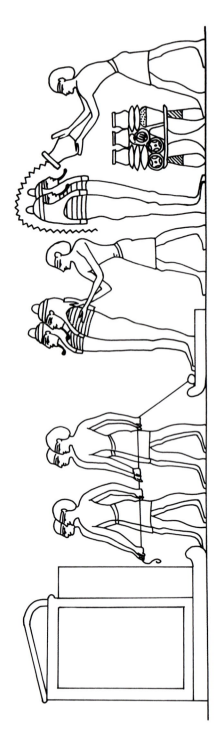

Figure 2 A Theban tomb scene showing priests moving mummies into a container for transport to the cemetery, after they have offered food and poured a libation over the mummies. After John Gardner Wilkinson, *A Popular Account of the Ancient Egyptians* (1878), II: pl. 486.

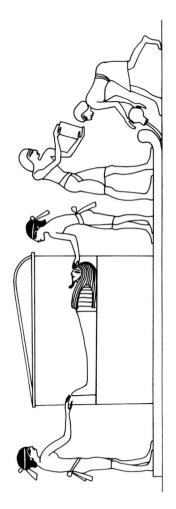

Figure 3 A Theban tomb scene showing a mummy and coffin being moved on a sledge. A man pours out liquid in front of the sledge, to facilitate its movement. After J. G. Wilkinson (1878), II: pl. 494.

Other major projects on the West Bank have included the clearing, recording and interpreting of the scenes and inscriptions on the walls of the mortuary temples, which has provided evidence about the royal funerary cult and divine worship in the New Kingdom; excavations undertaken by the Italian archaeologist E. Schiaparelli (1856–1928) of the tombs of Queen Nefertari and the princes Khaemwese and Amenhirkhopshef in the Valley of the Queens; and the discovery and excavation of the royal necropolis workmen's town at Deir el-Medina, where Schiaparelli made another major discovery when he uncovered the intact tomb of the architect Kha and his wife.

Much work remains to be done at Thebes. Although the emphasis is now placed on salvage archaeology, conservation, restoration, epigraphy and publication rather than searching for treasure, the possibility of discovering a new tomb cannot be entirely dismissed. Scientific instruments and methods now exist to assist in extracting more information even from uninscribed tombs, but the effects of pollution, climatic conditions, theft and vandalism, and the increasing numbers of tourists all pose their own problems. Some projects have attracted considerable public interest, such as the recent rediscovery of Tomb KV5 where the firstborn sons of Ramesses II were buried, and the international scheme to restore the superb Tomb of Nefertari so that it can now be opened to the public on a limited basis.

Tombs and pyramids originally contained funerary goods which were regarded as necessary for the owner's use in the next world. These objects sometimes had a strictly funerary purpose, such as the ushabtis (servant figures), canopic jars (used to store the viscera which had been removed from the body during mummification), amulets (sacred items of jewellery inserted between the mummy bandages to bring protection and good luck to the owner), and funerary masks, chest and foot covers, and coffins which encased the body. However, other items provide insight not only into funerary customs but also into everyday existence. Cosmetic containers, beauty aids, clothing, toys and games, vessels for food and drink, and even food offerings enable us to learn more about their lives and daily activities. In addition, models of houses, estates, servants, brewers, bakers, and agricultural and textile workers were placed in the tomb, in the belief that these could be magically activated by the tomb owner to provide him with benefits in the next life. These models represent many of the activities of the workforce and provide information about people's ordinary tasks and skills.

Many of these funerary goods have survived, although the tombs were frequently ransacked and robbed in antiquity. T. E. Peet (1882–1934) studied and translated papyri which dealt with tomb robberies at Thebes in later Ramesside times (*The Great Tomb-Robberies of the Twentieth Egyptian Dynasty* (1930)); these accounts demonstrate how the robberies had been organised and how the culprits were caught and punished.

Nevertheless, despite widespread plundering of the royal tombs, sufficient quantities of funerary goods have survived to supply knowledge of beliefs, artistic ability, and the abundance of natural resources. Many of these objects have been studied either as individual pieces or as categories of objects within important museum collections. Stylistic criteria and translation of inscribed texts help researchers to date these pieces and authenticate them. Today, the use of computers greatly facilitates the work of cataloguing and organising these collections.

Funerary goods, tombs, and wall scenes not only contribute to our understanding of Egyptian life and death, but also provide material for the study of architecture and art. As with most developments in ancient Egypt, technological advances were first introduced for funerary architecture and tomb goods, and this knowledge and expertise were then used to enrich people's general standard of living. However, statuary and sculpture were primarily produced for tombs or temples, and related studies have relied heavily on examples found in these contexts. Some scholars have made Egyptian art their speciality; they include J. Capart (1877–1947), the Belgian Egyptologist who wrote many books on the subject, including *Egyptian Art: Introductory Studies* (trans. W. Dawson, 1923); and I. Woldering (1919–1969), a German Egyptologist and art historian who produced an important study entitled *Egypt, the Art of the Pharaohs* (trans. A. E. Keep, 1963). Major works were also written by the American Egyptologist W. Stevenson Smith (1907–1969), including *A History of Egyptian Sculpture and Painting in the Old Kingdom* (1946, rev. 1981), and *The Art and Architecture of Ancient Egypt* (1958; reprint 1981). Another monumental study was written by K. Lange and M. Hirmer, and entitled *Egypt: Architecture and Painting in 3,000 years* (1956). Some Egyptologists have concentrated on particular aspects of art; C. Aldred (1914–1991), a British Egyptologist and art historian, produced a general account entitled *The Development of Ancient Egyptian Art* (1952), and also a specialised study, *Jewels of the Pharaohs* (1971). His researches on the Amarna Period included an important assessment of the distinctive art of that time. B. W. von Bothmer (1912–1993) became a leading authority on the sculpture of the Late Period and, among other works, produced, with E. Riefstahl, a definitive catalogue, *Egyptian Sculpture of the Late Period* (1960) which accompanied an exhibition of sculpture at the Brooklyn Museum.

However, it is probably the interpretation of Egyptian tomb paintings proposed by H. Schäfer (1868–1957) which has most profoundly influenced the modern understanding of Egyptian art. In his *Principles of Egyptian Art* (trans. and ed. J. R. Baines, 1974, 1980), Schäfer defined two fundamental types of art: 'conceptual', which represents in pictorial form what a person or object *is*, and is primarily concerned with the essential character, features and parts of an object rather than its outward appearance; and 'perceptual' art, which presents a specific view of how a person or object appears from the standpoint of an individual artist, and introduces elements such as perspective, use of light and shade, and the rendering of different textures.

'Conceptual' art, which gives a kind of diagram of the person or object, basically means all art that does not use or recognise the principles of perspective which the Greeks introduced in the fifth century BC. Schäfer described all art that we now regard as 'conceptual' as 'pre-Greek', and concluded that Egyptian art represented its most mature and sophisticated form. Indeed, Schäfer was able to demonstrate that Egyptian art was not inferior to the later perceptual (perspective) art, but was based on established religious concepts which demanded that figures and objects should be represented in this diagrammatic way. This was to ensure that all the elements in the wall paintings could be 'brought to life' by means of magic, to serve the owner in the next life. The elements could only be activated in this way, if they were fully visible in the painting. To a large extent, Schäfer's theories explain many apparently peculiar features of Egyptian art, and they remain the basis for our modern interpretation of the scenes. He and others have also shown that the human figure was drawn according to a canon which ensured that the proportions of the parts of the body always remained constant in relation to each other. The result of this conservatism has meant that there is little variation in the art over thousands of years.

This constancy in representing the figures and objects was a major feature of state and religious art. There are exceptions, such as the distinctive art of the Amarna Period, and the panel portraits which were used as part of the funerary equipment of the Greek settlers in Egypt in the Roman Period, when they adopted the Egyptian practice of mummification. The first of these portraits were brought back to Europe from Saqqara in 1615 by Pietro della Valle, when it was already recognised that they would be important for studying ancient painting techniques. In the late nineteenth century, further discoveries were made by T. Graf (1840–1903), an Austrian antiquities dealer, and by Flinders Petrie. Painted on thin wooden panels, these portraits were placed over the faces of the mummies as part of the protective cover for the head.

They may have been painted during the owner's lifetime and even hung in the home. Some of them at least appear to be genuine likenesses of their owners (a fact revealed in recent studies in which X-rays and scientific techniques have been used to reconstruct the faces from the evidence provided by the mummified heads). The portraits are important because they combine an Egyptian funerary use with a Hellenistic painting style and technique. Unlike Egyptian Pharaonic art, they are examples of perceptual art, using shading, highlighting, depth and perspective to give realism to the portrait. Because of their funerary use and the climatic conditions in Egypt, these portraits have survived, whereas similar examples, which were undoubtedly produced for various non-funerary purposes in other areas of the Hellenistic world, have perished. Thus, as the earliest and only surviving examples of this type of painting, the Egyptian portraits represent an important development in the history of early art.

In addition to the tombs, artwork, artifacts and mummies which continue to provide so much information about funerary beliefs and customs, ancient Egypt also has an extensive literature, a large part of which was concerned with the afterlife. An important proportion of these texts deals with the individual person's attempts to gain entry to the next world and to ensure that he had all the necessities for a comfortable afterlife.

The Pyramid Texts were inscribed on the interior walls of some pyramids of Dynasties 5, 6 and 7 at Saqqara, where they were first discovered in 1881 AD by Gaston Maspero; subsequently, in 1920 and 1936, Gustave Jéquier identified further texts. By this period, economic pressures had forced the kings to reduce the size of their pyramids, and therefore they came to rely increasingly on alternative means of securing their burials and ensuring that they would ascend to heaven and continue to rule there as kings. The most important method was to inscribe a series of magical spells – the Pyramid Texts – on the interior walls of the pyramid. Translation of these texts has provided a wealth of information about the earliest religious beliefs and about the predominant cults of the gods Re and Osiris. The Pyramid Texts were only intended for royal use, but during the Middle Kingdom, following a period of far-reaching democratisation of religious beliefs and customs, the spells (now known as 'Coffin Texts') were modified and inscribed on the coffins of the nobility, to provide them with similar benefits. During the New Kingdom, these spells became even more widely available and formed the basis of the Theban funerary texts, particularly the Book of the Dead.

In addition to these funerary spells, the literature also contains funerary hymns and other texts which comment on the Egyptian perception of death and the afterlife. These are of particular interest because they sometimes present a viewpoint which contradicts the evidence of the monuments and artifacts. For example, in the so-called Pessimistic Literature, which was largely composed at a time of social and political upheaval when the accepted values and stability of the Old Kingdom were overthrown, there is a text of outstanding significance. Known as 'The Dispute between a Man and his Soul', it is regarded as a masterpiece in the literature of the ancient world. It presents a unique theme by addressing the personal conflict of a man whose life has been devastated by the collapse of society. It is written in terms of a dialogue between the man and his soul: the man, because of his personal problems, longs for death and perhaps even contemplates suicide, but his soul eventually persuades him to live and await the advent of a natural death. By contrast, most of the Funerary Hymns (which were inscribed on the tomb wall and formed part of the burial service) contained general reassurances for the tomb owner by emphasising the certainty that he would experience eternal life and the joys of the next world. However, in the Middle Kingdom, a new scepticism emerged in these hymns which now encouraged the person to enjoy life while it lasted, and even questioned the existence of an afterlife. These concepts obviously reflected the general attitude found in the contemporary Pessimistic Literature, and were the result of the same political and social upheaval. These disturbing sentiments are expressed in a funerary hymn known as the 'Song in the Tomb of Intef', where it is suggested that even a well-provisioned tomb could not guarantee personal survival. Although later hymns attempted to counteract this pessimism, and reassert the reality and joy of the afterlife, this literature provides a unique insight into the doubts and uncertainties that the Egyptians felt about death and eternity, and contrasts strongly with the apparently unwavering belief in an afterlife that the archaeological evidence seems to imply.

Future studies of the literature, and research on the tomb scenes will enable scholars to continue to demonstrate the wealth and complexity of Egyptian concepts of death and survival.

CHAPTER III

THE RELIGION OF THE LIVING

—— •◆• ——

There was no ancient division between the funerary customs and the religious practices of the living. In both spheres, the Egyptians sought to influence the gods and gain the benefits they desired.

There have been a number of important general studies of ancient Egyptian religion, including H. Frankfort (1897–1954), *Ancient Egyptian Religion: An Interpretation* (1948) and *Kingship and the Gods* (1948); H. Kees (1886–1964), *Der Götterglaube im Alten Ägypten* (1941, rev. 1956), a monumental work which is considered to be one of the most significant and comprehensive studies in this field; and J. Vandier's (1904–1973) standard reference work *La Religion égyptienne* (1944, 2nd edn 1948). A leading authority on Egyptian religion, S. Morenz (1914–1970), who was both an Egyptologist and a theologian, was able to bring an added dimension to these studies. He explored the interaction between the history of Egyptian religion and Hellenistic studies in *Ägyptens Beitrag zur werdenden Kirche* (1946), and produced a widely read general account, *Egyptian Religion* (trans. A. Keep, 1973). The book by J. Černy (1898–1970), *Ancient Egyptian Religion* (1952), which he described as a 'sketch of the ancient Egyptian religion', in fact provides an informative introduction to the subject. These, and other more specialised accounts of particular aspects of the religion, including E. Hornung's *Conceptions of God in Ancient Egypt: The One and the Many* (1971), have been able to draw on evidence obtained from monuments, artifacts and inscriptions, to illuminate this vast and complex subject. Knowledge has greatly increased over the past century, so that accounts written by early scholars, such as the work by K. A. Wiedemann (1856–1936), entitled *Religion of the Ancient Egyptians* (1897), provide a substantially different interpretation of the subject.

The temples were one of the most important aspects of divine worship. They were central and crucial to the relationship between men and gods, and there is currently sufficient knowledge to enable us to determine the purpose and function of these buildings. It was Auguste Mariette, the first director of the Egyptian Antiquities Service, who began a programme to clear and restore the great temples which had become partly submerged under sand and were frequently occupied as dwellings by local inhabitants. Discovery and subsequent identification of these temples (made possible by Champollion's decipherment of hieroglyphs) had often been recorded by earlier travellers and archaeologists such as Belzoni, but when his efforts freed these buildings from the sand and rubble, Mariette enabled later generations of archaeologists and epigraphers to excavate the complete monument and record the wall scenes and inscriptions. Subsequently, it has been possible, from the archaeological and textual evidence, to determine the type and function of each building, and also to identify the various uses to which the different areas of the temples were dedicated.

Although studies in this field continue, and new information is still becoming available, it has already been possible for Egyptologists to determine that there were several distinct types of temple in ancient Egypt. In the predynastic villages, an image or symbol of the local deity was worshipped in a simple hut shrine which was constructed of reeds and mud. In later dynastic times, two types of temple developed from these shrines, and today, these are referred to as 'cultus' and 'mortuary' temples.

Cultus temples, of which the Temple of Luxor and the Temple of Amun at Karnak are good examples, were intended as places of great sanctity where the king, on behalf of Egypt, could approach the god's statue with presentations of food and other offerings and, in return, receive bounty for Egypt, prosperity for his people and success for his own ventures. The mortuary temple, on the other hand, was originally part of the pyramid complex, providing a location where the king could receive worship and offerings after his death, in order to ensure his continued well-being in the next world. However, when, in the New Kingdom, the pyramid was replaced by a rock-cut tomb in the Valley of the Kings, there was no space adjacent to the tomb where the mortuary temple could be accommodated. Subsequently, these temples were built separately from the tomb, usually at Thebes, on the plain between the necropolis and the river, although there are also examples at Abydos, Egypt's greatest religious centre. These New Kingdom mortuary temples provided a location where the reigning king could worship the resident deity and also perform rituals on behalf of the royal ancestors (all the previous legitimate rulers of Egypt), in order to gain their support and acceptance. There would also be provision within the temple for the king to receive a cult after his death (which was apparently performed even in his own lifetime), in order to ensure his continuation as a ruler after death.

The cultus and mortuary temples shared a number of basic functions and features: they represented the 'House of the God' and also re-created the original 'Island of Creation', the mythological location where life had first come into existence. A major study by E. Reymond (1923–1986), entitled *The Mythical Origin of the Egyptian Temple* (1969), based on the translation of inscriptions in the Temple of Edfu which were known as the 'Building Texts', revealed for the first time that this was the most important ancient explanation of the role of the temple.

The exterior and interior walls of each temple were decorated with reliefs and accompanying inscriptions. Studies of these have shown that, although some areas have formal or historical scenes depicting, for example, the coronation ritual or the king's powers in battle, in other parts, the scenes, arranged in registers on the walls, represent the sequence of rites that was regularly performed in that hall or chamber. Several epigraphic expeditions have recorded temple scenes and inscriptions in detail, providing the basic evidence for studies on the rituals and festivals, so that it is now possible to understand the ritual use of these buildings. There have been many important studies in this field, including that by A. Moret (1868–1938), *Le Rituel du culte divin journalier en Égypte* (1902), the series of publications by A. Blackburn (1883–1956) and H. W. Fairman (1907–1982), and the account entitled *Egyptian Festivals* (1967) by C. J. Bleeker (1898–1983).

As well as being centres of ritual, the temples were also places of instruction, and healing; in addition, they became a major economic force and employer in Egypt. Information on these functions of the temple has been derived from many sources, including the discovery and excavation of the sanatorium at the Temple of Denderah where the sick were treated, and translation and study of administrative documents such as Papyrus Harris No. 1, which probably formed part of a great temple archive. The temples were organised and run by priesthoods who were among the most powerful men in the land. The high-priest of each temple was responsible for performing the rituals on a regular basis, deputising for the king who, at the most, enacted the daily rites in the main temple of his dynasty's chief state-god. The French Egyptologist, S. Sauneron (1927–1976), who produced several major studies on the inscriptions and scenes in the Temple of Esna, also wrote an account of the priesthood, entitled *Les Prêtres de l'ancienne Égypte*; G. Lefebvre (1879–1957) published a major work on the same theme, *Histoire des grands prêtres d'Amon de Karnak* (1929). Another researcher, S. Schott (1897–1971), who published widely on Egyptian religion, dealt in particular with the symbolic meaning and religious functions of the different elements of the Old Kingdom pyramid complex, with special reference to the pyramid temple from which the New Kingdom mortuary temple later developed.

As well as the cultus and mortuary temples, the Egyptians developed a distinct type of building which was a focal point of the sun-cult. There are two separate versions of these solar temples: the Aten temples built at Karnak, Amarna, and possibly elsewhere at the end of Dynasty 18, to accommodate the cult of the sun-disc; and the temples introduced in Dynasty 5 to emphasise the close association between the rulers of that dynasty and the cult of the sun-god, Re. Six of these early temples were apparently built at Abu Ghurab, but only the two constructed in the reigns of Userkaf and Niuserre have been found. They follow the layout of a typical pyramid complex, with a valley building, causeway, and the equivalent of a mortuary temple and pyramid, but in these complexes, the pyramid was replaced by an open court with a squat stone obelisk, mounted on a platform. This imitated the Benben-stone, the cult-object which stood at the centre of the solar temple at Heliopolis.

The sun-temple of Userkaf, which was partly explored by L. Borchadt at the beginning of the twentieth century, was later thoroughly excavated by H. Ricke and G. Haeny for the joint expedition of the Swiss and German Institutes. The temple of Niuserre was excavated by L. Borchadt and H. Schäfer for the Deutsche Orient-Gesellschaft in 1898–1901, and it revealed a wealth of magnificent reliefs (now in the Cairo and Berlin Museums) which provided information about the god's cult. H. Ricke (1901–1976) published this excavation in *Das Sonnenheiligtum des Königs Userkaf*, I-II (1965–9). The account by L. Borchadt (1863–1938), *Das Re-Heiligtum des Königs Ne-woser-re (Rathures)*, Part I, appeared in 1905; H. Kees (1886–1964) (with von Bissing) produced Part II (1932) which, together with Part III (1928), gave a detailed account of the scenes and inscriptions found in the temple.

Work on pyramid complexes and temples continues today. At Abusir, the Czech expedition has discovered a hitherto unknown pyramid complex attributed to a Queen Khentkaus, and an unfinished pyramid complex of a Dynasty 5 king, Raneferef, with a mortuary temple which has the earliest archaeologically documented hypostyle hall from ancient Egypt. Other new material found here includes some fine statues of the king, and papyri from the king's temple archive which add to knowledge of the organisation of royal mortuary cults. At Deir el-Bahri, Thebes, research undertaken in recent years by D. Arnold has indicated that the funerary temple of Neb-hepet-Re Mentuhotep did not in fact incorporate a pyramid, as originally suggested by Édouard Naville and H. R. H. Hall. The large pedestal on which Naville and Hall believed a pyramid had once stood is now interpreted as a mound-like structure which probably represented the mythical 'Island of Creation'.

During the twentieth century, there have been many studies on the concept and nature of the gods in ancient Egypt. Some of these have provided specialised accounts of the nature and functions of particular deities, whereas others have attempted to explain how the Egyptian pantheon was organised and how it functioned. Again, available source material includes monuments, artifacts, and a wealth of inscriptional evidence, although, in general, the complexity of the subject still places limits on our understanding of beliefs in ancient Egypt. However, it is evident that, as a basic principle, the Egyptians had a multi-faceted approach to their faith, and considered that solutions and answers could be sought in a variety of ways.

In predynastic times, most of the evidence for religion comes from the graves. So far, no chapels or centres of worship have been clearly identified, as they would have been constructed of perishable materials, and there are no extant texts to provide insight into their religious beliefs at this period. However, from funerary provisions found in the graves, it is apparent that they already had a well-developed concept of a continued existence after death. Also, each community appears to have worshipped its own local deity, but as the villages gradually joined together to become larger political units, the gods of each community were amalgamated into groups who eventually protected the nome, an extensive geographical district. This process is known as 'syncretism'. In time, the god of the community that had seized local political power would become the chief deity of the nome, so that the religious practices in fact mirrored political reality.

This amalgamation eventually brought the scattered communities together, first as two kingdoms and then as a united country. By the Old Kingdom, however, this process had produced a pantheon which was unstructured and confusing, and the major priesthoods therefore attempted to organise the principal gods into family groups, or associations of eight (*ogdoad*) or nine (*ennead*) deities. These groups were directly linked to particular centres of worship, although some achieved a more universal recognition, and the various priesthoods promoted a number of different cosmogonies (creation myths), to explain the origin and supremacy of their particular god and cult centre.

Although there were hundreds of deities in the Egyptian pantheon, they can be classified as state, local, or household gods. Also, although a multitude of gods was believed to exist, each worshipper probably devoted his prayers to one local god or group of gods.

The state gods held the most important place at the top of the pantheon. They were worshipped throughout Egypt, although some had special associations with particular cult centres. Most exerted their influence continuously throughout the dynasties, but a few were only important when one particular line of rulers seized power and subsequently exalted their local god to become the supreme deity and royal patron of that dynasty. The state gods were worshipped in cultus temples, and were usually considered to have very little personal impact on the lives of ordinary people.

Local gods also received divine cults in temples and had their own priesthoods, but they were significant only in their own districts, and did not achieve a universal status throughout Egypt. The third group – household gods – played an important part in the lives of the general population. They did not receive temple worship, but people prayed to them at the shrines which they set up in their own homes. The most popular were Tauert, the hippopotamus goddess of childbirth and fecundity, and Bes, the god of marriage and jollification.

The state religion was primarily established to secure, through ritual offerings, the continuation of the universe, the prosperity of Egypt, and the gods' acceptance of the king. However, it was the household gods who provided direct help and comfort for most people, and there is firm evidence of a personal religion in Egypt. In addition to the divine statues and shrines found in the houses of the royal necropolis workmen, evidence of individual faith and piety is provided by a particularly interesting set of inscribed stones (stelae). Most of these memorials were set up by the workforce in the local chapels at Deir el-Medina. The texts on them express humility, and gratitude for recovery from illness or affliction which, they believed, was the gods' punishment for the person's own sins. This concept of personal salvation is unprecedented in Egyptian religion, and when the inscriptions were first translated by G. Battiscombe Gunn (1883–1950) in 1916, they aroused a great deal of scholarly interest. One theory was that such ideas were new to Egypt, possibly introduced in the New Kingdom by Syrian immigrants; however, others speculated that this concept of salvation had always existed as part of popular belief, but that it was only written down at this time because these workmen had a high degree of literacy. Another source which provides information about personal ethics and morals are the Instructions in Wisdom. These contained didactic or contemplative concepts which were handed down as instructions for life, by a sage to his charges or a father to his son. They provided practical advice on the correct behaviour which would ensure advancement in life, and were an important means of educating the young men who would eventually become the country's leaders.

In the Predynastic Period, many gods were represented with animal forms, perhaps to ensure that the deity would possess the power and skill associated with that animal. At this period, there were animal burials in the cemeteries, and statuettes and palettes in the form of animals were placed in the human graves. The worship of animal deities continued until the end of ancient Egyptian history. However, in the early dynastic period, there was a gradual anthropomorphisation of the animal gods, who began to be represented with animal or bird heads on human bodies or even with fully human forms. Further evidence for the study of animal worship, which is such a prominent aspect of the religion, has been supplied by W. B. Emery's discovery of the Sacred Animal Necropolises at Saqqara, by the excavation by S. Gabra (1892–1979) of the animal necropolis at Tuna el-Gebel, and by work undertaken on mummified animals in museums, especially the catalogues produced by C. A. Gaillard (1861–1945) and C. L. Lortet (1836–1909) of the Cairo and Lyon collections.

The life and personality of Akhenaten, described as the 'heretic pharaoh', provides one of the best examples of how interpretation based on contradictory or partial evidence can vary over time. The Aten – the god whom he promoted – has also been the subject of much discussion and controversy: was this cult simply a development of an earlier religious tradition which had been fostered by Akhenaten's father, Amenhotep III, and his grandfather, Tuthmosis IV, or was it an entirely new concept, a religious 'revolution' which was brought about by Akhenaten himself? Atenism (the term Egyptologists now use to describe the worship of the Aten) has also been interpreted in different ways. Some scholars have suggested that it was derived from a foreign tradition, perhaps introduced into Egypt by the Mitannian princesses and their entourages who came to the royal court of Amenhotep III. According to another theory, the similarity between the Hymn to the Aten and Psalm 104 in the Bible has led to speculation that both were derived from a common source. However, yet another inter- pretation suggests that Atenism was in fact a development of earlier Egyptian traditions, and that there is no need to explain it in terms of external influences.

Texts relating to Atenism emphasise the role of the Aten as: the sole creator of all mankind, animals, birds and plants; the possessor of a unique nature; and a universal deity who created and was worshipped by foreigners as well as Egyptians. When these religious texts were first translated, scholars interpreted them as evidence of original ideas which had been developed by Akhenaten, as the visionary founder of a new religion. More recent studies, however, have indicated that earlier New Kingdom litera- ture such as the sun-hymns and Hymn to Amen-Re (the powerful god whom the Aten briefly replaced) had already promoted these ideas, and that the Aten hymns in fact contain little that was not previously attributed to other gods.

The source for most of our information about Akhenaten is the city of Akhetaten which the king built and briefly occupied towards the end of Dynasty 18 (on a site often known today by the modern name of Tell el-Amarna). Situated on both banks, mid-way along the river, it consisted of the main city on the east bank, encircled by cliffs where the rock-cut tombs of the courtiers and officials were located; and the cultivated area on the west bank which supplied food for the population. The city was divided into three main districts – the northern, central and southern areas – where temples, palaces, administrative quarters, and houses were built to accommodate the royal family, court, officials and workers who had moved from the old capital of Thebes to the new site. Here, Akhenaten could vigorously pursue the cult of the Aten and establish his new political and religious capital. Important buildings in the central city included the Great and Smaller Temples, the Great Palace, which functioned both as a royal residence and administrative centre, and the Records Office, which housed the archive of correspondence between the Egyptian rulers – Amenhotep III, Akhenaten and Tutankhamun – and the leaders of states in Syria, Palestine, Mesopotamia and Asia Minor.

Also in the Central City, there were houses and artisans' workshops where archaeologists have found some of the finest examples of Amarna sculpture. The major building in the Northern City was the North Palace where, according to one theory, Akhenaten's wife Nefertiti resided for a period. In the Southern City, the Maruaten (Summer Palace) provided further royal accommodation; it was decorated with painted scenes and pavements, and featured a lake and flower gardens. About halfway between the southern and northern groups of officials' rock-cut tombs, there was a workmen's village which housed the families of those engaged in building Akhetaten. This had much in common with the other royal necropolis workmen's villages at Kahun and Deir el-Medina. Finally, in a remote mountain valley about 9 km from Akhetaten, a royal tomb was built for Akhenaten and his family, although it was probably never actually used for the king's burial.

Following a counter-revolution, the site of Akhetaten (Tell el-Amarna) was abandoned at the end of the Amarna Period. The buildings were desecrated; some were dismantled and the blocks removed to other sites, especially to nearby el-Ashmunein (Hermopolis). Several early travellers mentioned the site, and it was eventually excavated by Flinders Petrie (from 1891 to 1892), by the Egypt Exploration Society (in the 1920s and 1930s), and by Borchadt (from 1907 to 1916) for the Deutsche Orient-Gesellschaft. In recent years, the Royal Tomb (studied earlier by Percy Newberry, A. Barsanti, U. Bouriant and J. D. S. Pendlebury) has been re-examined by G. T. Martin, and excavations in the main city and at the workmen's village have been undertaken by B. J. Kemp for the Egypt Exploration Society.

Petrie's initial interest in the site was aroused when he visited it in 1886. A few months later, a peasant woman, who was digging in the mud-brick remains to obtain sebakh (soil) for use as fertiliser for the fields, found several inscribed clay tablets. These were ultimately sold on through agents and dealers, and some came to the notice of Wallis Budge of the British Museum, who accurately identified them as genuine pieces. Petrie's excavations at Amarna ultimately revealed that they were part of the archive of foreign correspondence found at the Records Office.

The initial expedition undertaken by the Egypt Exploration Society in the early twentieth century included, among others, H. Frankfort, T. E. Peet, C. L. Woolley and F. Ll. Griffith. It also benefited from the expertise of J. D. S. Pendlebury (1904–1941), a British archaeologist and Minoan scholar who worked at Amarna until 1936, excavating the central city and the main buildings. With R. Lavers, he was able to reconstruct the layout of the Great Temple and the Great Palace. He also located the administrative areas, and his knowledge of Minoan archaeology enabled him to use excavated objects to demonstrate that associations existed between Egypt and the Aegean world.

In addition to Amarna, monumental and inscriptional evidence about this period has come from other sites. G. Roeder (1881–1966) directed excavations at Ashmunein (Hermopolis) between 1929 and 1939, where he discovered many blocks which had apparently been moved from Amarna, following the counter-revolution and restoration of traditional religious beliefs. During the 1960s and 1970s, a study (named the 'Akhenaten Temple Project') was undertaken to examine the 36,000 decorated blocks which had originally formed part of several buildings at Thebes, including temples, which Akhenaten had erected before he and the Royal Court moved to Amarna. They were dismantled by later rulers who used them as infil in the Temples of Luxor and Karnak; when these buildings were restored in modern times, these distinctive blocks were once again revealed.

In 1839, the French Egyptologist Prisse D'Avennes (1807–1879) was the first scholar to notice the Aten blocks in the Horemheb pylons at the Temple of Karnak. Some eventually found their way into museums, while others remained at Karnak. Because of the vast number of blocks available for study, the Akhenaten Temple Project (founded and directed by Ray Winfield Smith from 1965 to 1972) used a computer to piece together the elements of the blocks and to reassemble the content of the scenes and inscriptions. The project provided important and previously unrecognised facts about the Amarna Period, including the importance of the early years of Akhenaten's reign (he was then known as Amenhotep IV) at Thebes, and the significance of Aten worship at this period, despite the fact that the new cult had its centre and sacred buildings near to those of the traditional supreme deity, Amen-Re. The evidence also indicated that Nefertiti became a major focus of the Aten cult and, although she was a queen, experienced unprecedented importance in this role, possibly becoming as significant as the king.

Since the rediscovery of Akhetaten in the nineteenth century, the so-called Amarna Period has constantly aroused interest and controversy. The existing evidence has been used to present different, and sometimes diametrically opposed, interpretations of various aspects of Akhenaten's reign and his religion. Initially, historians regarded him as a 'failed Messiah' who had given his people a new, monotheistic religion which promoted a universal god who loved and cared for his creation; however, he was unable to succeed against the traditional, polytheistic, and counter-revolutionary forces. In more recent years, however, Atenism has been explained in terms of an evolution of earlier religious traditions rather than as a 'revolution', although Akhenaten's attempt to create a 'monotheistic' cult that excluded the state worship of other gods is still accepted as an innovative venture. Furthermore, some historians have explained his actions in terms of political expediency, suggesting that his promotion of the Aten, and the disbanding of all other cults and their priesthoods, was an attempt to reassert the king's own political power and to dispense with the control over the kingship that the priesthood of Amen-Re in particular had come to exert. Perhaps, however, Akhenaten cannot be viewed strictly in those narrow terms, as *either* a religious visionary *or* a political opportunist, but instead should be considered within the context of his own society, where religion and politics, and the motives that drive them, were inextricably interwoven.

Other aspects of the king's life have also aroused discussion. There has been speculation about his family background – for example, was he the father or half-brother of Tutankhamun? His supposedly monogamous relationship with his wife Nefertiti, which earlier scholars proposed, has since been overturned by evidence that he married two of his daughters and had at least one other wife, Kiya. It was also originally claimed that he was a pacifist who devoted himself to pursuing his religion at Akhetaten while neglecting to protect his empire abroad. This theory was based on archival evidence at the Records Office, discovered in letters sent by foreign vassal rulers. They had sought Akhenaten's help in vain, in an attempt to combat predatory neighbours, and the king's refusal to act was initially interpreted by Egyptologists as a new pacifist approach on his behalf. However, this foreign policy is now regarded simply as a continuation of the strategy which was followed earlier by Amenhotep III, who preferred to use gold subsidies and foreign marriage alliances rather than rely on force to retain his international supremacy. It has also been suggested that some reliefs from Amarna, which show armed soldiers in attendance on Akhenaten, may indicate that he needed to be protected in his own capital, possibly against threats to his rulership by some factions of society.

Finally, since it is likely that the king's body has never been found (although some have claimed that this was the mummy discovered in Tomb 55 in the Valley of the Kings), we have to rely on the art representations of the period (the so-called 'Amarna Art') to give some indication of Akhenaten's appearance. This art provides the only known major break with traditional forms during the Pharaonic Period. Statues and reliefs of the king show him with certain physical abnormalities; these were also extended to art representations of members of his own family, and even courtiers and other personnel who were not related to him. When C. L. Chevrier (1897–1974) initially discovered the colossal statues of Akhenaten at Karnak, they displayed an abnormal physique which was in marked contrast to the usual idealised royal figures. There has been much debate as to whether these statues depict the king's actual physical condition or whether they were simply an expression of the new art concepts that the king had promoted. If Akhenaten really possessed these characteristics, then it is necessary to seek a medical explanation for this condition, and various theories have been proposed, including the possibility that he suffered from a disorder of the endocrine glands.

In recent years, therefore, there have been many studies of Akhenaten and his reign, including works by C. Aldred, H. W. Fairman, J. Samson and D. Redford. The existing evidence has been almost continuously reworked and reassessed and, perhaps more than for any other period, the facts have been interpreted in a variety of ways, to support very different theories. However, until new evidence emerges, perhaps from the current excavations at Amarna, many questions must remain unanswered, and Egyptologists can only speculate about Egypt's most controversial ruler.

CHAPTER IV

EVERYDAY LIFE

——— .◆. ———

In the nineteenth and twentieth centuries, excavation in Egypt has provided an essentially one-sided view of the civilisation because it has been directed towards funerary sites, rather than domestic buildings, and consequently, a disproportionate amount of evidence has been derived from this source.

Nevertheless, a great deal of information has survived about everyday existence. Some of this comes from the tombs, where wall scenes depict many aspects of daily life and work; by magically activating these, the tomb owner could continue to enjoy his earthly pleasures and an abundance of food and drink in the afterlife. For the same reason, objects of everyday use and models of workers were placed with the burial, which again provide evidence of various secular activities.

However, there have also been important excavations of settlement sites which supply first-hand details of domestic buildings and their contents. Some of these have been on royal sites, such as the city of Akhetaten which was only occupied for a short time. This is one of the few town-sites that have been excavated and studied in detail and, because there were no subsequent layers of occupation, archaeologists have been able to plan its layout. Gurob, another town with royal associations, was excavated by Flinders Petrie from 1888 to 1890. This became an important centre in the reign of Tuthmosis III in Dynasty 18. Archaeologists originally considered that it was a royal necropolis workers' residence town, but the excavations indicated that it had not been constructed for a specific purpose. The main reason for the town's development was its location in the Fayoum, a place of natural beauty, which the kings liked to visit. A palace and royal harem were built there, and these had their own staff and administration. When the king was absent from Gurob, the residents continued to function as a community, and the people engaged themselves in agriculture, fishing, tool-making, and various crafts. The major industry, however, was weaving, which came under the direct jurisdiction of the royal harem. There have been various detailed studies of the textile industry in Egypt which once produced the finest quality linen in the ancient world. G. M. Crowfoot (1878–1957), a British archaeologist, made a special study of early textiles and wrote many articles on the subject, including a monograph on the tunic of Tutankhamun (1914). She gained first-hand experience of primitive weaving techniques from the Bedu in the Sudan, which gave her insight into these ancient skills. In 1921, she wrote *Models of Egyptian Looms* with

H. L. Roth (1855–1925), a British weaving expert who also published a study on ancient Egyptian and Greek looms.

To return to domestic architecture, perhaps the most important archaeological evidence is provided by the towns which were built to house the royal necropolis workmen and their families. It has been suggested that true urban development never existed on a widespread scale in Egypt, and that, because the country's political stability and the natural barriers of deserts and mountains protected most settlements, there was no need for walled towns, except on the trade routes where goods entered Egypt. This theory argues that there were modest district centres which housed the local administrators and officials, as well as the state capital which moved from one location to another in different dynasties. The two most important capital cities were Memphis and Thebes. The kings also had several residences around the country which they visited periodically. However, other Egyptologists support a different concept of urbanism, and claim that there was indeed an ordinary pattern of town development, with major cities established at various locations, in addition to the main capitals. They have also claimed that there were walled towns of various sizes and levels of importance, which housed local officials and administrators, craftsmen and agricultural workers. Sometimes, these were built on the government's instruction, to provide accommodation for the personnel associated with particular temples or royal projects.

Unfortunately, limited excavation of settlement sites and the lack of inscriptional evidence has not yet provided conclusive evidence about the quality, importance and spread of towns and villages, but it is clear that two main types of domestic settlement evolved. There was the natural and unplanned growth of those centres that grew out of the predynastic villages, and this was dictated by factors such as the religious or political importance of a particular location, or the fact that it lay on a trade route. Then, there were the planned towns which were built for specific reasons at identified locations, and then abandoned at a later date. These towns were not natural choices for continuing occupation because their location primarily depended on proximity to the site of the project. Therefore, when these towns were eventually vacated, they were not levelled down for resettlement, and thus they provide the archaeologist with the opportunity to excavate a site which does not have multiple levels of occupation.

The most important of these purpose-built towns were constructed to house the families of the men who built, decorated and maintained the king's burial place and its associated temples. The royal workforce consisted of labourers who were conscripted peasants, but also employed professional architects and craftsmen. The labourers were housed in barracks near the building site, for the few months of each year when they were engaged on the pyramid or tomb. It has been suggested that, during this period, they were unable to carry out their agricultural duties because the fields were

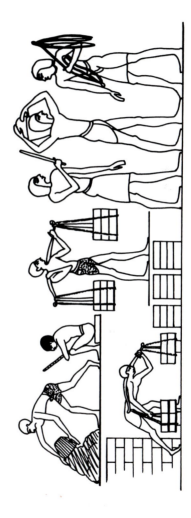

Figure 4 Making mud-bricks for building projects. Based on a scene in the tomb of Rekhmire at Thebes. After J. G. Wilkinson, *A Popular Account of the Ancient Egyptians* (1878), II: pl. 433.

Figure 5 Builders' tools from Kahun, *c.* 1890 BC include a mud-brick mould (top), butterfly clamps (left), and a plasterer's float (traces of plaster still remain on the handle). The site of Kahun, discovered by Flinders Petrie in the 1890s, provides unique information about everyday existence.

under water as a result of the inundation. However, the second group – the craftsmen and officials – were separately and permanently accommodated, together with their families, in purpose-built towns.

There were probably several of these towns, but so far only three have been excavated. The sites date to different periods, but the towns had a common function and were built with many similar characteristics. Each was built to a predetermined plan, and enclosed within a thick mud-brick wall. The sites for the towns were chosen because of their proximity to the royal burial place, and because they were isolated and could be guarded. These considerations outweighed even the need to build near to a good water supply, and the towns were all located on the desert edge. Within the enclosure wall, there were rows of terraced houses for the workforce, and at two of the sites, there were also larger houses for officials. The three towns – at Kahun, Deir el-Medina and Tell el-Amarna – were occupied for different lengths of time and the number of houses varied at each place. For example, Deir el-Medina, which had the longest period of occupation (some four hundred years), also accommodated the largest number of houses, and there was further random building outside the boundary walls.

The towns provide important information about early town-planning and also about the working lives and conditions of the royal gangs.

Figure 6 A brush, sandal and rush basket containing a workman's tools, from Kahun, *c*. 1890 BC. The excavator, Flinders Petrie, preserved all types of evidence, however mundane, for further study.

Although the towns had much in common, they also display some individual and unique features. Kahun, the earliest example, was built *c*. 1895 BC to house the workforce engaged in constructing the pyramid of Senusret II at nearby Lahun. There were a hundred houses and villas for the workers and officials, and it was occupied for about a hundred years. Around the nucleus of the workforce, a community soon developed which had administrative, legal, educational and medical functions and facilities.

The site was excavated by Petrie in the late nineteenth century. This was the first example of town-planning to be discovered in Egypt. Here, Petrie also found the famous archive of literary, mathematical, medical, veterinary, legal and administrative documents, which was translated by F. Ll. Griffith, and revealed important aspects of the community's life, and the organisation and composition of the workforce. The inhabitants appear to have abandoned the site suddenly, and left their possessions behind in the houses. Studies of these items have revealed unparalleled information about living conditions and technological advances at this time. A Canadian expedition is currently surveying and re-examining this site, which is a rich source of unique information.

The town and cemetery at Deir el-Medina once housed the families of the royal necropolis workmen who were engaged in building and decorating the tombs in the Valley of the Kings at Thebes. The town was built in the reign of Tuthmosis I, and was occupied throughout Dynasties 18, 19 and 20, until the royal necropolis was finally moved to Tanis. Although here there was not the wealth of artifacts and objects of daily use that Petrie had found at Kahun, the archaeologists who explored the town's rubbish heaps found documents which gave detailed information about the social and legal arrangements of the community, as well as about the organisation and working arrangements of the royal labour force. These include the earliest extant references to industrial action undertaken by these workers during the Ramesside Period, when their food payments were delayed. The literary evidence shows that the community enjoyed considerable legal and religious autonomy, and the discovery of ostraca (limestone flakes or potsherds), decorated with the workmen's own off-duty sketches, has revealed their often satirical view of their own society.

The site has been excavated by the Institut Français d'Archéologie Orientale since 1922, and studies of the buildings and artifacts and translations of the texts have been undertaken by many scholars, including B. Bruyère, G. Nagel, E. Schiaparelli, G. Möller, and J. Černy.

The third town was built at Akhetaten (Tell el-Amarna), for the workmen engaged in constructing Akhenaten's new city. It had seventy-four houses and, as at Kahun, there was an internal wall inside the boundary wall which divided the town into two unequal sections. The town was probably designed and built by one architect; it could be readily controlled and guarded although, as with the other towns, water had to be transported from some distance away. The site was abandoned when Akhetaten ceased to be occupied and the court returned to Thebes; at this time, the Amarna workmen probably returned to live at Deir el-Medina. Part of the site was cleared by the Egypt Exploration Society in the 1920s, but a survey undertaken in the 1970s indicated the great potential for further work, and the society has subsequently continued its excavations there under the direction of B. J. Kemp. The current project has continued the process of excavating the remaining houses, and has studied the artifacts and organic remains. This modern, multidisciplinary expedition has extracted much new information from the site, including evidence that this workforce, although based at the centre of the monotheistic worship of the Aten, nevertheless appears to have retained religious independence and worshipped traditional gods such as Hathor, Tauert and Bes.

The royal family, as well as their subjects, lived in mud-brick dwellings. Few examples of palaces have survived, but those at Amarna provide most information because the site has only one level of occupation. There are also significant royal buildings at Malkata, south-east of the Medinet Habu temple complex at Thebes, where Amenhotep III built a town that incorporated a large palace known as the 'House of Joy'. Here he lived during his reign, and his son Amenhotep IV/Akhenaten spent his early years at

Malkata before he and the royal court moved to Amarna. Malkata was investigated in 1901–2 by R. de Peyster Tytus and Percy Newberry, and in 1910–18 by H. Winlock and A. M. Lythgoe for the Metropolitan Museum, New York.

Sufficient evidence has survived from the sites to indicate that it was customary for each king to build a new palace, and that these buildings contained both private, royal apartments and state administrative head-quarters. They were adorned with colourful wall paintings and decorative tiles, and contained beautiful and elegant furnishings. Some palaces were built near to temples; a notable example is that of Ramesses III at Medinet Habu where the uncharacteristic stone tower (but not the rest of the palace, which was presumably built of mud-brick) has survived.

In addition to the excavation of domestic sites and related archaeolog-ical studies, there have been a number of detailed works about various aspects of daily life which have been based on the tomb wall scenes, artifacts and literature. In this context, the researches of Alfred Lucas (1867–1945) should be mentioned: his important analyses of the materials and substances used by the ancient Egyptians formed the basis for his major publication, *Ancient Egyptian Materials and Industries* (1926). Ancient Egyptian music has been studied by H. Hickmann (1908–1968), a German musicologist who examined ancient and modern music and musical instruments in the Near East, and produced the catalogue of musical instruments in the Cairo Museum (1949). Works on mathematics and astronomy have been written by O. Neugebauer (1899–1990), a mathematician, and R. A. Parker (1905–1993), an American Egyptologist. They co-operated on three volumes of *Egyptian Astronomical Texts* (1960–69), and Neugebauer produced *The Exact Sciences in Antiquity* (1952).

However, despite specific knowledge about various branches of ancient Egyptian learning, there is no clear definition in the papyri of their educa-tional methods. The Greeks expressed high regard for the Egyptian system, which apparently involved training of the 'complete person' and sought to produce an individual who had self-control, good manners and morals, and who would contribute to the society. Most evidence highlights the educa-tion of the upper and middle classes, who were trained to become officials, lawyers, doctors, and architects. They were taught reading, writing, and the study of literature, as well as foreign languages for those who planned to enter the diplomatic service, and mathematics for those training to become architects. Pupils were trained to write by copying out long compositions which were then corrected in the margins by the master. This taught them the required spelling and grammatical skills, and the content of the texts was chosen for its uplifting moral and ethical wisdom.

Two main literary sources have survived which demonstrate the concepts and teaching methods which dominated education. The Instructions in Wisdom (or Wisdom Texts) were initially written for the sons of the

Figure 7 A multicoloured sock (late third century AD), knitted for a child, divides in two at the toe to accommodate a thonged sandal. It was found at Oxyrhynchus by Flinders Petrie, and is a rare example of early knitting.

nobility and upper classes in the Old and Middle Kingdoms, to provide them with practical advice and training for their future careers. Later, in the New Kingdom, the training of scribes (learned persons) had been extended to include the middle classes and, to reflect this change, other Wisdom Texts were added. The second literary source for education is provided by the Schoolboy Exercises which mostly date to *c.* 1250 BC. In some cases, these schoolboy copies of moral compositions and letters have preserved texts which have not survived anywhere else. However, the boys sometimes made errors in understanding and copying the original texts, which consequently caused many mistakes, and these have produced considerable difficulties for the translator. Some of the compositions were written on papyri, and are now preserved in museum collections, while others were inscribed on writing boards or tablets. Others occur on ostraca, such as those found near the mortuary temple of Ramesses II at Thebes, discarded by pupils studying at a school situated within the temple precinct.

The legal system has also been the subject of specialist studies. Compared with other ancient societies, Egyptian law has yielded very limited evidence of its institutions. There was no formal law code, but cases were largely decided on precedent. The earliest extant evidence of legal transactions is provided by inscriptions in tombs and on stelae dating to the Old Kingdom, and these suggest that the system was already well developed by this time, and must have had a considerable history behind it.

Many of the legal transactions dealt with funerary property. There were arrangements to ensure that the tomb continued to be provisioned after the owner's death and, although there were no wills as such, a document of transfer could be prepared with regard to a house and any valuable property which the owner might wish to pass on during his lifetime or after death. Ownership and transfer of property were carried out as either crown or private transactions, and although in theory the king had absolute rights over his subjects, it was often possible to deal with matters on a private basis.

A major section of the law was concerned with social customs and behaviour. Men and women of all classes were treated equally, and the laws were generally designed to protect the family and to safeguard the economic status of women and their children. The kingship probably passed down through the ruler's chief queen (the Great Royal Wife) to her eldest son, who became heir apparent, and similarly, for commoners, the law ensured that property was handed on through the matrilineal line. After marriage, and even following a divorce, a woman retained her own property; she was also paid compensation by the husband after divorce. Within the royal family, the kings had many wives, but for other people, polygamy and even bigamy were rare, although in some cases (for example, if a wife could not bear children), the man acquired a serf-concubine.

The legal system was administered through law courts which admitted and considered all kinds of evidence. There were local courts (*kenbet*) which sat under a chairman and dealt with most types of case; and there was the High Court at the capital, headed by the vizier (chief minister), where serious cases were tried, particularly those carrying the threat of capital punishment. Cases did not end when judgment was passed; it was necessary for the defeated party to admit guilt. Punishments were severe, and included beatings, forced labour in the mines or quarries, amputations, and various forms of the death penalty.

Despite these deterrents, which were designed to prevent further offences, the law was generally fair and relatively even-handed, when compared with other contemporary systems. Pharaonic law continued to be universally applied in Egypt until the Ptolemies and Romans became rulers, when they introduced their own systems for the Greek and Roman immigrants, while Egyptian law was reserved for the indigenous population. The major source of our knowledge of Egyptian law is a variety of inscriptions which include texts in tombs, the archives from royal necropolis workmen's towns and other sites, and documents relating to the tomb robberies and to a trial associated with the harem conspiracy in which the women of the Royal Court plotted to assassinate Ramesses III. The document describing this conspiracy and trial, now preserved on papyri in the collection of the Turin Museum, may have been housed originally in the temple-library at Medinet Habu. Important research on the tomb robberies was published by T. E. Peet in

The Great Tomb-robberies of the Twentieth Egyptian Dynasty (1930) and in *The Mayer Papyri A + B* (1920). To further advance knowledge of ancient Egyptian law, an Egyptian lawyer, I. Harari (1919–1989), established an association in Paris in 1984, to study the ancient Egyptian legal system, and he has contributed himself to publication in this field.

Egypt developed one of the earliest known medical systems in the world. In addition to the great potential now available to discover evidence of disease from the multidisciplinary study of mummified remains, there are also a number of Medical Papyri which provide some details of diseases and their treatment. These documents may have once served as handbooks for doctors' daily use, or outlines for medical lectures, or notes taken by students at lectures or for their clinical notebooks. Some papyri may have fulfilled more than one purpose; possibly they originated as notes taken by a doctor when he was a student which he then retained for reference in his later career.

The papyri are not books or even continuous texts with any unity of composition or subject-matter, but include information on a variety of subjects. The texts describe treatments which use either 'rational' methods, or magical or 'non-rational' formulae, and the proportion of these treatments in any one papyrus varies considerably. For example, the London Papyrus contains only magical formulae, whereas the Ebers Papyrus has 12 magical and 867 rational prescriptions. Most of the papyri date from the New Kingdom onwards, although many were probably copied from earlier works. Some are clearly compilations of smaller collections, and bring together a wide range of practical knowledge and experience which may have been handed down orally and then compiled by a physician for his own use or for teaching others. One document, the Hearst Papyrus, was probably a reference book for a local doctor in a provincial town, whereas others such as the Ebers Papyrus appear to be more systematically organised and were possibly used by the priests in one of the temples. They all appear to contain compilations of knowledge rather than first-hand accounts of clinical medicine, apart from the Edwin Smith Papyrus, which may describe actual case studies. Since only ten major medical papyri (and some less important texts) have been identified to date, it seems probable that they represent only a small proportion of similar documents which were once in existence, but even these examples demonstrate the range and great complexity of diagnosis and treatment.

Four of these papyri are called after the people who purchased them in modern times: Edwin Smith, Chester Beatty, Carlsberg and Hearst. Three are named after the cities where they are kept in museum collections: London, Leiden and Berlin. Two – the Kahun and Ramesseum Papyri – carry the names of the sites where they were discovered, and the Ebers Papyrus is called after the scholar who first edited the text.

G. M. Ebers (1837–1898), a German Egyptologist who also wrote successful novels, bought the Ebers Papyrus from Edwin Smith, and in

1875 published a facsimile of it with an introduction and glossary. It was translated in 1937 by B. Ebbell (1865–1941), a Norwegian doctor, and published as *The Papyrus Ebers*, and this became the basis for modern understanding of Egyptian medicine until further knowledge was added when the Edwin Smith Papyrus was published in 1937. The Ebers Papyrus contains extracts from different sources, and dates to the ninth regnal year of Amenhotep I (*c.* 1550 BC). It provides the most important account of Egyptian pathology, and describes the concept of the *metu*, the Egyptian explanation of how the physiological system functioned.

Some case studies and prescriptions are repeated in two or more of the papyri. For example, the Berlin Papyrus (*c.* 1300 BC) includes paragraphs which are also found in the Ebers and Hearst Papyri, and contains sections on rheumatism, gynaecology and the prediction of the sex of unborn children, as well as a treatise on the vessels of the heart.

The earliest extant papyrus comes from the archive found at the pyramid workmen's town of Kahun (*c.* 1895 BC). Translated by F. Ll. Griffith, this is the world's earliest treatise on gynaecology, and provides information about pregnancy, sterility, sexing unborn children and gynaecological cases, as well as contraception and aphrodisiacs. Again, it contains much that is repeated in the Berlin, Ebers and Ramesseum Papyri.

The Ramesseum Papyri (IV and V) date to *c.* 1900 BC, while the London–Leyden Papyrus was written *c.* 300 AD. The latter contains sixty-one prescriptions of which only twenty-five are concerned with medical treatment while the others include spells to cause illness, or recipes for ointments and sleeping potions. In terms of its content, this stands halfway between the other medical papyri and the Turin 'Book of Magic' (*c.* 1165 BC) which is essentially a compilation of magical spells but also contains the earliest known detailed list of payments to a physician.

The Chester Beatty Papyri (IV and V) date to *c.* 1300 BC and contain magico-medical spells, while the Hearst Papyrus, which contains 260 cases, probably dates to the same period as the Ebers Papyrus and was excavated from a house at Deir el-Ballas which was probably owned by the local doctor. It was translated by G. A. Reisner in 1905 and, with the Ebers Papyrus, provides our principal source on ancient Egyptian pharmacology.

Perhaps the most interesting document, however, is the Edwin Smith Papyrus. This may have been the reference book of a practising physician and, although this copy dates to the seventeenth century BC, on the evidence of the vocabulary it contains, it is probably derived from an Old Kingdom source. The papyrus was purchased in 1862 by Edwin Smith (1822–1906), an American dealer, and is now in the New York Academy of Medicine. In 1930 it was translated and published by J. H. Breasted as *The Edwin Smith Surgical Papyrus*.

Breasted speculated that it could have been written by Imhotep, the vizier of King Djoser and architect of the Step Pyramid at Saqqara in

Dynasty 3, whom later generations of Egyptians regarded as the founder of medicine. As the world's earliest known surgical treatise, the papyrus deals with general surgery and surgery of the bones. It also demonstrates how the author was attempting to create new technical terms such as 'brain', to describe parts of the body he was discussing in the text. The papyrus is devoid of magical prescriptions, and reveals a scientific mind at work, providing the earliest recorded evidence of observation and conclusion. In terms of organisation and content, this is far superior to the other papyri, although they were compiled at a later date.

The Medical Papyri have provided insight into the skills and practices of the ancient physicians. Various major studies have produced valuable commentary on these texts, and on the history of medicine in ancient Egypt. F. C. Madden (1873–1929), an Australian surgeon who was professor of surgery in Cairo, wrote *The Surgery of Egypt* (1919) which, although a commentary on modern practice, is useful in studying the ancient texts. H. Grapow (1885–1967) produced (with H. v. Deines and W. Westendorf) a major, six-volume study of the medical texts, *Grundriss der Medizin der alten Ägypter* (1954–9). F. Jonckheere (1903–1956), a Belgian doctor who autopsied a mummy in 1942, wrote many articles on Egyptian medicine, including a study of schistosomiasis (1944), and an account of the Chester Beatty Papyrus (1947). W. Wreszinksi (1880–1935) published widely on Egyptian medicine, including commentaries on the Berlin, London, Hearst, and Ebers papyri. P. Ghalioungui (1908–1987), an Egyptian doctor, wrote several books and articles on Egyptian medicine, and a recent book by J. Nunn, entitled *Ancient Egyptian Medicine* (1996), provides a concise but detailed account of current knowledge on this subject.

In the future, studies on mummified remains will help us to re-examine and possibly to revise the translation of some of the treatments and terms found in the Medical Papyri. It is many years since these papyri were translated, and ultimately it will be necessary for new translations and commentaries to be prepared which will take account of evidence obtained from research on the mummies. Egypt is uniquely placed in that it can provide both written evidence and well-preserved human remains, and these will eventually form the basis for a comprehensive study of this ancient medical system and the diseases that it attempted to combat.

CHAPTER V

LITERARY SOURCES

—— •◆• ——

The Egyptians had one of the great literatures of the ancient world. The earliest texts can be traced to the Old Kingdom and they reveal that there was already a long history of oral tradition. The literature extends over 3,000 years and includes religious texts, stories, didactic writings, historical accounts, and love poetry, as well as legal, medical and scientific records. When Champollion deciphered hieroglyphs (see Chapter 8), he gave Egyptologists the unprecedented opportunity to gain a greater insight into the thoughts and beliefs of the Egyptians, by enabling scholars to study their literature. Today, despite some difficulties in translating the texts, knowledge of the literature greatly enhances our understanding of the civilisation, amplifying and modifying the information that can be gained from monuments and archaeological remains.

Religious texts are found inscribed on tomb and temple walls, on papyri and on artifacts. In the temples, the wall scenes and accompanying inscriptions preserve the rituals that were once performed there. One particularly important genre of religious writings are the Funerary Texts. The earliest of these, the Pyramid Texts, comprised a series of spells that were inscribed on the walls of several pyramids at Saqqara which date from Dynasties 5 to 7. They were placed there to ensure that the deceased king was able to reach the sky where he took his rightful place among the gods, in the company of his father, the sun-god Re. The first edition and translation of the Pyramid Texts was produced by Gaston Maspero, but Kurt Sethe's six-volume study (1935–62) was the earliest standard work. J. Garnot (1908–1963) wrote an important account in 1946, and S. A. B. Mercer (1880–1969) provided the first complete translation and commentary in English, entitled *The Pyramid Texts* (1952). Subsequently, R. O. Faulkner (1894–1982) has produced another translation and commentary, *The Ancient Egyptian Pyramid Texts* (1969). These texts pose great difficulties in translation, and there are also problems in interpreting the religious allusions which, in some instances, may reflect predynastic beliefs and customs. However, the later studies have drawn on additional texts from other pyramids and later non-royal tombs, as well as sarcophagi, and from these sources it has sometimes been possible to restore and translate those portions of the Pyramid Texts which are missing or damaged in the inscriptions found in the Saqqara pyramids.

By the First Intermediate Period, Egypt was undergoing a process of democratisation, and the Pyramid Texts (designed exclusively for royal use in the Old Kingdom) were now modified and inscribed on the coffins of non-royal persons (hence, they are referred to as the 'Coffin Texts'). These spells protected the owner and ensured that he would pass unscathed through the dangers of the underworld and achieve an individual immortality. A. de Buck and A. H. Gardiner edited a study of these, *The Egyptian Coffin Texts* (1935–61), and more recently, Faulkner produced a translation and commentary in *The Ancient Egyptian Coffin Texts* (1973–8).

In their final form, which was introduced in the New Kingdom, these texts re-emerged as the so-called 'Funerary Books', of which the most famous is the Book of 'Coming Forth by Day', known also as the Book of the Dead. These texts, which continued the idea of magically protecting the owner and ensuring his safe passage to the next world, included various spells associated with the Day of Judgement.

The Funerary Books were often written on papyrus, and could be purchased by commoners and placed in their tombs. However, during the New Kingdom the subject-matter also appears as the content of the wall decoration found in the royal tombs at Thebes. There have been many accounts of these texts, including E. W. Budge's publications, especially *Book of the Dead* (1920), and P. Le Page Renouf's study of the Papyrus of Ani in the British Museum (1890), and his translation of the Book of the Dead, which was completed and published by Édouard Naville in 1907. Naville also produced work on the Sun Litany and texts in the tombs in the Valley of the Kings, and, later, A. Piankoff wrote extensively on the decoration and inscriptions in these tombs, including his work entitled *The Tomb of Ramesses VI* (1954). E. Schiaparelli also produced a major publication on the funerary papyri and the Book of the Dead (1881–90).

One important aspect of Egyptian belief revolved around the concepts regarding the creation of the universe and mankind. It was thought that creation had been brought about by the sacred force of the divine word. In the Old Kingdom, the most powerful priesthoods developed individual theologies which each provided a unique mythological explanation of how their chief deity had created the universe. The most important of these creation myths (cosmogonies) was developed at Heliopolis and emphasised the role of Re, the sun-god, as creator. The Pyramid Texts are the main source for this version. At Memphis, the god Ptah was regarded as the supreme creator, bringing the universe into existence through divine utterance; this version is preserved in a text known as the 'Memphite Theology', which occurs on the Shabaka Stone. Now in the British Museum, this is probably the world's oldest surviving example of a philosophical treatise. Two major studies have been written about this text, but they disagree about its purpose. The text poses many problems in translation, and one scholar, H. Junker, did not agree with another interpretation by K. H. Sethe that it was a dramatic play, accompanied by prose narrations. A third cosmogony was associated with Hermopolis, where the priests presented a mythological explanation which included several different forms of creation.

The Wisdom Texts were another important literary genre which developed in the Old Kingdom. These were written to provide instructions for the young on how they should behave in society, and together with the Schoolboy Exercises (see page 38) which the pupils copied out, they provide the most important source for understanding the education system. Although most Wisdom Texts date to the Old or Middle Kingdoms, some were written in the New Kingdom and later periods, and reflect different political and economic conditions. In one late example, known as the Instruction of Ankhsheshonq (a priest of Re at Heliopolis), Ankhsheshonq writes to his son from prison; in earlier texts the instructions were always conveyed in the form of an address by an eminent wise man, sometimes the chief minister or even the king, but the later texts clearly take a less elevated stance. A study of this papyrus by S. R. K. Glanville was published as *The Instruction of 'Onchsheshonqy (British Museum Papyrus 10508)* (1955).

Another important later Wisdom Text – the Instruction of Any – was probably composed in Dynasty 18, while the Instruction of Amenemope, which probably dates to the Ramesside Period (*c.* 1250 BC), is a particularly interesting example in which a close parallelism has been observed between some of its passages and those found in the biblical Book of Proverbs. The style and content of Amenemope is closer to Hebrew literature than any other Egyptian text, and this parallelism was explored in E. Drioton's *Le Livre des proverbes et la sagesse d'Aménémopé* (1959).

The Great Hymn to the Aten, written in the Amarna Period, and the biblical Psalm 104 also display similarities. The doctrine of Atenism was set out in two hymns which were inscribed on the walls of the courtiers' tombs at Amarna. Written in beautiful and dignified language, these remain the basic source for knowledge of the tenets of Atensim. However, although the earliest translations and studies of these hymns suggested that they contained some startling and innovative ideas, it is now known that almost all of these concepts were present in earlier hymns addressed to other gods. Literature from the Amarna Period has been translated by M. Sandman in *Texts from the Time of Akhenaten* (1938).

Other important religious texts relate to Osiris, one of Egypt's greatest gods. The most complete version of the myth of Osiris is found in Plutarch's *De Iside et Osiride*, which preserves a Greek rather than an Egyptian tradition. However, some earlier Egyptian inscriptions also include references to the myth, such as the Pyramid Texts and the texts that accompany temple scenes of rituals performed at the time of the annual festivals of Osiris.

In Plutarch's version of the myth, Osiris is described as a human king who was murdered by his brother Seth, but whose dismembered body was later magically put together again by his wife Isis. She posthumously conceived his son, Horus, who eventually avenged his father's death and killed Seth in a frenzied conflict. When their dispute was brought before the tribunal of gods, the judgment favoured Osiris (who was resurrected to become king and judge of the dead in the underworld) and Horus (who was henceforth identified with the King of Egypt, and became ruler of the living on earth). Seth, who was now identified as the Evil One, became an outcast. This story of the triumph of good over evil and life over death became the foundation of many Egyptian beliefs about the afterlife, including the opportunity for the individual who had worshipped Osiris and tried to live a blameless life to enjoy an individual eternity after death. Although Plutarch's version may not provide an entirely Egyptian account, it nevertheless probably preserves the main features of the myth. E. A. Budge produced an account of the god's mythology and attributes in his *Osiris and the Egyptian Resurrection* (1911) in which he tried to draw parallels between Osiris and other nature gods of the Near East and Greece. This idea is now largely discounted, and more recent studies, such as J. G. Griffiths, *The Origins of Osiris* (1980) and *Plutarch, De Iside et Osiride* (1970), incorporate later research in this field.

Some categories of literature contain both texts which express personal attitudes and religious beliefs, and those which describe historical events. The so-called 'Pessimistic Literature' probably reflects events which occurred towards the end of the Old Kingdom, when the political structures and social order were overturned. Two texts, the 'Prophecy of Neferti' and the 'Admonitions of a Prophet', may actually describe the appalling economic conditions of that period, while the 'Dispute between a Man and his Soul' and some of the contemporary funerary hymns express the personal disillusionment and despair of people who lived in those times. As noted above, they present a stark contrast to the archaeological evidence, which indicates an absolute confidence and belief in eternal life.

The Egyptians have also left historical texts which give us some insight into their political and military undertakings. One of the most significant personal accounts is the autobiography of a soldier, Ahmose, son of Ebana, which is inscribed on the walls of his tomb at el-Kab. This describes the part he played in the conflict against the Hyksos at the start of the New Kingdom and provides a unique historical source for this period. However, most historical texts were formal inscriptions, placed on the walls of the great New Kingdom temples; they described the prowess of kings such as Tuthmosis III, Ramesses II or Ramesses III in military conflicts with their enemies. In some cases, the same events are recorded in more than one version in different temples. The accompanying scenes provide a vivid depiction of the kings' exploits, although the 'facts' that are presented in the inscriptions, regarding individual royal successes or the numbers of the enemies who were killed or captured in battle, cannot be regarded as reliable accounts.

The historical inscriptions were relentlessly propagandist and always presented Egypt and its rulers as outright winners. J. H. Breasted collected a corpus of historical inscriptions which eventually numbered 10,000 manuscript pages. He was able to use these for his great compilation of ancient Egyptian historical texts which, when it was published as *Ancient Records of Egypt* (1906–7), made this material available to Egyptologists for the first time.

The Egyptians not only composed propagandist texts for their temple inscriptions. There is an early example, in the Westcar Papyrus, where a popular story (sometimes known as 'King Cheops and the Magicians') is used as a means of political and religious propaganda to justify the claims of the early rulers of Dynasty 5 to be the rightful kings. Public storytellers would have narrated the tale as an oral tradition in the towns and villages, and the text uses a range of techniques to make the story appealing and interesting to a general audience, in order to gain people's attention and put its message across.

Another famous text, the Story of Sinuhe (sometimes regarded as the greatest masterpiece of Egyptian literature) was composed as an autobiographical text to be placed in the tomb, although it may in fact recall actual historical events. It relates the story of Sinuhe's life and describes the many tribulations he suffered and his eventual success, but these events appear to be set within a real historical context. Storytelling was already well developed by the Middle Kingdom (when this text was composed), but in the New Kingdom more complex plots and ideas were added. The range now included mythological tales, stories which had human and divine locations and personalities, and accounts which were placed within a historical setting. Another literary form which is first encountered in the New Kingdom are the love poems, which were written to be performed as short songs.

Translations in English of selected texts from Egyptian literature are available in A. Erman's classic account, *The Literature of the Ancient Egyptians* (trans. A. Blackman, 1927) and produced in an updated version, with an introduction by W. K. Simpson, as *The Ancient Egyptians: A Sourcebook of their Writings* (1966). Another major anthology has been compiled by M. Lichtheim, and is published as *Ancient Egyptian Literature* (1975–80).

Generally, the study of Egyptian literature has contributed enormously to current understanding of the civilisation. Problems with translation, and the considerable number of texts that await translation, still impose limits on this. However, the existence of extensive literary sources allows us to enter into, and at least partially comprehend, the mind and psyche of the ancient Egyptians.

PART 2

THE DEVELOPMENT OF EGYPTOLOGY

CHAPTER VI

CLASSICAL AND MEDIEVAL
INTEREST IN EGYPT

———— •◆• ————

The earliest extant history of ancient Egypt is preserved in the writings of Manetho, an Egyptian priest (*c.* 300 BC) who lived at the Temple of Sebennytos in the Delta. As a priest, he had intimate knowledge of the religious beliefs and customs and temple rituals, and he could read both Greek and Egyptian hieroglyphs.

When Egypt became a province of the Roman empire in 30 BC, travellers and writers began to regard the country as a safe place to visit. They travelled from distant parts of the empire to marvel at the ancient monuments and to gain a first-hand impression of this strange and exotic civilisation. Several writers of this period have left us their personal accounts and descriptions of Egyptian culture, and these remained the major source for studying the history, geography, art, religion and customs, until hieroglyphs were deciphered in the nineteenth century.

However, even before Egypt was absorbed into the Roman empire, the most famous Classical eye-witness account was written by Herodotus (*c.* 484–430 BC), who today is regarded as the 'Father of History' because he was the first commentator who seriously attempted to separate fantasy and speculation from reality. Born at Halicarnassus in Asia Minor, Herodotus wrote his works in Greek.

Herodotus' *Histories* describes the great conflict between Greece and Persia. When he retired to Thurii in Italy, he added to this work, including a digression from the main theme (Book II, 'Euterpe') which was devoted to the examination and interpretation of the history and geography of Egypt.

One of the most significant aspects of Herodotus' career as a writer and historian was his personal involvement in his subject-matter: he actually visited the places and people that he described. In *c.* 450 BC he travelled to Egypt, which was then under Persian domination, and was thus able to give his own first-hand description of the monuments he saw there, and to draw on the 'facts' which were relayed to him by the priests and other people he encountered on his travels.

He provides most information about the northern sites in Egypt, describing the Giza pyramids (which he correctly identified as royal burial places), and places in the Fayoum district such as Lake Moeris (now Birket Qarun) and the great temple and administrative complex known as The Labyrinth which, he claimed, must have cost more in labour and money than all the

Figure 8 A painted panel portrait of a man, *c.* 200 BC. Placed over the face of the mummy in the Roman Period, such panels represent the earliest extant evidence of realistic portrait painting. This, and many other examples, were discovered by Flinders Petrie at Hawara.

walls and public works of the Greeks put together. He also discussed important sites on the Delta such as the royal tombs at Sais and the city of Bubastis (Tell Basta) where there was a fine temple which, according to Herodotus, although 'other temples may be larger, or have cost more to build . . . none is a greater pleasure to look at'. It was joined to a nearby temple dedicated to Hermes by a stone-paved road which was 'lined on both sides with immense trees – so tall that they seem to touch the sky'.

Since Herodotus' account concentrated mainly on the northern districts, and he did not even describe the monuments of Thebes (the southern capital), this has prompted modern speculation about the extent of his travels in Egypt and caused scholars to question his claim that he went to the south. However, he may indeed have reached the First Cataract on the Nile.

There is no doubt that his writing conveys his own amazement and wonderment at the facts he gleaned during his visit to Egypt. The landscape was a subject of great interest to him, and he speculated about the source and the inundation of the Nile. The priests had given him no information about this, although they told him that the country had been built up by the Nile silt. He observed: 'for I am convinced – and the Egyptians themselves admit the fact – that the Delta is alluvial land and has only recently (if I may so put it) appeared above water'. He then went on to speculate why, if they had no place in which to live, the Egyptians had claimed that they were the oldest race on earth. However, he concluded that they must have had another homeland and that they only moved into the Delta after it was gradually created from the Nile silt.

Herodotus also discussed the flora and fauna of the country, and related some strange stories about the behaviour of the hippopotamus, ibis, crocodile, and the mythical phoenix. He claimed that some Egyptians worshipped the crocodile, particularly around Thebes and Lake Moeris. 'In these places', he says,

> they keep one particular crocodile, which they tame, putting rings made of glass or gold into its ears and bracelets round its front feet, and giving it special food and ceremonial offerings. In fact, while these creatures are alive, they treat them with every kindness and, when they die, embalm them and bury them in sacred tombs.

However, elsewhere, particularly in the vicinity of Elephantine, Herodotus claimed that crocodiles were not regarded as sacred but were eaten.

The mythical phoenix bird (which, Herodotus stated, he had only seen in paintings) was said to be a rare visitor to Egypt, appearing only every five hundred years when the parent-bird died. Some Egyptians apparently would not sacrifice goats because they venerated them, but pigs were considered to be unclean: 'If anyone touches a pig accidentally in passing, he will at once plunge into the river, clothes and all, to wash himself.' However, pigs were sacrificed both to the moon deity and to Dionysus, at the time of the full moon; afterwards, the flesh was eaten on the day of the full moon, but they would not sacrifice pigs on any other festivals or eat the flesh on any other occasion. Swineherds were regarded as a group apart who were only allowed to marry each other's daughters and were forbidden to enter the temples.

There is also an interesting account of how the sacred Apis-bulls were selected: the priest appointed for the purpose would seek out an animal to replace a deceased bull, examining the creature's markings and physical features. Subsequently, these bulls were revered, and anyone who sacrificed such an animal was put to death. Eventually, when the sacred bull met a natural death, it was mummified and buried with considerable ceremony.

Herodotus also described the general treatment of animals which, without exception, the Egyptians regarded as sacred. The animals were fed and cared for by specially appointed guardians who passed the office and its duties down through the family. In particular, cats were revered and protected: when a cat died of natural causes, the occupants of the house where the animal had lived shaved their eyebrows and, after death, many cats were taken to Bubastis (Tell Basta), the city where the cat goddess Bast was worshipped. There, Herodotus stated, 'they are embalmed and buried in sacred receptacles'.

Generally, Herodotus regarded the Egyptians as a most religious people, and he described their religious beliefs and customs, their festivals, magical rites, dream interpretations and cults. With regard to mummification, he and another Classical writer, Diodorus Siculus, provide the only major extant literary accounts of the procedure, to which there are only brief and passing references in the Egyptian religious texts. Herodotus described the distinctive features of the embalmer's profession, and gave details of the three basic methods of mummification. These, available according to cost, included the 'most perfect process', which involved the evisceration of the body and subsequent dehydration of the body tissues by means of natron; a second-quality treatment when the intestines were not removed, but oil of cedar was injected into the body to liquify the internal organs so that they could be easily expelled from the body; and a third method by which the intestines were cleared out with a purge, and the body was dehydrated by treating it with natron for a period of seventy days. Scientific investigations carried out in the late twentieth century have mainly supported the accuracy of Herodotus' description of mummification.

Herodotus was the first foreign observer to write a factual account of Egypt which has survived. For the later historical periods, when the archaeological evidence is absent or scarce, his information is still uniquely important. However, some scholars have questioned the veracity of some of his 'factual evidence', claiming that it was mainly provided by priests who were either ignorant of the facts, and fabricated answers to please him, or who consciously gave him false information so that they could preserve the secrets of their religion. Sometimes, also, the events and procedures they described were not contemporary or were in decline by this late period. For example, mummification was still practised in the fifth century BC, but had undoubtedly declined from the highest standards achieved some six hundred years earlier. In particular, Herodotus' account of pyramid construction and of the personalities and actions of Cheops and Chephren, who built the largest pyramids at Giza, is likely to be exaggerated and inaccurate since it was based on the accounts of the priests he met who were alive some 2,400 years after these events had occurred. Herodotus reported that Cheops 'brought the country into all sorts of misery', and closed the temples and forced his people to work as slaves at his pyramid site. The work was arranged in three-monthly shifts, with a hundred thousand men in each shift, in order to build the track along which the quarried stone blocks were dragged for constructing the pyramid. It was claimed that this task took ten years, while the pyramid itself was built over twenty years; when Cheops died, he was succeeded by his son, Chephren, whose reign was equally oppressive.

However, despite the possible inaccuracies in his work, Herodotus has provided subsequent generations with a most important source; it became one of the few authorities to be relied upon by most medieval and Renaissance writers. This first-hand account, which combined the writer's own observations and an assessment of 'facts' which were related to him by other people, still remains an inspiring and unique view of Egypt. The modern reader, through Herodotus' own eyes and words, can glimpse something of the early traveller's amazement at encountering Egypt in the last stages of its pharaonic civilisation. The historian has provided us with his unique observations of customs, monuments and sites which, in many instances, have now totally disappeared.

Diodorus Siculus was another Greek writer, who lived in the late first century BC. He made a visit to Egypt between 60 and 57 BC, and used this experience as background for the book he wrote about ancient Egypt which was the first of the twelve volumes that comprised his *Universal History*. However, he also owed a great debt to earlier writers such as Hecataeus of Abdera, Agartharchides of Cnidus, and especially Herodotus, whose lead he followed in writing about subjects such as mummification (where Diodorus provides some additional details), animal worship, the cult and burial of the dead, medicine, the flora and fauna, and the cause of the Nile's inundation. He also provided information about law, education and the Osiris myth (although later Plutarch wrote much more fully about this).

Although Diodorus supplies some additional facts, and is a useful source for the later periods when other evidence is less abundant, the work nevertheless contains many inaccuracies, and lacks the original and forthright approach of Herodotus. It is essentially a derivative account which does not convey the same enthusiasm as Herodotus' own descriptions.

Once Egypt became part of the Roman empire, tourists and travellers began to move around there freely, visiting the major ancient sites en route. They usually landed at the still-renowned port of Alexandria, and then crossed by land to Giza, site of the famous pyramids, and to Memphis, the earliest capital of Egypt. Some then travelled southwards to the site of ancient Thebes and the nearby Valley of the Kings, before proceeding up the Nile to the island of Philae and its famous temples, situated near the First Cataract on the river.

Among these travellers was the geographer Strabo (64 BC–22 AD) who accompanied his friend, the Roman prefect Aelius Gallus, on an expedition through Egypt in 25/24 BC which probably took them as far south as the First Cataract. Strabo was born in Pontus, and lived at Alexandria in Egypt for some years. His journey included a visit to the tombs at Thebes in 27 BC, where he also observed the famous Colossi of Memnon – two enormous stone statues which had once flanked the entrance to the mortuary temple of Amenhotep III. He was the first writer to comment on the supposed phenomenon of the 'singing' which had been attributed to the northern statue. The strange sounds that came forth from this huge seated statue in the early morning were an attraction to tourists who identified them either as human voices or as musical chords. However, Strabo was sceptical about these explanations, and sought to find an alternative solution. He surmised that the priests, ever anxious to increase their power and influence, may have installed some kind of device that would produce the sound. However, it is now generally accepted that this 'wonder' (which had first occurred after 27 BC, when an earthquake damaged the statue) was actually an internal vibration within the statue, caused by this disturbance and by the sudden changes in humidity and temperature at dawn. However, the singing ceased after 199 AD when the crack was repaired, following a visit by the Emperor Septimius Severus in 202 AD. On this occasion, the statue refused to 'sing' for the emperor, who consequently attempted to win the god's favour by initiating the repair and restoration of the statue.

Strabo also referred to the Serapeum at Memphis, located 'in a spot so sandy that the wind causes the sand to accumulate in heaps'. Under the sand, he claimed, they could see many sphinxes which were either partially or completely buried. Nearly two thousand years later, the French archaeologist Auguste Mariette recalled this literary passage when he discovered a solitary head of a sphinx projecting out of the sand at Saqqara, and this led him to excavate and reveal the site of the Serapeum.

Strabo also provided one of the earliest references to the Valley of the Kings when he referred to the 'tombs of kings which are stone-hewn'. He stated that they numbered about forty, and were finely constructed and worthy of a visit. However, although he described sites at Thebes and the famous Nilometer at Elephantine, he gave most information about Alexandria and the Delta. He was interested in many aspects of Egypt, and devoted the last book in the seventeen volumes of his *Geographia* to a short account of the geography of Egypt. The *Geographia* was written in Greek, and brought together a great many facts about the Roman world; in his final volume, Strabo primarily provides a topographical list of ninety-nine towns, settlements, and resources, and within this context, includes references to pyramids, tombs and temples as well as historical facts and comments on religious cults. Strabo was critical of Herodotus and other writers for attempting to enliven their accounts with fantastic tales, but his own 'facts' are not always correct, although his geographical details are generally sound.

Another Roman writer, Pliny the Elder (23–79 AD), also provides useful information about Egypt in his *Historia Naturalis*, although his information is largely drawn from earlier writers. There is a description of mummification which augments the accounts of Herodotus and Diodorus Siculus, and he discusses human inventions, material objects not manufactured by man, and monuments within Egypt (he was one of the first Roman writers who described the Great Sphinx at Giza) as well as those which had been exported and set up elsewhere, such as the obelisks that had been moved to Rome at the emperor's request.

The Greek writer Plutarch (*c.* 50–120 AD), who came from Chaeronea, has provided us with the most complete version of the Egyptian myth of Osiris and Isis (*De Iside et Osiride*). This work is preserved in Plutarch's *Moralia*, and it is important because, during the medieval and Renaissance periods, it was one of the very few detailed texts about Egyptian religion which provided European scholars with a clear insight into the beliefs of ancient Egypt. In fact, this text preserves the only complete account of Egypt's most important myth, since no extant Egyptian version has survived, although it is often referred to in Egyptian texts found on papyri, and in tomb and temple wall inscriptions.

The myth, which relates how the ancient king of Egypt, Osiris, eventually defeated his wicked brother Seth, epitomises the eternal conflict between good and evil, and glorifies the ultimate triumph of life over death, with the resurrection of Osiris as the king and judge of the afterlife. Although the version that Plutarch provides may present a Greek viewpoint which possibly differs in some respects from the original Egyptian tradition, the main events of the story and its underlying philosophy are probably fairly accurate.

Finally, the Jewish historian Flavius Josephus (*c.* 70 AD) was also a source of information about Egypt which was used by Renaissance scholars. Josephus included edited extracts from Manetho's history, and he also commented on personalities and events such as the Hyksos and those with biblical associations, including Joseph, Moses and the Exodus.

However, since source material for the Hyksos period is very limited, there is insufficient evidence to refute or confirm most of Josephus' comments on this period. According to his account, he quoted the exact words of Manetho about the Hyksos' actions, but this cannot be proved. He stated that the Hyksos were an obscure race who came from the east and invaded Egypt in the reign of an unidentified ruler named Tutimaios. The Hyksos were able to seize the land without striking a blow, and subsequently they ruthlessly burnt cities and razed temples to the ground, and massacred or enslaved the whole native population. Then a Hyksos leader named Salitis (the names of whose successors Josephus also lists) was made king, and he ruled from Memphis and built a new capital at the site of Avaris in the Delta (for discussion of the location of Avaris, see page 153).

Josephus mistakenly interpreted the hieroglyphic word for the Hyksos to mean 'shepherd kings' or 'captive shepherds', although it is now known that this word should be translated as 'chieftains of foreign lands'. He concluded that the Hyksos invasion represented the descent of the Hebrews into Egypt, and that the period of Hyksos rule should be equated with the Hebrews' sojourn there; finally, he identified the biblical Exodus with the final expulsion of the Hyksos by the local princes of Thebes, who founded the New Kingdom. However, there is no other evidence to support this theory, and apart from the chronological problems it poses, there is also a major discrepancy in that the Hyksos were driven out of Egypt, whereas the Exodus represented a flight by people who desperately wished to leave Egypt and its pharaoh.

The Classical authors have therefore provided unique accounts which preserve details of a civilisation that they observed first-hand. These writings remained the most reliable source of literary evidence (and were extensively used by medieval and Renaissance scholars) until Champollion deciphered hieroglyphs in the nineteenth century. Even today, they supply details which would otherwise remain unknown or have subsequently been destroyed, and this is particularly true for the later periods of Egyptian history when other evidence is lacking or scanty. However, these historical and geographical accounts must be used with caution, as the information they provide and the theories they promote are sometimes only based on fantasy and speculation.

During medieval and Renaissance times, little factual evidence was added to the Classical descriptions, although there was considerable European interest in Egypt during the Renaissance, when travellers began to make quite extensive journeys. In earlier years, however, the monuments and inscriptions suffered damage and destruction because they were considered to be unimportant, or even worse, to be an affront to the later religions. The early Christians in Egypt (fourth–fifth centuries AD) defaced the figures of gods and the sacred inscriptions in the temples because they regarded them as idolatrous; sometimes, the wall scenes were plastered over and decorated with paintings of Christian themes, when whole areas of the temples were converted into churches. Sometimes, houses were built inside temples or on top of their walls – a custom which continued until the clearance of the temples, in recognition of their significance as archaeological sites, in the nineteenth and twentieth centuries. In addition, the great stone blocks from which the temples had been constructed now provided a readily available supply of building materials, and some of these monuments were used as quarries.

Few travellers visited Egypt in medieval times, although some pilgrims who went to the Holy Land also passed through Egypt, mainly to see the sites which were associated with Christianity and the period when the Holy Family stayed there. However, these travellers assumed that the pyramids and other pharaonic monuments were in fact associated in some way with the biblical accounts. The earliest known description by a European which tells of a visit to the ancient sites is recorded in a manuscript which was discovered at Arezzo in Tuscany in 1883. The author was Lady Etheria, a nun from Gaul, who travelled around Egypt between 379 and 388 AD, with the purpose of identifying sites she had read about in the Bible. Her travels took her to Alexandria, and to Saft el-Henna in the Delta, which she correctly identified as the site of ancient Tanis, and to the southern area of the country, around Thebes.

In 640 AD, Amr ibn el-'As, the general of Caliph Omar, conquered Egypt, achieving his objective with fewer than 4,000 troops. He was an enlightened and sensible man who decided to build a new Moslem capital (el-Fustat), just to the north of the old foundation of Babylon-in-Egypt, which had become a centre for Christians and Jews. Fustat was also called 'Misr' or 'Masr el-Fustat' by the Arabs who, in addition, gave the name 'Misr' to Egypt itself. The name 'Fustat' means 'tents' and tradition relates that when Amr prepared to move on from this area in order to conquer Alexandria, he found two doves nesting in his tent. He decided to leave his tent standing until after he returned, and a new city began to grow up around the tent. When he came back from his victorious campaign, he built the first mosque in Egypt at the spot where his tent had stood, and a mosque survives on the site (in Cairo) today, although no visible traces of this first building are preserved.

El-Fustat was founded as a military headquarters and a seat of government. Amr had acted on behalf of the Umayyads, an Arab dynasty which had its residence in Damascus, and for much of the Middle Ages Egypt became a province of the empire of the Caliphs. The Caliph was the temporal head of the true believers – the Moslems – and their champion in the holy wars of Islam. It was necessary that the Caliphs (or deputies of the Prophet Mohammed) should be the descendants of the Arab tribe to which the Prophet Mohammed and the early Caliphs had belonged. The history of medieval Egypt centres around the power of the Caliphs and their decline and subsequent dependency on the Mamluks, slaves who were purchased by the Turkish Sultans and trained as soldiers to become bodyguards and to form the nucleus of the army.

Amr had established el-Fustat (this was later destroyed, apart from Amr's mosque, but marked the location where the modern city of Cairo was founded in 969 AD), in order that he would have a base in Egypt for the

Arab campaigns against Byzantium and the conquest of North Africa. Under the Umayyad dynasty (658–750 AD), Arab tribes were settled in the Nile valley, and the government of Egypt now became based on the Arab model. The country was ruled successively by dynasties of foreign caliphs, with a brief period of independence under the Tulunids (868–905 AD).

Against this historical background, there was little interest in Egypt's ancient past. The Arabs who came to Egypt found an indigenous population who knew little about their past, and since the ability to read the hieroglyphs had been lost, there was no opportunity to gain knowledge through the texts. The Arabs believed that the monuments had been built by giants or magicians, and their main interest in them was as a potential source of treasure. One explorer, Ma'mun (who was the son of Caliph Harun er-Rashid) undertook a typically vain quest for treasure when he entered the Great Pyramid at Giza in the ninth century AD, forcing his way through the masonry in a vain quest for treasure. In addition to general neglect and treasure-seeking, the ancient monuments also suffered during this period because they were used as quarries. In particular, limestone casing blocks on the Giza pyramids were dismantled and removed to Cairo to be utilised in the many new buildings that were being constructed there.

Some foreign travellers still visited Egypt, despite the difficulties. In 870 AD, Bernard the Wise and two monks made the journey, and in 1165–71 AD, Rabbi Benjamin ben Jonah left his home at Tudela in Navarre, and was able to provide a first-hand account which, for the first time, accurately reported on the source of the Nile and identified the seasonal rains in the Abyssinian highlands as the cause of the river's annual inundation.

However, the most significant traveller and writer of this period was an Arab doctor from Baghdad, named Abd' el-Latif. He taught medicine and philosophy in Cairo around 1200 AD, and had the opportunity to visit Giza and Memphis during that period. At Giza, he was able to enter the Great Pyramid, and he saw the Great Sphinx when it was still intact. His account is of unique interest because he was travelling around the country at a time when, because of the political situation created by the Crusades, Europeans were not often able to visit the monuments in this area. Some of the ancient sites were relatively well preserved when Abd' el-Latif saw them, but have subsequently suffered damage or destruction, so his account has preserved some details which are no longer visible. However, perhaps his most important contribution is that he provided an objective report on the monuments because, as a Moslem, he did not attempt to interpret them from a biblical viewpoint, as the early Christian travellers had done. Unfortunately, his writing had no impact on later European authors, as it was not translated from the Arabic until the nineteenth century.

With the end of the Crusades, and the renewed opportunity to travel more freely in the Middle East, there was increased interest in Egypt. Several pilgrimages are reported, with Christian travellers making their way by land

and sea to Jerusalem, Egypt and St Catherine's monastery in Sinai. During this period, hand-written copies of travel books began to appear, although they were still rare, but the most popular guidebook for the pilgrimage to the Holy Land was supposedly written by Sir John Mandeville, a man who did not even exist. This fourteenth-century work, entitled *The Voiage and Travaile of Sir John Maundevile, Knight*, was probably written by Jean d'Outremeuse of Liege, but he himself had never visited Egypt, and the book simply drew upon earlier works, including the Classical authors, for its information. However, the credentials of the book remained unchallenged for several centuries, and its erroneous statements (for example, that the pyramids were Joseph's granaries) continued to be reported as established facts by later writers.

The Renaissance in Europe brought to an end many of the attitudes that had been prevalent in medieval times. More relaxed religious attitudes, and an increased interest in the Classical civilisations and their religious beliefs and philosophies inevitably led travellers and scholars to turn their attention to ancient Egypt. However, it was events in Egypt that now established the country as a province of the Turkish empire, and made it a safer place for merchants, diplomats and pilgrims to visit.

In 1517 AD, the Osman ruler Sultan Selim I of Constantinople took Cairo by storm, and soon established Egypt as a Turkish governorate or pashalik. This situation lasted until 1798 AD, when Napoleon Bonaparte was able to take advantage of the declining power of the Osman Sultans and invade Egypt. However, it was under Selim I that Egypt was finally opened up to the outside world; an earlier treaty which had allowed the French and Catalans to trade there was now reaffirmed, and merchants were given religious protection in Egypt. They now led the way, and were soon followed by others, including pilgrims who came to visit the holy sites and antiquarians and collectors who wished to gain access to Egypt's ancient monuments and antiquities.

CHAPTER VII

THE RENAISSANCE PERIOD

—— •◆• ——

Political conditions, namely the end of the Crusades and the conquest of Egypt by the Turks, and a new enthusiasm for the ancient civilisations ensured that the period from the Renaissance until the expedition of Napoleon Bonaparte to Egypt in 1798 saw a considerable increase in the number of visitors to the country. In fact, more than two hundred accounts survive which were written by travellers who visited Egypt between 1400 and 1700. These are important because they provide first-hand contemporary narratives which augment the earlier Classical descriptions.

The Renaissance was a time when men sought information and enlightenment about the civilisations of ancient Egypt, Greece and Rome. One of two Classical texts rediscovered in the fifteenth century, which added to the existing literature, was Horapollo's *Hieroglyphica* (fourth century AD). This claimed to be Egyptian in origin and attempted to show that hieroglyphs were essentially symbolic (rather than a language system); the work was also believed to contain wisdom and truths of great significance. The other work, known as the Hermetic Corpus, included a series of philosophical texts which were also believed to preserve ancient Egyptian wisdom.

Renaissance interest in antiquities led scholars to Rome, with its wealth of Egyptian antiquities which had mostly been imported there in the early years of the Roman empire. These included seven obelisks, the finest of which had once belonged to Tuthmosis III and now stood in the Lateran Palace in Rome. This major group of antiquities in Rome was a readily available source for the study of ancient Egypt, and encouraged scholars to travel further afield and visit Egypt to see the monuments for themselves.

However, in addition to the travellers and scholars who went to Egypt because of their desire to see and study the country and ancient sites, others now realised the great potential that existed for the acquisition of antiquities which could be sold to private collectors in Europe. From the seventeenth century, some of the great private collections started to be developed. The most enthusiastic collectors were the kings of France, and during this period, the foundations were laid in France and Italy for the great national collections of later years. In England, the British Museum was established by an Act of Parliament in 1756; here, the important Egyptian collection was gradually built up from a group of objects assembled by the physician, Dr Hans Sloane.

It soon became a fashionable pursuit for wealthy European patrons – often royalty or nobility – to collect Egyptian artifacts. Agents were sent to Egypt to obtain curios such as coins, manuscripts and antiquities. Officials in the embassies and consulates in Egypt also now started to play a role in this trade. In addition to their diplomatic role, they also began to act as local agents who acquired antiquities for wealthy patrons. Some of these collections were to become a major resource for study. However, at this time, no one could read the inscriptions because hieroglyphs had not yet been deciphered, although the antiquities were undoubtedly admired as objects of artistic excellence.

Another result of the intensified interest in acquiring antiquities was the desire on the part of foreign collectors to conduct their own excavations. Once they had obtained permission from the Turkish rulers, they were able to remove inscriptions, statuary and tomb contents from burials and temples. This developed into 'treasure-hunting' in later years, when an intense rivalry grew up between excavators and agents from different countries. These men were largely driven by the wish to make a profit from supplying their wealthy patrons with the finest pieces.

The foreigners who now visited Egypt for the sake of seeing or buying the antiquities were either travellers, tourists, scholars, or the agents who supplied antiquities, although individuals were sometimes compelled to make this journey for more than one reason. Their accounts preserve a wealth of detail about the sites and monuments, and also about the joys and privations of Renaissance travel.

One of the earliest travellers of the seventeenth century was George Sandys (1578–1644), an Englishman who was the youngest son of Edwin Sandys, Archbishop of York. In 1610, he set out on a tour to visit France, Italy, Turkey, Egypt and Palestine, and he returned via Rome. Several years later, in 1621, he published an account in four books about this journey entitled *Sundys' Travells: A Relation of a Journey begun An. Dom. 1610.* However, although he gained first-hand knowledge of the monuments and was able to describe the pyramids at Giza and relate how he climbed the Great Pyramid and entered its interior, he nevertheless added little that was new. He relied heavily on Classical sources, and discussed earlier traditions regarding the pyramids, concluding that they were indeed the burial places of ancient kings and not the granaries of Joseph.

One location that Sandys did not visit, but for which he relied on the account given by Herodotus, is Lake Moeris (now Birket Qarun) in the Fayoum, where he mentions 'two Pyramides, in the middle, on each a colossus of stone, the Sepulchres of King Moeris and his Wife, that Herodotus saw'. Herodotus' account was shown to be correct in 1888, when the archaeologist Flinders Petrie was able to identify huge blocks of masonry at Biahmu as the pedestals of two colossal statues, surrounded by courts.

Figure 9 An early account of travelling in Egypt was provided by George Sandys. This plate, from his book *Sundy's Travells: A Relation of a Journey Begun An. Dom. 1610* (1621), shows his party visiting the Giza pyramids.

About the same time, an Italian nobleman, Pietro della Valle (1586–1652), visited Egypt as part of his travels around the eastern Mediterranean (1614–26). He described the interior of the Great Pyramid, the smaller monuments, and the Great Sphinx. He was also an avid collector and brought antiquities back to Italy. These included important Coptic manuscripts (grammars and vocabularies), used by the scholar Athanasius Kircher (1602–1680) who later in the century made one of the earliest attempts to decipher hieroglyphs. Also, at Saqqara, Pietro della Valle acquired some mummy portrait panels which were the first to reach Europe, and demonstrated the significant contribution that Egyptian antiquities could make to the understanding of ancient art.

In contrast to accounts of travels that produced few new insights, the study by John Greaves (1602–1652) was the first scientific attempt to investigate the facts about the Egyptian monuments and compare this new assessment with the often fantastical stories that had been written previously.

Figure 10 Early travellers to Egypt found the temples partly submerged in sand. This early photograph of the Temple of Khnum at Esna, Upper Egypt, shows the sand reaching almost to the top of the columns.

Greaves was an English mathematician, astronomer and orientalist who had studied philosophy and mathematics and had also learnt to read several oriental languages, so he was able to understand texts on astronomy in Greek, Arabic and Persian. He became professor of astronomy at Oxford, and in 1646 published a major work entitled *Pyramidographia, or a Discourse of the Pyramids in Aegypt*. This work drew on his experience of Egypt, which he had visited in 1638–9, when he stayed for four months in Alexandria, and then proceeded to Cairo. He visited Giza on two occasions, and took mathematical instruments with him so that he could make measurements of the pyramids for the first scientific and systematic survey of these monuments that had ever been undertaken.

Greaves climbed the Great Pyramid, measured the sizes of the stones, and explored the inner chambers. Although his measurements were not all entirely accurate, he established scientific methods which were unprecedented. He correctly claimed that the pyramids were burial places, and noted the remains of other buildings adjacent to the pyramids; he also accurately identified the foundations of a building near to the Great Pyramid as its associated funerary temple.

In addition to Greaves's conclusions about the monuments, his work also included a critical assessment of the writings of ancient authors, with special mention of medieval Arabic sources. This comparison of some earlier descriptions of the pyramids with his own first-hand observations produced a unique piece of scholarship which, in terms of its methodology and consideration of both literary and archaeological evidence, is now regarded as a landmark in the study of ancient Egypt.

Several French travellers also made significant journeys in the earlier part of the seventeenth century. In 1605, François Savary, the French ambassador to Constantinople, reached the pyramids at Giza. Another interesting account was left by Jean de Thévenot (1633–1667), who is regarded as the first modern explorer of Egypt. In 1656, his travels took him from Turkey to Egypt, when he visited the Delta and Cairo. A second journey was made in 1663, when he visited other parts of the East. These experiences formed the basis of his *Voyage au Levant* (1664) and the five volumes of *Voyages de M. Thévenot*, which were published in 1689, after his death.

Another explorer who made a significant contribution to the study of ancient Egypt in the eighteenth century was Benoît de Maillet (1656–1738). He was a French diplomat who became the French consul-general in Egypt from 1692 to 1708. This gave him the opportunity to travel within Egypt, and he made extensive investigations, including entering the Great Pyramid at Giza more than forty times. He acquired a considerable number of antiquities which were sent back to France to be added to royal and noble collections there, and he also bought Coptic and Arabic manuscripts. His interest in ancient scripts led him to observe that some of the cursive signs on the mummy bandages were different from the hieroglyphic letters – which was an important statement in terms of the study of the Egyptian scripts and language system. However, his most important contribution was to suggest that there should be a proper scheme for the scientific exploration of Egypt; this was later developed and put into practice by the *savants* included in Napoleon's expedition in 1798.

Another French antiquary and traveller, Paul Lucas (1664–1737), was sent to Egypt in 1714 as the official traveller of Louis XIV. His instructions from the royal librarian were to examine the monuments at Thebes and near Lake Moeris, as well as the Labyrinth in the Fayoum, and to open and enter a pyramid to discover its contents. He visited the temples at Denderah and Armant; the latter was later demolished, so his contemporary plan and description is of particular importance. He also visited the mummy-pits at Saqqara, which contained large numbers of birds buried in pots. Lucas claimed that this was a new discovery, although in fact they had been mentioned nearly forty years earlier by a German traveller, J. B. Vansleb, who had been instructed by Louis XIV's chief minister to travel to Egypt to copy the hieroglyphic inscriptions and to collect antiquities for the king. Lucas was not a scholar, and his books – three volumes of *Voyage dans la Turquie, L'Asie, Sourie, Haute et Basse-Égypte* (1719) – were prepared by others for publication in several languages. Nevertheless, Lucas demonstrated his ability both as a writer and an antiquarian, and showed that he had good powers of observation.

One of the most important travellers of this whole period was Father Claude Sicard (1677–1726), a French Jesuit who was professor at Lyons before going out to Syria as a missionary. In 1707, he moved to Cairo to become superior of the Jesuit Mission. He spent the rest of his life in Egypt where his main task was to convert the Copts to Roman Catholicism. However, as he had an excellent intellect and was an Arabic scholar, the Regent, Philippe of Orléans, ordered him to undertake a survey of the ancient Egyptian buildings and make plans of them.

He visited Upper Egypt four times, in 1708, 1712, 1720 and 1721, primarily to visit Coptic communities and attempt to convert them, but he also used this opportunity to explore and examine the ancient sites. He visited el-Ashmunein (the Hermopolis of the Greek period), which was very well-preserved at that time, although subsequently, in the 1860s, the buildings were demolished to provide materials for the construction of mills and factories.

Sicard was also the first modern traveller to identify the site of Thebes, and to confirm that the temples of Karnak and Luxor had been part of this ancient capital. He also correctly identified and described the Colossi of Memnon and the Ramesseum, the funerary temple of Ramesses II. In the Valley of the Kings, he was able to identify ten of the tombs from the total of forty-seven that are mentioned in the writings of the Classical author, Diodorus Siculus. In fact, it was the Classical descriptions of the monuments that formed the basis for Sicard's identification of the major sites. He was also the first European traveller who is known to have reached Aswan, and he left descriptions of Philae, Elephantine and Kom Ombo. Altogether, he visited twenty-four complete temples, over eighty decorated tombs and twenty principal pyramids, and amassed more information about ancient Egypt than any previous traveller. However, although he left a complete list of all the monuments he visited, his work was never published during his lifetime and, subsequently, no manuscript has ever been discovered. His reputation as an early traveller and scholar rests on a few surviving letters and a map prepared to accompany the missing manuscript. The map, now in the Bibliothèque Nationale in Paris, is very accurate for its date, and the surviving letters confirm his abilities as an accurate observer of his surroundings.

Another account, very well illustrated with maps and plates, was produced by the Reverend Thomas Shaw (1694–1751). He was an English traveller and antiquary who visited Egypt, Sinai and North Africa in the

1720s. His book, *Travels or Observations Relating to Several Parts of Barbary and the Levant* (1738), includes a description of his visit to the pyramids at Giza.

Two visits were made to Egypt by Dr N. Granger, a French physician from Dijon, who arrived in Cairo in 1730, at the invitation of his friend, the French consul. In the following year, he travelled through Middle and Upper Egypt, visiting the Fayoum, Beni Hasan, Abydos (where he discovered the almost complete Temple of Sethos I), Thebes, Edfu and other sites. An account of this journey was given in *Relation d'un voyage fait en Égypte en l'année 1730,* published posthumously in 1745. Granger also visited Cairo on a second occasion in 1733.

There is another important account of the monuments by the Reverend Richard Pococke (1704–1765), an English traveller and clergyman who made an extended foreign tour before he became Bishop of Meath in 1765. He visited Egypt in 1737–8, and went to Busiris and Saqqara in the north, and also travelled along the Nile to Aswan, Denderah and Thebes. At Thebes, he visited Qurna on the West Bank and viewed the Valley of the Kings, where he referred to 'many entrances into the rocks, which were probably of the nature of grottoes'. He also provided the first description of a decorated, private (non-royal) tomb, although he wrongly believed that these tombs were the dwelling places of the living, located underneath the 'king's palaces' (as he incorrectly identified the royal mortuary temples on the West Bank).

Pococke's clear plans of the tombs in the Valley of the Kings enabled later scholars to identify some as specific burial places of the Saite Period. It was Pococke's detailed and comprehensive descriptions of the sites and monuments that he had visited which made his book, *A Description of the East, and Some Other Countries* (1743–5), such an important account which provides much more detailed information than other contemporary records. It also preserves facts about the monuments which were later obliterated and had often disappeared altogether by the time that later full recordings were being made. Even in the mid-eighteenth century, however, he had occasion to comment on the damaged state of some of the monuments: 'They are every day destroying these fine morsels of Egyptian Antiquity, and I saw some of the pillars being hewn into mill-stones.'

Pococke had an important contemporary, Frederick Lewis Nordern (1708–1742), a Danish naval marine architect and traveller who was sent by the king of Denmark, Christian VI, to explore Egypt and produce an accurate account of the country. His expedition set forth in 1738 and continued for almost a year, in which time he managed to reach Derr in Nubia. His *Travels* (first published in 1751, and subsequently reissued several times and translated into French and German) was the first significant attempt to produce a comprehensive description of Egypt which made detailed information available both to scholars and to general readers. It was illustrated with his own excellent drawings and accurate plans of the monuments. When he arrived at Luxor a few days ahead of Richard Pococke, he was able to provide the earliest known reference in modern times to the private tombs on the West Bank, which he called 'grottoes'.

In the eighteenth century, the increased numbers of travellers who reached Egypt had the result of increasing an awareness of ancient Egyptian civilisation among both scholars and the educated public. In response to this interest, important, multi-volume works were produced, such as those published in 1719–24 by Bernard de Montfaucon and in 1752–64 by Baron de Caylus, a French antiquarian who travelled widely in Italy, Greece and the Near East. He acquired a great collection of antiquities, which formed the basis of his seven-volume publication, *Recueil d'antiquités égyptiennes, étrusques, grecques et romaines.*

Other instructive memoirs were produced by the great traveller James Bruce (1730–1794), who reached Egypt in 1768 and proceeded to sail up the Nile. Bruce came from Stirlingshire in Scotland, and was originally employed in a wine merchant's office in Portugal, but when he was twenty-four, after his wife's early death, he began travelling. He studied oriental languages, including Arabic, and made journeys through parts of North Africa, holding the post of British consul in Algiers for a time. He undertook archaeological and geographical investigations, and finally set himself the task of reaching the source of the Nile. When he travelled in Egypt, wearing Arab dress, he took the opportunity to examine the ancient monuments along his route. He visited Luxor and Karnak, and reached the Valley of the Kings in January 1769, where he repeated the error made by other travellers by identifying the caves in the mountainside as private dwellings. However, he discovered and cleared the tomb of Ramesses III in the Valley of the Kings, although its ownership was not identified at that time, since hieroglyphs had not yet been deciphered and the king's name could not be read. Subsequently, it was often referred to as 'Bruce's Tomb', in honour of its discoverer.

After Egypt, Bruce continued on his travels and explored Abyssinia, before returning to Aswan in 1772 and eventually arriving back in Britain in 1773. His memoirs, which he dictated, were published in five volumes in 1790, under the title *Travels to Discover the Source of the Nile*. Only one part of these is devoted to his description of Egypt, and he added little that was new about ancient Egyptian civilisation, although his memoirs provide a very informative travel narrative.

By the end of the eighteenth century, the study of ancient Egypt had reached a watershed. Many travellers and scholars had made extensive journeys throughout the country, and all the principal monuments above ground were known. In many cases, these had been correctly identified with the ancient sites. Some travellers had even engaged in archaeological exploration, at the tombs in the Theban necropolis opposite Luxor and at the pits containing the mummified birds at Saqqara.

The quantity of literature about Egypt and its ancient civilisation had also increased dramatically. In addition to the Classical accounts, there were now several well-informed, first-hand, contemporary descriptions by Renaissance travellers. These were often well illustrated and contained accurate information about the geography and ancient monuments, and increasingly, they came to replace the older travel books which had often repeated inaccurate information from earlier sources.

During the eighteenth century, a considerable antiquarian enthusiasm also developed which encouraged the great collectors who lived outside Egypt to try to obtain antiquities. This in turn led to an accelerated destruction of some of the Egyptian monuments, and to an avid quest for treasure which hastened the removal of ancient artifacts from Egypt. These objects were frequently separated from their archaeological contexts and, consequently, much information about their date, provenance and purpose was lost. However, on the other hand, these great collections of inscribed objects which were now being built up outside Egypt began to provide scholars with a considerable resource of material for their continuing studies.

One scholar, Georg Zoëga (1755–1809), produced important works which epitomised the best type of research carried out towards the end of the eighteenth century, in the years before hieroglyphs were deciphered. He was a Danish antiquarian and scholar who prepared a treatise on Egyptian obelisks, *De Origine usu Obeliscorum* (1797). He had secured the patronage of Cardinal Stefano Borgia (1731–1804), an Italian prelate whose Egyptian antiquities and Coptic codices eventually became the nucleus of the Egyptian collection in the Naples Museum. Zoëga learned the Coptic language and script to assist his attempts to understand hieroglyphs, and he made several important discoveries in recognising that the direction in which hieroglyphs faced within an inscription was significant, and that cartouche-shaped rings contained royal names.

It was customary for most Renaissance scholars to produce theories about the monuments (particularly the pyramids) and about hieroglyphs which are now regarded as ludicrous. In order that the study of ancient Egypt could develop and progress, and that these misconceptions could be corrected, it was now essential that scientific archaeology should replace the random treasure-seeking that was being carried out on behalf of wealthy clients and collectors, and that hieroglyphs and the related scripts of hieratic and demotic should be deciphered, so that the inscriptions on the monuments and artifacts could be read and understood.

The unlikely event which brought about the right circumstances for these developments to happen, and which provided the impetus for Egyptology to be established as an academic discipline, was the military adventure which Napoleon Bonaparte now embarked upon in Egypt.

CHAPTER VIII

THE DECIPHERMENT OF
EGYPTIAN HIEROGLYPHS

—— •◆• ——

There had been many attempts to decipher and understand the ancient Egyptian texts, but most scholars misconstrued the basic principle of hiero-glyphs and claimed that the signs were symbols, representing individual ideas. In reality, some of the signs (which we now call phonograms or 'sound-signs') were alphabetic and provided the individual sounds of a word, while others (ideograms or 'sense-signs') were placed at the ends of words to convey their meaning, but were never pronounced. This basic error in understanding how the hieroglyphs worked prevented scholars from realising that they were a written version of the language of ancient Egypt. Until this was appreciated, no progress could be made in reading the inscrip-tions in order to gain new knowledge about the history of the civilisation, the names and chronological order of the kings, the religious beliefs, and many aspects of daily life, including law, medicine and education.

Among the earliest writers to promote the concept of hieroglyphs as symbols were the Greeks Chaeremon and Horapollo, whose *Hieroglyphica* (written in the fourth century AD) was rediscovered in the fifteenth century. However, perhaps the most renowned exponent of this theory was the Jesuit scholar Athanasius Kircher (1602–1680). He left Germany, where he was professor of philosophy, mathematics and oriental languages at Wurzburg, and eventually became professor of mathematics at the Roman College (1635–43). He undertook studies in several fields, including the sciences, philosophy, oriental languages, and archaeology. He made notable contributions to the study of Coptic (which represented the final stage of the Egyptian language), including the translation of a Coptic–Arabic vocab-ulary that the traveller Pietro della Valle had brought back from Egypt. Kircher also wrote a series of books on Coptic, with information that proved valuable to scholars once hieroglyphs had been translated. His major work, in four volumes, was entitled *Oedipus aegyptiacus* (1652–4), and this generally created considerable interest in ancient Egypt. However, any assessment of his work is influenced by the fact that, because he continued to regard hieroglyphic signs purely as symbols, he was able to contribute nothing to the decipherment of the language. He attempted in vain to read the royal names and inscriptions on the obelisks which had been removed from Egypt and set up in the capital of the Roman empire.

Others who supported the symbolic theory of hieroglyphs included an English physician, William Stukeley, who was the founder (1741) of the first recorded Egyptian Society in London. He opposed the view promoted by some scholars that Chinese was derived from Egyptian hieroglyphs, but still claimed that the hieroglyphs were symbolic and therefore could not be understood completely. Among early scholars, only William Warburton (1698–1779), an English bishop and renowned scholar, did not subscribe to the symbolic theory. In his literary work entitled *Legation of Moses* (first published in 1738, and translated into French in 1744), Warburton included an essay on the decipherment of hieroglyphs which is considered to be the only study before Champollion's to recognise that hieroglyphs were a written language and that there was evidence of a correct procedure for reading the signs.

The symbolic theory still continued to hold sway, although a few individuals made some progress, among them the Swedish diplomat and orientalist, Johan David Akerblad (1763–1819), who had studied oriental languages and travelled in the Middle East. He made some initial progress in reading names and words in the demotic, but made no further advances because he wrongly concluded that demotic was an entirely alphabetic system.

The final discoveries in deciphering and understanding the structure of the Egyptian languages are attributed to an Englishman, Thomas Young (1773–1824) and to the French scholar, Jean François Champollion (1790–1832). Crucial to their work was the Rosetta Stone, a black basalt stone with three horizontal panels, each inscribed in a different script: Greek, hieroglyphs and demotic. The Greek was readily translated, and scholars immediately recognised that the content of this inscription was repeated in the other two texts. It was a decree by the priesthoods of Egypt in honour of King Ptolemy V Epiphanes (196 BC), issued in Greek, the official language of Egypt at that time, in hieroglyphs, the ancient sacred writing of Pharaonic Egypt, and in demotic, a cursive script derived from hieroglyphs and used for business and legal matters.

The stone had originally been set up in Memphis, but it was moved, at an unknown date, to Rosetta on the coast of the Delta, where it was discovered in 1799, as an indirect result of Napoleon Bonaparte's military adventures in Egypt. Its geographical location made Egypt significant both to Britain and to France. Egypt was an important stage on the overland route to India, where the British were anxious to protect their empire. Also, the weak rule which the Turkish sultans exercised over Egypt might have encouraged the British to attempt to invade the country. It was not difficult, therefore, for Napoleon Bonaparte, the youthful and ambitious French leader, to persuade his government of the need for military intervention. The French encountered few difficulties in defeating the local Mamluke army in the Delta and at the Battle of the Pyramids, and they proceeded victoriously into Upper Egypt and pushed the Egyptian troops further south into Nubia.

However, the British quickly recognised the danger that the French presence posed in Egypt, and were soon engaged in attempts to drive the French out. Nelson's fleet successfully defeated the French at the Battle of Aboukir, and was able to cut off Napoleon's army, and then, by joining forces with the Turks, the British finally managed to remove the French from Egypt.

As part of this confrontation, the French had attempted to consolidate the coastal defences of the Delta against the British navy. As they were gathering stones to strengthen the ramparts at Fort Rachid, near Rosetta, one of the men dug up a stone which was carved with strange inscriptions. He showed this to Lieutenant Pierre François Xavier Bouchard, an engineer and officer who was in charge of the exercise. Bouchard commendably realised that the stone might be of interest and importance, and sent it to the Institut d'Égypte that Napoleon had established in Cairo, as a centre where scholars and scientists from a variety of disciplines could share their knowledge through seminars and discussion. The Rosetta Stone thus came to the attention of experts who were soon aware of the crucial role it could play in the decipherment of the Egyptian scripts. Copies of the inscriptions were made and circulated among scholars, and although initial progress was slow because of the continuing belief in the symbolic theory of the hieroglyphs, the stone was to be of the utmost importance to Champollion, the man who would ultimately decipher hieroglyphs. At the time of its discovery, however, he was still a child living in France.

The Rosetta Stone was eventually ceded to Britain in 1801, as part of the conditions of capitulation reluctantly accepted by the French. In fact, it was the only study item that they relinquished to Britain. Once it had been transported to London, it was placed in the British Museum as a gift from King George III. Under the original terms of capitulation, the French had agreed to hand over to the British all the natural history specimens and antiquities that their Commission had collected in Egypt, but finally they refused to transfer these items, stating that they would prefer to burn them. The British general eventually conceded to their demand, and with the exception of the Rosetta Stone, members of the Commission sailed from Alexandria in 1801 with their study collections intact.

The discovery of the Rosetta Stone now provided the first real opportunity to decipher two stages of the Egyptian language – hieroglyphs and demotic. As already indicated, scholars had considered hieroglyphs to be symbols or representations of individual ideas rather than the written version of the language used and spoken in Egypt for thousands of years. They did not understand that some signs were alphabetic, spelling out the sounds of a word, whereas others were placed at the end of a word to determine or depict its meaning. These had been the flawed conclusions of Kircher, Stukeley and others, whose main contribution had been to arouse and maintain interest in the process of decipherment. An important concept

– that the cartouches or ovals seen in the hieroglyphic texts contained royal names – was recognised by a number of scholars. Abbé Barthélemy (1716–1795), a French antiquarian and numismatist, was the earliest to identify this fact in a paper he published in 1761, although the discovery is also attributed to Joseph de Guignes (1721–1800), who was a professor of Syriac at the Collège de France, and to the Danish scholar Georg Zoëga (1755–1809). Zoëga produced a corpus of all the hieroglyphic signs he could find, but he made no attempt to decipher them. However, he introduced a systematic approach to the study of hieroglyphs, and made the important discovery that the direction in which the hieroglyphs faced in an inscription was significant (ultimately, it was discovered that this indicated the direction and order in which the individual hieroglyphs should be read). Strange ideas were still prevalent, however, and scholars such as Guignes produced outlandish theories, claiming that there was an association between Egyptian and Chinese characters, based on his belief that China had been an Egyptian colony.

Even with the discovery of the Rosetta Stone, there was no immediate breakthrough in deciphering the texts. Nils Gustaf Palin (1765–1842), a Swedish diplomat, produced several books on the Rosetta Stone, and claimed that he had deciphered the hieroglyphs, but his work made no real contribution. Another Swedish diplomat, Johan David Akerblad (1763–1819), made some progress although, as already indicated, he still supported the symbolic theory of hieroglyphs. He obtained a copy of the Rosetta Stone (wax impressions had been taken and were circulated among scholars in various European countries), and attempted to decipher the demotic text by identifying in it the proper names he had read in the parallel Greek text. He was able to identify some other alphabetically written words in the demotic, and he discovered the cardinal numbers in the hieroglyphic text. Akerblad had prepared himself for this work by studying oriental languages, as well as Coptic, the final stage of the Egyptian language; also, he had previously attempted to decipher Phoenician and runic inscriptions. He held a post at the consulate in Paris, and used this opportunity to study in 1801–2 with the leading French scholar, Silvestre de Sacy, to whom he addressed his *Lettre à M. de Sacy* (1802) in which he described the important advances he had made in deciphering demotic. However, he made little further progress, mainly because he clung to the erroneous idea that all demotic writing was exclusively alphabetic.

Silvestre de Sacy (1758–1838), a leading French orientalist who eventually became Champollion's professor, was himself engaged in studies on the Rosetta Stone. He worked on the Greek and demotic texts and, in 1802, he concluded that certain sign groups in demotic could be identified as the names of Ptolemy and Alexander, which were easily recognisable in the Greek. Thus, he is credited with being the scholar who could first read Egyptian words in the ancient texts, but despite his intellectual capacity, he made no further progress because, like others, he held on to the mistaken concept that the Egyptian system was purely alphabetic and did not include ideograms. Perhaps de Sacy's most significant contribution was to encourage others to work on the decipherment of Egyptian, and in particular, to support the studies undertaken by Young and Champollion.

Before considering the major contribution made to the decipherment of Egyptian by Young and Champollion, it is necessary to briefly outline the various scripts that were developed and used in Egypt over a period of some three thousand years. The earliest form, hieroglyphs, developed from pictorial representations of the flora, fauna, buildings, people, and objects of daily use that surrounded early man and formed his world. All writing systems originally evolved from pictorial images of the features which comprised primitive man's environment; in this simplest form of written communication, each picture conveyed a particular idea. Such pictures would be easily recognised and identified by anyone, regardless of his place of origin or spoken language, as they conveyed universal ideas (for example, a picture of a man catching an animal would be a widely understood image). However, later there developed the need to convey a spoken language (words or sentences) in a written form, and the pictographs then came to have specific meanings, and were used to convey a distinctive language with its own grammar and vocabulary. Their meaning and message could now only be understood by the people who spoke and used that particular language. This system had already been developed and was in use in Egypt before the beginning of Dynasty 1 (*c.* 3200 BC). Evidence for this is provided by palettes, inscribed with hieroglyphs, which archaeologists have found and dated to this period.

The way in which writing first developed in ancient Egypt remains obscure. One proposal is that the concept of writing was introduced to Egypt from elsewhere, perhaps as early as *c.* 3400 BC. It has been argued that foreign immigrants (the so-called 'dynastic race') may have entered Egypt from another area, perhaps Mesopotamia, and brought the idea of writing with them, as well as the techniques of monumental brick architecture and advanced skills in arts and crafts.

In Mesopotamia (the 'Land between Two Rivers', the Tigris and Euphrates), the Sumerians, who arrived there *c.* 3500 BC, had founded an early civilisation centred around the idea of the city-state. An important factor in these people's success had been the introduction and use of a writing system which could be employed to organise commercial and economic, as well as literary and religious activities. This writing system was similar to Egyptian hieroglyphs in that it used pictographs (pictures of things or objects), but whereas Egyptian hieroglyphs always retained their truly pictorial form (they were written with pen and ink on papyrus or wood, or carved in stone), Sumerian pictographs became stylised and bore little resemblance to the objects from which they were derived. This was because they were engraved with a reed stylus on clay tablets, which produced lines and wedge-shaped (cuneiform) impressions on the wet clay. The cuneiform writing system was later employed for writing the languages of the other peoples – Akkadians, Babylonians and Assyrians – who conquered and replaced the earliest inhabitants of the region.

The influence of cuneiform on Egyptian hieroglyphs remains unclear; there is evidence of cuneiform texts that pre-date Egyptian hieroglyphs but this may simply be due to the difference in the writing materials used in Egypt and Mesopotamia. Clay tablets would probably have survived better than the papyrus and wood on which the earliest hieroglyphic texts would have been written. However, the earliest hieroglyphs that have been found in Egypt clearly represent purely Egyptian forms and objects, and it is evident that a distinctive writing system had been developed prior to this date. If Egypt did adopt the idea of writing from elsewhere, it was presumably only the concept which was taken over, since the forms of the hieroglyphs are entirely Egyptian in origin and reflect the distinctive flora, fauna and images of Egypt's own landscape.

As already stated, the Egyptians used a system that combined phonograms (sound-signs that spelt out the word, that is, an alphabetic system) with ideograms (sense-signs that were added to the spelled-out word, to depict its meaning). They never developed an entirely alphabetic system. In the various attempts made at decipherment prior to the work of Young and Champollion, little headway was made because the scholars mistakenly supported the idea that the Egyptian scripts were either symbolic or represented a purely alphabetic system; they did not realise that the system was more complex, and combined both sound-signs and sense-signs.

In fact, although hieroglyphs had developed from pictures and always retained their pictorial form, they provided a script which was used for over 3,000 years to convey a fully developed language which had its own syntax, grammar and vocabulary. However, although hieroglyphs had this basic and undisputed function, they were also regarded as an art-form, and the Egyptians used them to decorate monumental wall surfaces in tombs and temples, as well as objects and papyri. Scribes were trained to acquire skills in producing and copying hieroglyphs, and much attention was devoted to the shape and detail of the individual forms, as well as to the symmetry of their arrangement on the wall or page.

The importance of the written word went beyond the visual aspect, however, and texts were inscribed not only on surfaces where they would be beautiful and impressive to the viewer, but they also adorned funerary goods and tomb walls that were intended to be visible only to the deceased owner. The real significance of the written word was that it provided a channel through which concepts or events could be 'brought into existence'. The Egyptians believed that scenes and accompanying texts in temples and tombs could be 'brought to life' by means of magic, so that they would continue to have existence for eternity. A ritual known as the 'Opening of the Mouth Ceremony' was performed by a priest when the tomb or temple was handed over to its owner on the day of burial or the occasion of the consecration of the temple for the resident deity. Once the priest had touched the figures in the wall-scenes and the statues in these buildings, it was believed that they, together with the inscriptions, would be activated for the owner's use throughout eternity. Thus, the primary purpose of writing was to provide a vehicle through which certain magico-religious objectives could be achieved. Of course, writing was also decorative and it had literary and commercial functions, but the Egyptians always retained a firm belief in the magical and religious significance of writing.

Although hieroglyphs were retained for religious and secular uses, and inscribed on papyrus, wood and stone for more than 3,000 years, there was evidently a need for a simpler script which could be employed on a regular, daily basis. Early in the historical period, a cursive script was developed in which each character was a simplified version of a hieroglyph. This script, known today as hieratic, was widely used alongside hieroglyphs until *c.* 800 BC, for religious, literary and business texts. It provided a more rapid alternative to hieroglyphs which were largely, although not exclusively, retained for formal or religious texts. Since hieratic texts were inscribed with pen and ink, it was customary to use papyrus, and cheaper writing materials such as leather, wood, and ostraca (potsherds and limestone flakes) for these texts. Occasionally, hieroglyphic and hieratic texts are found together on the same object. By *c.* 700 BC, another cursive script we call demotic had evolved from the hieratic; for nearly a thousand years, business, legal and literary inscriptions were written in demotic, while hieratic continued to be employed for religious texts, and hieroglyphs were mainly used for monumental stone inscriptions.

With the conclusion of the pharaonic period, when Alexander the Great of Macedon conquered Egypt in 332 BC, the country came to be ruled by a line of Macedonians (the Ptolemaic dynasty) before it became part of the Roman empire in 30 BC. During this Ptolemaic era, many Greeks took up residence in Egypt, and Greek was imposed as the language of governance and administration. The Egyptian language continued to be employed by the indigenous population, and hieroglyphs were still used for religious inscriptions, especially for the decoration of the Egyptian temples. This stage of the language and writing, which has its own particular grammatical forms and vocabulary, is known as 'Ptolemaic Egyptian'.

Finally, when Egypt (as part of the Roman empire) adopted Christianity, the last stage of the Egyptian language, known as Coptic, replaced the use of hieroglyphs, hieratic and demotic. Coptic preserved the ancient Egyptian language but it was now written in Greek characters, with a few new signs taken from the demotic which served to convey the Egyptian sounds that were not present in Greek. Coptic was important for several reasons. First, as the script used for the translation of the biblical texts in Egypt, it was of great significance in the early development and spread of Christianity throughout the country. Second, it played an important role in defining the identity of Egyptian Christianity, and it remained the language of the Copts (Egypt's Christian population) for many centuries after the Arabs invaded the country in the seventh century and introduced Arabic as the official language. Today, the Copts still retain Coptic as the liturgical language of their Church.

In addition, Coptic played a particularly important role in the decipherment of the ancient Egyptian scripts. Once scholars recognised that it did indeed form the final stage of the ancient Egyptian language, it was possible to use Coptic to gain insight into some aspects of Egyptian grammar and vocabulary. When knowledge of the earlier scripts gradually disappeared, Coptic survived as the last remnant of the Egyptian language system. Also, Coptic was of particular significance because, whereas hieroglyphs, hieratic and demotic preserved only the consonantal sounds of each word in their written forms (like early Hebrew and Arabic), Coptic conveys both the consonant and vowel sounds through use of the Greek characters. Thus, Coptic can be used to 'fill out' the skeleton of the language which occurs in the hieroglyphic, hieratic or demotic texts, because it can provide clues about the pronunciation of individual words. However, the Egyptian language was in use for over 3,000 years, and there would have been many changes and variations in pronunciation over that period, so any modern vocalisation can only provide an approximation of how the words were spoken in antiquity.

Today, since Egyptologists sometimes need to be able to pronounce words in the texts, they have developed a convenient and generally accepted system of vocalisation. This addition of vowels to the consonants is, however, artificial, and merely provides scholars with a working system; it probably bears little resemblance to the way in which the ancient Egyptians actually pronounced their words, although the evidence provided by Coptic has undoubtedly played an important part in this reconstruction and vocalisation of the language.

The decipherment of Egyptian hieroglyphs is generally attributed to the French scholar Champollion, but there is little doubt that an Englishman, Thomas Young, also made a significant contribution. Young (1773–1824) was a physician and physicist who had a wide-ranging knowledge of many languages, and had also carried out medical and scientific research, where his major discoveries were made in the area of physiological optics. However, in middle age he became involved in the decipherment of hieroglyphs, and, having obtained copies of the Rosetta Stone, he applied his formidable talents to studying the texts.

He made several major discoveries. First, he recognised that some of the demotic characters, as well as linear hieroglyphs and hieratic, were derived from hieroglyphs; this was significant because it showed that demotic was not an entirely alphabetic script (an erroneous conclusion that had prevented other scholars from making much progress). It enabled Young to be the first to realise that the Egyptians used both phonograms (alphabetic signs) and ideograms (sense-signs) alongside each other in the same text.

Earlier researchers had independently and correctly stated that the cartouches (ovals) seen in the hieroglyphic inscriptions contained the names of kings and queens. In the parallel Greek inscription on the Rosetta Stone, Young was able to read the name of Ptolemy and also that of Berenice on another royal decree. He then attributed the known sound values of the Greek letters in those names to the hieroglyphic signs within the cartouches. He was able to compile a list of thirteen signs in these two names; six of these identifications were ultimately proved to be correct, three were partly right, and four were wrong, but he was able to use this list to read the name of Ptolemy in the hieroglyphic text.

He had further success in identifying some other names in the hieroglyphs, and he correctly suggested that there was a close relationship between hieroglyphs and Coptic, thus opening up the possibility that study of Coptic inscriptions might provide insight into the earlier texts. He began a comparison of Greek, demotic, and hieroglyphs, and indicated correctly that demotic was a cursive form of hieroglyphs.

His conclusions had a profound influence on the decipherment of hieroglyphs, although his contribution has probably never received full acknowledgement. Financial problems and ill-health finally forced him to curtail his interest in Egyptology. He had received encouragement in his work from such notable scholars as de Sacy, but de Sacy later decided that it was Champollion's results which were correct, and supported his system and conclusions.

Jean François Champollion (1790–1832) was born at Figeac in France. He was the son of an impoverished bookseller. From an early age, he showed evidence of a remarkable intellect. He taught himself to read when he was five years old, and had learnt at least nine oriental languages by the age of seventeen, in order to prepare himself for his self-appointed task of deciphering Egyptian hieroglyphs. This interest may have been aroused by a visit he made when he was eleven to the mathematician Jean Baptiste Fournier, who had accompanied Napoleon's expedition to Egypt. In addition, his elder brother, Jacques Joseph Champollion, who was a historian with a great enthusiasm for Egyptology, undoubtedly had a profound effect on his life. He was responsible for his young brother's early education, and later devoted much of his life to his work, assisting with the process of decipherment and with the preparation and publication of research.

Champollion the younger became a student at the Lyceum in Grenoble where, when he was only 16, he presented a paper at the Academy, in which he claimed that Coptic was the same as the ancient language of Egypt, although it was written in different characters. His considerable talents were further developed when, in 1807, he began his studies in Paris with Sylvestre de Sacy. By 1818, he was appointed to the Chair in history and geography at the Royal College at Grenoble, and in 1831, the first Chair in Egyptian history and archaeology was created for him at the Collège de France in Paris.

Champollion's earliest attempts at deciphering Egyptian hieroglyphs were unsuccessful, because he initially supported the old belief that they were purely symbolic in purpose, and concluded that the writing was not alphabetic; both demotic and hieroglyphic characters, he claimed, were representative of 'things' and did not express 'sound-values'. This view (which opposed Young's claim that some signs were alphabetic) was presented in his *De l'écriture hiératique des anciens Égyptiens* (1821). However, he soon changed his opinion on this, and adopted Young's alphabetic approach, since he discovered that this enabled him to make considerable progress in deciphering the royal names. He now began systematically to compile a hieroglyphic alphabet.

In September 1822, Champollion made a discovery when he was studying copies of an inscription from the temple at Abu Simbel, which was a major breakthrough in his search for the key to reading the hieroglyphs. By using the phonetic principles which had been established by Young's work and his own endeavours, he found that he could identify the name of the Egyptian pharaoh, Ramesses II. He suddenly realised that the Egyptians had used hieroglyphs not only to write the names of foreigners who ruled their country, such as Ptolemy, but also for the names of their own kings. Thus, for the first time, he recognised that many hieroglyphs were in fact phonetic, and not symbolic as previously supposed, and this was a landmark in his understanding of the writing system. He presented his conclusions in his famous *Lettre à M. Dacier, secrétaire perpétuel de l'Académie Royale des Inscriptions et Belles-Lettres, relative à l'alphabet des hiéroglyphes phonétiques* (1822).

This was followed in 1824 by the publication of Champollion's *Précis du système hiéroglyphique,* which claimed that Egyptian hieroglyphs combined both phonetic and ideographic signs – the breakthrough in understanding the writing system which had eluded so many scholars for hundreds of years. This revelation would ultimately enable the Egyptian texts to be read and translated in the same way as any other language. In later works – his *Grammaire* (1836–41) and *Dictionnaire* (1841–4) – Champollion further underpinned and developed his initial discoveries.

However, Champollion's claim to have deciphered Egyptian hieroglyphs did not receive universal acceptance. Gustavus Seyffarth (1796–1885), a German archaeologist who later emigrated to America, was the most extreme example of those who opposed Champollion's theories. He claimed that he himself was the true decipherer of hieroglyphs, and that all theories after Young were based on Seyffarth's own conclusions. Essentially, he believed that the Egyptian language and scripts were based on ancient Coptic which he claimed was derived from Hebrew; he stated that the Egyptian alphabet had 630 hieroglyphic signs, and that it had no ideograms. As Champollion's ideas gained credibility, Seyffarth found it increasingly difficult to get his work published, and he left his academic post and emigrated to America in 1854.

However, other scholars also questioned Champollion's claims, and the extent to which he had appropriated (but not given credit to) Young's earlier discoveries was also disputed. His system was only finally acknowledged and accepted in 1837, when the great German scholar, Karl Richard Lepsius (1810–1884), wrote a letter to Champollion's pupil, Ippolito Rosellini, in which he stated that he accepted Champollion's conclusions. Lepsius also added his own comments and corrections to Champollion's work, and emphasised the close relationship of some grammatical elements in Egyptian and Coptic. Lepsius followed his major expedition of 1842–5 by a visit in 1866 to the Suez area and the eastern Delta, where he discovered the bilingual Decree of Canopus at the site of Tanis. This stone was important because it enabled Egyptologists to check and confirm the results which, until then, had been achieved by using only the texts on the Rosetta Stone and the system proposed by Champollion.

Gradually, therefore, Champollion's system gained acceptance. Even while scholars were debating the rival systems, Samuel Birch (1813–1885), Keeper of Oriental Antiquities at the British Museum, supported Champollion's results and ensured that they gained credibility in Britain. To provide further evidence for his discoveries Champollion needed access to more examples of inscribed material, and so, in 1824, he examined the collection built up by Bernardino Drovetti in Turin, and also visited other collections in museums in Rome, Naples, Florence and Leghorn. Finally, in 1828, he led an expedition to record the monuments in Egypt.

Champollion's brief life ended in January 1832, when he suffered a stroke. His unfinished books were prepared for publication by his brother, and other scholars now continued the language studies he had initiated. His contribution to Egyptology is unequalled, in that it enabled the modern world to read one of the earliest and most comprehensive literatures, and to gain an insight into the ideas and beliefs of people who lived some 5,000 years ago. His discoveries ensured that the literature could now be studied in addition to the architecture and the artifacts.

Despite this great achievement, however, the decipherment of hieroglyphs at first made little impact beyond the confines of the scholarly world, and it now became the task of a few men to carry Champollion's ideas forward. One of the most significant of these was Vicomte Emmanuel de Rougé, a French nobleman who first studied Semitic languages but later was inspired by reading Champollion's *Grammaire*. He subsequently pursued studies in hieroglyphs, and eventually succeeded to Champollion's Chair in 1860. He has been credited with developing Champollion's own work by establishing the rules of Egyptian philology. He was the first to set in place the correct system for reading and translating the hieroglyphic texts, and to be able to translate a continuous text; in addition, he was able to demonstrate the scope and quality of the hieratic texts in Egyptian literature, with his own studies of two texts, the *Tale of Two Brothers* and *Poème de Pentaur*. His work built on the foundation of Champollion's successful decipherment, and he also ensured that his knowledge was conveyed to the next generation of students. One of these was François Chabas (1817–82), a French wine-merchant, who began his studies under de Rougé in 1852. He worked on his own, refusing the offer of the Chair when de Rougé died, but he corresponded with many leading philologists of the day, and was able to make important contributions to the study of texts.

Elsewhere, other scholars were making major discoveries. An Irish clergyman, the Reverend Edward Hincks (1792–1866), produced work of considerable significance in the fields of Egyptian hieroglyphs and cuneiform texts, although his contribution has not been fully recognised. From 1833, he wrote many articles, including one entitled 'An attempt to ascertain the number, names and powers of the letters of the hieroglyphs, or ancient Egyptian alphabet, etc.' (1846). He discovered that Egyptian grammar was Semitic in form, and he was also the first person to use a correct system of transliteration for Egyptian. Transliteration is the process of identifying and transcribing individual hieroglyphs into modern written characters. It is an essential stage in translation, providing scholars of different nationalities with a common system of dealing with hieroglyphs, before they translate the text into their own language (French, English, German and so forth). Thus, Hincks made a major contribution to the process of decipherment and translation, by providing the first systematic approach to working through the various stages of identifying, transliterating, and then translating the hieroglyphs.

Meanwhile, a group of German scholars now began to have a major impact on the development of philological studies. Heinrich Brugsch (1827–1894) became Professor of Egyptology at the University of Göttingen in 1867, and Director of the School of Egyptology in Egypt which had been established by the Khedive. Brugsch was honoured by the Khedive with the titles of bey in 1870 and pasha in 1881. He made great contributions in many areas of Egyptology, but was regarded as one of the pioneers of grammatical studies in hieroglyphs and demotic, establishing a systematic approach to these language studies. His most important works were the *Grammaire démotique* (1855), and the *Dictionnaire hiéroglyphique et démotique* (1867–82) which was published in seven volumes and is noteworthy because, unlike many other dictionaries, it was the work of a single author.

The career of Adolf Erman (1854–1937) marked the beginning of the so-called 'Berlin School' in Germany. He was Director of the Egyptian and Assyrian departments in the Berlin Museum from 1884 to 1914, and Professor of Egyptology in the University of Berlin from 1884 to 1923. His work was extremely important in establishing a methodology for the teaching of grammar and philology. His students included U. Wilcken, Georg Steindorff, Walter Crum, Georges Jéquier and G. A. Reisner, and his influence on modern philological study was probably unparalleled. In particular, he pioneered scientific philology, and was the first to classify the ancient Egyptian language according to three periods, namely Old, Middle and Late Egyptian. Through Erman's teaching, the work of his students, and his many publications, the Berlin School came to have a profound effect upon the development of Egyptian philology and Egyptology generally. His published works included his *Ägyptische Grammatik* (1894), which also appeared in three later editions, and studies in Coptic and in literary texts. His anthology *Die Literature der Ägypter* (1923) was translated into English as the *Literature of the Ancient Egyptians* in 1927, and still enjoys popularity today as a sourcebook for studying and enjoying the wide range of Egyptian literature.

However, his greatest work was undoubtedly the dictionary which he edited jointly with H. Grapow. The *Wörterbuch der ägyptischen Sprache* was published in five volumes (1926–31) and a further two volumes were added in 1957–63; in addition, there were five volumes of *Belegstellen* (references). The *Wörterbuch* was based on material collected by many scholars; Herman Grapow (1856–1967), who had studied with Erman and Steindorff and became Honorary Professor in the University of Berlin in 1928, was responsible for amassing the data for this dictionary, which was arranged on slips (*Zettel*). Grapow assisted with the sorting and arrangement of one-and-a-half million *Zettel* and, in addition, ensured that the publication of the volumes of the dictionary was successfully completed. He also worked on his own studies, making a particular contribution to research on ancient Egyptian medical texts. Others who assisted Erman with major projects, especially the *Wörterbuch*, included Hermann Ranke (1878–1953), Ludwig Borchadt (1863–1938) and Kurt Sethe (1869–1934). Sethe, who had studied with Erman, later became Professor of Egyptology at the University of Göttingen in 1900, and then succeeded Erman at the University of Berlin (1923). Sethe's achievements in Egyptian philology were considerable; he and Erman were regarded as the leading scholars in the field of Egyptian philology during this century, and Sethe's contribution has even been compared with that of Champollion or Brugsch.

Sethe's reputation rests on the discoveries he made in many areas of philology, ranging from early dynastic texts through to demotic and Coptic. A major achievement was his collation and re-editing of the Pyramid Texts; he also collected and arranged a large number of historical texts, published as *Urkunden der 18. Dynastie* (1906–9), which provided scholars with access to a whole range of historical literature. His studies in Egyptian grammar were extremely important, and his most significant work was *Das aegyptische Verbum in Altaegyptischen, Neuaegyptischen and Koptischen* (1899–1902).

However, despite its outstanding contribution to Egyptology, the work of the Berlin School was not universally accepted. Karl Piehl (1853–1904), professor of Egyptology at Uppsala, Sweden, was engaged in his own study of texts of the Late and Roman periods, and he strongly opposed the methods of the Berlin School. Sir Ernest Wallis Budge (1857–1934), Keeper of Egyptian and Assyrian antiquities at the British Museum, collected papyri inscribed in many different scripts and brought them to the attention of many scholars, but his own translations did not incorporate the new grammatical theories which were being developed in Berlin. In another instance, the *Wörterbuch* project had a major impact on the work of Victor Loret (1859–1946), a French scholar who became Director-General of the Antiquities Service in Egypt (1897–9). In 1884, he had begun, singlehandedly, to produce the material for a dictionary, but when he realised that it would be superseded by the Berlin project, he began to rework the material for a thesaurus. His data, collected in twenty-one notebooks, was unpublished at the time of his death.

Although many great advances were made in the general area of Egyptian philology, some scholars chose to specialise in specific stages of the Egyptian language, or in the Greek texts that were being found in Egypt. These various scripts had their particular problems and difficulties, but groundbreaking work again ensured that the literature written in these scripts could be translated, and this in turn illuminated many aspects of Egyptian civilisation.

One of the earliest and most notable decipherers of hieratic was Charles Goodwin (1817–1878), a British judge who made many contributions to the study of hieratic texts; his most important work was published in *Cambridge Essays* (1858) under the title of 'Hieratic Papyri'. A Dutchman, Willem Pleyte (1836–1903), who became the Director of the Leiden Museum in 1891, published many hieratic papyri in museum collections in Leiden, Paris and Turin, and Georg Möller (1876–1921), Assistant Director of the Egyptian collections in the Berlin Museum, also undertook important studies on the hieratic texts and palaeography.

One of the most outstanding scholars, and a leading philologist in Britain, Francis Llewellyn Griffith (1862–1934) had taught himself the Egyptian language, and then proceeded to make major advances in several fields, including hieratic, demotic, Old Coptic and Meroitic. He was initially employed as an assistant in the Department of British and Medieval Antiquities in the British Museum but his first wife's father, Charles Timothy Bradbury, provided him with an income so that he could devote himself entirely to his studies. Eventually this financial support formed the basis for the endowment with which he established the Griffith Institute in Oxford, opened in 1939.

One of Griffith's most important works was his study of the collections of papyri which Flinders Petrie discovered and brought back from the town sites of Gurob and Kahun. There were over a thousand fragments, many no larger than 2.5 cm square, which Griffith painstakingly pieced together. They were inscribed in hieratic, and represented the legal, medical and veterinary, educational and religious archives of these communities. Written in different cursive scripts, they were difficult and laborious to transcribe and translate, but Griffith was able to publish the texts in three volumes (1897–8), and to provide new evidence about the customs of the people who lived in these towns.

He was also the leading demoticist of his time, and published a translation of the *Stories of the High Priests* (1900). However, his most significant achievement was to decipher the Meroitic script which had been evolved from Egyptian hieroglyphs by the inhabitants of a kingdom to the south of Egypt, whose capital was located at Meroë (third century BC–fourth century AD). Griffith's work was published in two parts (1911 and 1912), under the title of *Meroitic Inscriptions*.

Later hieratic studies have included Jaroslav Černy's specialised work on the hieratic script of the late New Kingdom. Černy (1898–1970) studied with Lexa (see page 86) at Prague and Erman at Berlin, eventually becoming Professor of Egyptology at Oxford (1951–65). When the French archaeologists excavated the royal workmen's town at Deir el-Medina, Thebes, they discovered a wealth of documentary evidence which Černy was invited to translate, and this has provided a new insight into the lives and working conditions of the royal necropolis workforce. Other hieratic studies and translations have been undertaken by Ricardo Caminos (1915–1992), and Georg Posener (1906–1988), who worked on the literary hieratic ostraca from Deir el-Medina (1934–80).

Demoticists have also made a significant contribution to our understanding of Egyptian civilisation. An early pioneer was Eugène Revillout (1843–1913), Professor of demotic, Coptic and Egyptian law at the École du Louvre in Paris. Although his methods and conclusions have been criticised, he copied most of the demotic texts available at that time, and made other scholars aware of their existence. Another leading demotic scholar was Sir Henry Thompson (1859–1944), who lectured at University College London, and in Germany Wilhelm Spiegelberg (1870–1930), lecturer in the University of Strasbourg, produced excellent work in this field. He and Griffith were the foremost demotic scholars in Europe; Spiegelberg published many texts and produced a demotic grammar. He also worked on hieratic texts and made major contributions to Coptic studies, including his authorship of a Coptic dictionary which was the standard publication for many years.

Other notable works were produced by František Lexa (1876–1960), Professor of Egyptology at Charles IV University in Prague, who published seven volumes of a demotic grammar (1938–50); by the Italian demoticist Giuseppe Botti (1889–1968), who undertook an important classification of the collection of hieratic papyri in the Turin Museum; and by Stephen Glanville (1900–1956), who produced the catalogue of demotic papyri in the British Museum.

In Coptic studies, scholars have consistently worked to achieve a better understanding of the grammar and to make the texts available for further study. At an early date, the British scholar, the Venerable Henry Tattam (1788–1868), became a leading figure who acquired a large quantity of Coptic manuscripts. One of Erman's students, Georg Steindorff (1861–1951), who became Professor of Egyptology in Leipzig where he founded an Egyptian Institute, was also a pioneer in this field. An outstanding philologist, he established the rules for the vocalisation of Egyptian, and also wrote a Coptic grammar (1894) which is still a standard work.

Another outstanding Coptic scholar, the Englishman Walter Crum (1865–1944), studied all texts then available to him, and produced the standard Coptic dictionary, published in six parts between 1929 and 1939. Walter Till (1894–1963), an Austrian who lectured at the University of Manchester, made further contributions to the study of grammar.

Finally, there have been studies on the Greek papyri found in Egypt, most notably by the papyrologists Bernard Grenfell (1869–1926) and Arthur Hunt (1871–1934). Both were professors of papyrology at the University of Oxford, and together they edited the famous Oxyrhynchus Papyri which had been excavated at the site of Oxyrhynchus and then brought back from Egypt.

Gradually, therefore, advances have been made in many areas of philological studies. Some language specialists have worked and contributed in several fields, while others have pursued more specific studies. As well as these general developments, some scholars have produced translations of important texts or standard grammars and reference books which have further advanced language studies. It would be impossible to include a comprehensive list here, but a few publications are of outstanding importance.

The Russian scholar Vladimir Golenischeff (1856–1947), Professor of Egyptology in the University of Cairo from 1924 to 1929, published many important literary papyri, including the Story of Wenamun and the Story of the Shipwrecked Sailor, making these examples of Egyptian storytelling available to the modern reader. Important publications of the funerary texts which provided insight into early religious beliefs and practices included those by Pierre Lacau (1873–1963), who produced a series of articles on the Coffin Texts. Later, Adriaan de Buck (1892–1959), a Dutch scholar who had studied under Sethe, provided a more extensive work on these texts. By the time of his death, he had edited six volumes (1935–61), and some of the translation and commentary had also been completed; the seventh and final volume was also ready in manuscript. In addition, de Buck published an *Egyptian Reading Book* (1944) that has been used by generations of students who are learning to translate hieroglyphs. Other major contributions were made by Raymond Faulkner (1894–1982) with his translations of the Pyramid Texts, Coffin Texts, and the Book of the Dead. He also published a widely used English and Middle Egyptian dictionary.

Some scholars have utilised the advances made in understanding the language to produce grammar books for students' use. For many years, Erman's *Ägyptische Grammatik* was a leading publication in this field, and later Étienne Drioton (1889–1961), Professor of Egyptian philology and Coptic language at the Catholic Institute of Paris, produced a grammar for his own students. He also worked on Ptolemaic texts, written in the stage of the language which was in use when Egypt was ruled by the Ptolemaic dynasty (*c.* 332–30 BC). Other major advances in the study of Ptolemaic Egyptian were made by Aylward M. Blackman (1883–1956), Professor of Egyptology at the University of Liverpool.

In 1924, Battiscombe Gunn (1883–1950), later professor of Egyptology at Oxford (1934–1950), published *Studies in Egyptian Syntax,* which helped to explain the verbal system. The leading philologist of a later generation, Hans Jacob Polotsky (1905–1991), Professor of Egyptian and Semitic linguistics at the Hebrew University of Jerusalem, made major contributions to the study of Egyptian and Coptic grammar, and provided new insight into the Egyptian verbal system with his research on second tenses. New studies from scholars in Germany have included the work of Wolfgang Helck (1914–1993), Professor of Egyptology at the University of Hamburg who, together with E. Otto and W. Westendorf, produced the *Lexikon der Ägyptologie* (1975–92).

However, for generations of English-speaking students of Egyptology, the grammar which has been instrumental in teaching Middle Egyptian is Sir Alan Gardiner's *Egyptian Grammar*, first published in 1927. Gardiner (1879–1963) had a major impact on British Egyptology in several areas. Although he wrote on historical and other subjects, his specialisation was in philology; he worked on hieratic texts on papyri and ostraca, in collections in the British Museum (Chester Beatty Papyri), Turin and Leiden, and his discovery that the Sinaitic script was an alphabetic link between the Egyptian hieroglyphic and Semitic alphabets was of great significance. Gardiner had been instructed in philology by Griffith in London, and he also lived for several years in Berlin, where he studied and worked with Erman, helping with the preparation and editorship of the *Wörterbuch*.

Because of his family's wealth, Gardiner was able to support himself so that he could devote his time to research. He was also in a position to finance some publications produced by himself and other scholars, and to employ assistants such as B. Gunn, R. O. Faulkner and H. W. Fairman to work on his philological projects.

Since Champollion first published his decipherment of Egyptian hieroglyphs in the early 1820s, great advances have been made in understanding the Egyptian language in all its stages, including recognition that hieratic, demotic and Coptic were all stages in the development of one language which initially had been expressed in hieroglyphs, and that the Egyptian and Semitic grammar systems were closely linked.

Painstaking work has gradually enabled scholars to establish the rules by which the texts can be read, developing the systems of transliteration and vocalisation which are still key elements of current studies. Slowly, generations of Egyptologists have been able to increase knowledge of the various stages of the language, and produce the grammars and dictionaries which are the tools of the trade for research and instruction. Particular groups of scholars, such as the immediate successors of Champollion's legacy and the members of the Berlin School, have produced significant results, but those working on a more individual basis have also achieved notable successes. The study of Egyptian philology and grammar has flourished because, through an exchange of ideas and students, it has always been possible to adopt an international approach and to encourage co-operation between scholars from many countries.

Today, although scholars still try to achieve a better understanding of the grammar and syntax and to produce improved translations, it is accepted that the language in all its various forms can be read, understood and appreciated as readily as many other languages. Our ability to gain access to the written thoughts and ideas of the ancient Egyptians, even after a period of thousands of years, cannot be overestimated. The contribution made to this by Champollion and his successors remains one of the cornerstones of the study of ancient Egypt.

CHAPTER IX

RECORDING THE
MONUMENTS

——— •◆• ———

The first objective of Egyptologists was to understand and translate the language. In order to make advances in this field, it was necessary to acquire new texts, and therefore, from the earliest period, scholars set out to make exact copies of the inscriptions on the monuments. Since so many of the inscribed, standing monuments were exposed above ground, it was possible for Egyptologists to produce good copies of the inscriptions, and these epigraphic studies preceded scientific excavation. By the beginning of the twentieth century, techniques to record and publish the monuments had been satisfactorily developed.

Major projects have included the recording of tomb scenes and scenes and inscriptions on temple walls. In recent times there have been emergency rescue surveys of the monuments of Nubia, undertaken to record the buildings which would become submerged as the result of the construction of the two major dams at Aswan. There have been advances in recording techniques, although the painstaking methods developed in earlier years have never been superseded by photography, since the eye and knowledge of the epigraphist are vital to ensure that the recording of the inscription is as accurate as possible. Epigraphy is an essential tool of Egyptology, as it records for posterity the detail on the monuments which is often subsequently damaged or lost.

Epigraphic and recording surveys have sometimes been undertaken by large expeditions, but individual scholars and copyists have also made major contributions in this field. The earliest scientific survey of the country was undertaken as part of Napoleon's attempt to conquer Egypt. A Scientific and Artistic Commission was established to accompany Napoleon's military expedition. It consisted of 167 scientists and technicians, who were given the task of gathering cultural and technological information so that Napoleon would be well prepared to colonise and govern the country. Although his military objectives were never achieved, the Commission had a profound effect upon Europe's knowledge of the ancient civilisation of Egypt, and this marked the beginning of a scientific awareness of the monuments and artifacts.

The *savants* who were recruited for this task included antiquarians, writers, musicians, artists, mathematicians, astronomers, chemists, engineers, mineralogists, naturalists, botanists, surgeons and physicians. To assist them in their research, they took a library and a wealth of scientific equipment to Egypt. During the three years they spent there, the scholars visited different areas of the country, mapping the land and amassing information about the flora and fauna, the irrigation system, the customs of the population, and the monuments and antiquities. They also acquired a large collection of specimens and antiquities, which, with the exception of the Rosetta Stone – eventually ceded to the British as a spoil of war – was transported back to France. The intellectual ambitions of the French expedition were further emphasised by the establishment in Cairo of an Institut d'Égypte, where scholars met to read papers at seminars and to exchange ideas. Napoleon was the vice-president of this institute, which sought to foster an interdisciplinary approach and to encourage research in Egypt.

The work of the Commission had a profound effect upon the development of Egyptology, and was instrumental in establishing the concept of studying ancient Egypt as a scientific discipline. The information amassed by the expedition provided the basis for one of its major achievements – the publication in nineteen volumes of the *Description de l'Égypte* (1809–29).

Individual members of the commission also produced publications. The most famous was Vivant Denon (1747–1825), a French nobleman, scholar and artist who accompanied the expedition as an ex officio member. He travelled through the Delta and Upper Egypt, recording the monuments in detail. Many of the drawings were used to illustrate the *Description de l'Égypte*; most of the editing and production of this was undertaken by Edmé François Jomard (1777–1862), another member of Napoleon's Commission. However, Denon also used this material in his own account of the journey, published as *Voyage dans la Basse et la Haute Égypte* (1802). This very successful book was published in several editions and translated into English and German; it had a considerable influence on the European perception of ancient Egypt and inspired widespread scholarly interest in this new discipline. Denon also made a collection of antiquities during his stay in Egypt, and after his return to France, he became director-general of museums, and played an important part in developing the collections at the Louvre.

The next great expedition to Egypt, led by Champollion and his pupil, Rosellini, in 1828, included fourteen members, among them architects and artists. Ippolito Rosellini (1800–1843) became the founder of Egyptology in Italy. On this expedition he led a group of scholars and artists from Tuscany. The aim was to produce the first systematic survey of the monuments, and to copy the inscriptions in order to provide material for further language studies. It was this expedition that provided scholars with the first opportunity to be able to read the inscriptions correctly when they visited the monuments, since the recent decipherment of hieroglyphs provided them with the key to understanding the language. Royal names on the monuments could now be read correctly and identified for the first time,

Figure 11 Harvesting scenes from Theban tombs, showing reaping, gleaning, winnowing, threshing and recording the bushels. After J. G. Wilkinson, *A Popular Account of the Ancient Egyptians* (1878), II: pl. 367.

enabling the scholars to attribute the monuments to their correct historical and chronological contexts.

The expedition remained in Egypt for seventeen months, travelling as far south as Nubia. Ultimately, the scholars returned with large quantities of antiquities and many portfolios of drawings which formed the basis for Champollion's *Monuments de l'Égypte et de la Nubie d'après les dessins executés sur les lieux, sous la direction de Champollion le jeune* (1835–47). This appeared in four volumes which were published by Champollion's brother, after his death. The material brought back by the expedition also provided the basis for Rosellini's great work on the monuments of Egypt and Nubia, published in 1832–44. Nestor l'Hôte (1804–1842), a French draughtsman who accompanied the expedition, produced drawings which enhanced both of these great publications.

Attempts to decipher hieroglyphs and the need to acquire new texts for translation had also inspired the efforts of individual travellers. William John Bankes (1786–1855), an English traveller, collector and antiquarian, travelled in Egypt, Nubia and Syria between 1815 and 1819. He reached Abu Simbel, where he drew the temples and copied inscriptions, and he brought back an obelisk from Philae with a bilingual inscription. This had originally been acquired by the archaeologist Giovanni Battista Belzoni for the collector Henry Salt, but Bankes transported it to England and set it up in the park of his home at Kingston Lacy, Wimborne, Dorset. He disagreed with Champollion's decipherment results, and used the key to hieroglyphs that had been produced by Thomas Young, together with other inscriptions including a Greek text on the pedestal of his Philae obelisk, to read the name of Cleopatra which was written in hieroglyphs inside a cartouche.

Indeed, Bankes was only one of a number of serious travellers and scholars who went to Egypt in the nineteenth century in order to copy and study the inscriptions. The political background to this development was set by Egypt's new ruler, Mohammed Ali, who opened up the country to western ideas and technology and encouraged the involvement of foreigners. Mohammed Ali was a man of humble descent who came orig-inally from Macedonia, but his outstanding if ruthless personality enabled him to rise through the ranks of the Turkish army in Egypt, in which he served. Following the Anglo-Turkish defeat of Napoleon's expedition, Egypt was handed back to the Turks, and in 1805, Mohammed Ali became the virtually independent ruler of the country, although he still owed nominal allegiance to the Turks.

Mohammed Ali pursued an active programme of modernisation, real-ising that this was the only way forward for Egypt. An essentially medieval country was rapidly pushed forward into the nineteenth century: European technology was introduced, and the ruler welcomed foreign engineers, merchants, and diplomats. He also ensured that, for the first time, Egyptians

Figure 12 Views of the Great Gallery inside the Great Pyramid at Giza, showing its impressive architectural features. From *Description de l'Égypte* (1809–29), V: pl. 15.

were sent abroad to study medicine, engineering, agriculture and industry, so that they could return to develop these areas in their own country. New industries were established, such as cotton production, factories were built, and an infrastructure was put in place which allowed the irrigation system to be developed and communications to expand throughout the country.

This new political atmosphere, and the upsurge in economic and commercial opportunities for foreigners, provided the setting for travellers, epigraphists, archaeologists, antiquity dealers, and tourists to visit and even stay in Egypt in a way that had not been possible previously. With regard to treasure-seeking and excavation, this new openness led to problems, but travellers and epigraphists were not seriously affected by the restrictions which the government soon found it necessary to impose on excavations and collectors of antiquities.

During this period, travellers were still discovering spectacular sites. Frédéric Cailliaud (1787–1869), a French mineralogist, went to Upper Egypt and Nubia in 1816. Subsequently, he was employed by Mohammed Ali to find the emerald mines referred to by the Arab historians, and he travelled in Upper Egypt and followed the routes to the Red Sea; his discoveries included quarries and sites in the Eastern Desert and in the Kharga Oasis in the Western Desert. In 1819, he returned to Egypt and visited the Siwa Oasis, but his greatest journey in 1821 took him along the Nile, to the southern city of Meroë in Nubia. This was the subject of his account entitled *Voyage à Méroé au Fleuve Blanc, 1819–22* (1823), which was produced in four volumes of text and three volumes of plates. Around the same time, the Swiss traveller Johann Ludwig Burckhardt (1784–1817) was travelling in the East. A scholar who had studied Arabic at Cambridge, he adopted the name of Sheikh Ibrahim and wore Arab dress when he travelled around Arabia and Nubia. One of his greatest discoveries was the lost site of Petra, and during his travels in Egypt (1812–17), he was the first European to report the discovery, in March 1813, of the temples at Abu Simbel. The Italian Belzoni (see pp. 113–16) read his account and eventually visited this site.

Several independent travellers and copyists now made a major contribution to the work of recording the monuments. The most important of these was Sir John Gardner Wilkinson (1797–1875), who has been called the founder of Egyptology in Britain. Wilkinson had become interested in the decipherment of hieroglyphs and, with the support of a small private income, he was able to take up the study of the Egyptian language. He first went to Egypt in 1821, and remained there for twelve years; his travels took him to Nubia and the deserts, and he twice made the journey to the Second Cataract on the Nile. He learnt Arabic and Coptic to assist him with decipherment of hieroglyphs, and he made his own independent advances in these studies, recognising royal names and arranging rulers and dynasties in a correct order.

However, perhaps his most significant contribution to Egyptology was the survey he undertook of all the main sites in Egypt and Nubia; unlike the great expeditions of Napoleon, Champollion or Lepsius, this was carried out singlehandedly. Although the commissions of Napoleon and Champollion had visited and recorded a wealth of monuments, Wilkinson's survey covered sites that had never previously been documented. These included Tell el-Amarna, where he produced the first plan of Akhenaten's city. At Hawara he made one the of the earliest identifications of the

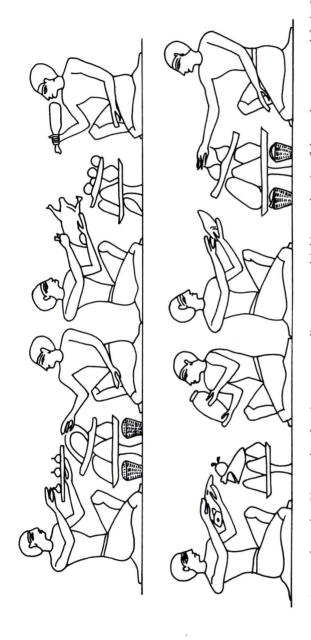

Figure 13 A scene from the Giza tombs, showing men at a dinner party, drinking, and eating fish, poultry, meat and fruit. John Gardner Wilkinson was the first Egyptologist to describe social activities and crafts in ancient Egypt. After J. G. Wilkinson (1878), I: pl. 196.

Figure 14 The pyramids at Gebel Barkal in the Sudan. From Cailliaud's *Voyage à Méroé au Fleuve Blanc* (1823).

Labyrinth, the religious and administrative complex attached to the pyramid of Amenemhet III at Hawara. At Beni Hasan, he was the first to make detailed drawings of the tomb scenes, and in Nubia he surveyed and mapped Gebel Barkal, following the path of Cailliaud, who had visited the site earlier. Because he had no government funding, he could not undertake the vast expeditions which some other scholars were leading, and so restricted his excavation activities to Thebes (in 1824 and 1827–8), where he attempted the first comprehensive survey of the region.

He recorded the wall paintings in the Theban private (non-royal) tombs which he had excavated, making detailed copies of the inscriptions, reliefs and paintings, and because he was one of the few artists who understood the conventions of Egyptian art, he was able to produce accurate results. His last visit to Egypt was made in 1855–6. Throughout the whole period he spent there, Wilkinson was able to provide a unique epigraphic record. His many drawings and coloured reproductions of tomb wall-scenes are probably unequalled in quality, and they preserve information about tombs which have since been damaged or destroyed or have become inaccessible. His copies are now in the Bodleian Library in Oxford where they provide a unique resource.

Illness forced Wilkinson to return to England in 1833, but this gave him the opportunity to use the information from the archaeological sites, papyri and inscriptions to produce three important books. In 1835, he published his first popular book, *The Topography of Thebes and General Survey of Egypt*, which was intended as a guidebook. This, however, included new information about his excavations at Thebes and the map of the area which

Figure 15 Tomb scenes from Beni Hasan, showing girls playing ball games. After J. G. Wilkinson, *A Popular Account of the Ancient Egyptians* (1878), I: pl. 217.

he had made (he was the first Egyptologist to produce a comprehensive plan of the ancient sites there).

Subsequently, he published *The Manners and Customs of the Ancient Egyptians* (1835), which brought him great scholarly and popular acclaim; it held its position as the best general account of ancient Egypt for nearly fifty years, and led to a knighthood for Wilkinson in 1839. The book, which appeared in three volumes, was the first serious study to use Egyptian evidence – derived from Wilkinson's own notes and drawings – rather than the accounts provided by Classical authors. With his own primary source material, he wrote the most comprehensive description of Egyptian civilisation, concentrating on daily life, religion and culture rather than political history and chronology. Although he used his original and scholarly research (mainly the tomb-scenes which illustrated many aspects of daily life), Wilkinson was a writer who very effectively produced his information in a way which appealed to a popular readership. For the first time, he described ancient Egyptian civilisation in terms of subjects, such as the social classes, architecture, furniture, arts and crafts, religion, and daily activities. Today, this is not an unusual approach, but at a time when the authors and editors of the great expeditions were describing their discoveries under the headings of sites, Wilkinson broke new ground in utilising his data to provide a comprehensive and easily understandable account of the ancient Egyptian civilisation. His *A Popular Account of the Ancient Egyptians* was published posthumously in 1878.

The early nineteenth century was a time of great activity for epigraphists in Egypt. A contemporary of Wilkinson, Robert Hay (1799–1863), first toured the Middle East in 1824, having briefly visited Alexandria in 1818. Hay was of Scottish descent and had independent means, so he was able to follow his interest in the Egyptian monuments, making drawings, plans, and copies of the inscriptions. In 1824–8 and 1829–34 he travelled through Egypt, amassing an invaluable collection of drawings and plans of the monuments which are kept today in forty-nine volumes in the British Museum, together with his letters and diary. Hay was accurate and systematic in his approach, and his collection is of great importance because it preserves details of the monuments which have subsequently been damaged or lost. Hay also employed various artists and scholars to accompany him and assist with the work. These included Joseph Bonomi (1796–1878), a British sculptor and draughtsman of Italian origin, who went to Egypt with Hay in 1924 and remained there for nine years. As an artist, Bonomi had a wide knowledge of Egyptian painting and he was also an excellent draughtsman. He helped Burton with his *Excerpta Hieroglyphica* (see below), was responsible for preparing the illustrations for Wilkinson's *Manners and Customs*, and also worked for Lane (see below).

James Burton (1788–1862), a British Egyptologist and traveller, started his career in Egypt as one of the foreign experts brought in by Mohammed Ali to modernise the country. His task was to search for sources of coal as part of the Geological Survey of Egypt. However, he met Wilkinson and travelled with him in the Eastern Desert in 1824, and then, the following year, he pursued his growing interest in Egyptology and accompanied another Englishman, Edward Lane, in a journey up the Nile. He helped to excavate tombs at Thebes, and published *Excerpta Hieroglyphica* (1825–8). During his travels in Egypt, he produced many accurate and skilful drawings and plans of monuments which remain important records; they are now in the British Museum.

Another contemporary, the British Arabic scholar Edward William Lane (1801–1876), went to Egypt in 1825 and then made journeys up the Nile in 1826 and 1827. He produced quantities of drawings and notes, but his most important contribution to Egyptology was the publication in 1836 of *Manners and Customs of the Modern Egyptians*. This described the lives of the contemporary Egyptians and complemented Wilkinson's study on ancient Egypt.

In the mid-nineteenth century, the Prussian expedition (1842–45) took place. This last of the great epigraphic and archaeological surveys was led by the German Egyptologist Karl Richard Lepsius (1810–1884), who is generally regarded as the foremost Egyptologist after Champollion. The expedition went up the Nile as far as Meroë, having initially explored the pyramid area near Memphis and the non-royal Old Kingdom tombs, which provided information about the daily lives of the ancient Egyptians. In the Fayoum, Lepsius sought out the location of Lake Moeris (now known as the Birket Qarun) and excavated the Labyrinth, producing stratified drawings of the site. In Middle Egypt, he visited Tell el-Amarna and the Middle Kingdom tombs, and the expedition ultimately proceeded through Nubia, reaching Napata and Meroë. On his return journey, Lepsius visited Sinai, where he found the inscriptions left by the ancient labourers sent to work in the copper mines in Wadi Maghareh and Serabit el Khadim; from these inscriptions, he was the first scholar to be able to demonstrate the nature and extent of Egyptian activity in this area.

This expedition, better equipped than any previous project, included skilled artists and draughtsmen, and was well prepared to achieve its main objectives of surveying the monuments and collecting objects. It also provided the source material for the publication of the largest Egyptological work ever produced, the *Denkmäler aus Aegypten und Aethiopien*. The first twelve volumes, which consisted of plates, appeared in 1859, while the text was published after Lepsius's death in a further five volumes (1897–1913) by Édouard Naville and others, using the notes left by Lepsius. The *Denkmäler* was the first accurate publication of a wide range of monuments, and included copies of inscriptions and wall scenes of every major site. Lepsius's expedition and subsequent publication was the last comprehensive topographical survey of the Egyptian monuments. The importance of the expeditions undertaken by Napoleon, Champollion and Rosellini, and Lepsius should be emphasised, because they provided original material which could be studied by scholars to increase existing knowledge about language studies and also about the historical and religious background of the civilisation. Additionally, their work preserved information about the monuments which were sometimes subsequently damaged or lost, and they increased people's general awareness of the wealth of the Egyptian heritage.

However, although these great expeditions undoubtedly played a crucial role in the development of the subject, they produced what were essentially superficial catalogues of the monuments which did not include any of the evidence provided by small objects such as tools, weapons, papyri, articles of everyday use, pottery and jewellery. Future studies in Egyptology, however, would pay increasing attention to the excavation of sites and to the artifacts that were found there, while more specialised topographical and epigraphic studies of particular sites or areas would replace the large-scale surveys.

Lepsius himself sent many Egyptian antiquities back to Germany, where, in 1846, he was appointed Professor at the University of Berlin. In 1865 he became Keeper of the Egyptian collection at the Berlin Museum. His illustrious career was of great significance, not only because of his own achievements but also because of the crucial support he gave to Champollion's system of deciphering hieroglyphs. In his letter to Rosellini (see page 81) he stated that, having studied all the counter-claims being proposed at that time, he nevertheless believed that the system proposed by Champollion was the correct one. This opinion persuaded Egyptologists that Champollion had indeed found the correct solution, and led to general acceptance of his theories.

In the years following Lepsius's expedition, several individuals made further contributions. Prisse d'Avennes (1807–1879), the French Egyptologist regarded as a pioneer in the subject, first went to Egypt in 1827 and was appointed as an engineer and a lecturer in military schools there. From 1836 to 1844, he set out on a project singlehandedly to copy the Egyptian monuments, and this resulted in the largest series of illustrations compiled by a Frenchman since Champollion's own work. Meanwhile, Johannes Duemichen (1833–1894), a German Egyptologist who became Professor of Egyptology in the University of Strasbourg, was one of the first to attempt to record complete monuments. He made frequent visits to Egypt from 1865 onwards, to copy inscriptions and texts which he subsequently published. However, the standard of epigraphic work undertaken at this time was variable, and less accurate results were achieved by Philippe Virey (1853–1920), who became a member of the French Archaeological Mission in Cairo in 1884 and copied the scenes and inscriptions in the Theban tombs. This work was published in the Mission's *Mémoires*.

The concept of recording complete monuments, pioneered by Duemichen and de Rochemonteix (see page 104) was now developed by Jacques de Morgan (1857–1924), a Frenchman who became Director-General of the Egyptian Antiquities Service in 1892–7. He initiated a *Catalogue des Monuments*, intended to include all the extant monuments in Egypt. Although the first three volumes of this were published (1894–1909), and included a comprehensive study of the Temple of Kom Ombo, the project was too ambitious and was not continued.

The next major initiative was the foundation of the Archaeological Survey of Egypt as part of the work of the Egypt Exploration Fund (later Society). The idea of an archaeological survey that would send trained archaeologists, Egyptologists and surveyors to Egypt to map, plan, photograph and copy the most important sites and monuments, in order to preserve and record this heritage, was the result of a campaign which had been started in England in the late nineteenth century.

The survey was led by Francis Llewellyn Griffith, then a young and promising scholar of Egyptology. He believed that, with the support of the Egyptian government, it would be possible to survey all the sites in Egypt, producing an index of the monuments and describing each ancient city as a whole, with a detailed account of its tombs and temples, rather than extrapolating information about architecture, scenes and inscriptions, and publishing this material separately. The time he allotted to this task was two years. The whole concept was over-ambitious, but it did set in motion a survey which continues until the present day. Griffith set out new criteria for studying the ancient buildings which involved not only recording existing monuments and seeking for new ones, but also using written sources, such as the accounts of earlier travellers, as a valuable background for this project.

The first members of the survey team were George Willoughby Fraser (1866–1923), a civil engineer, and the young Egyptologist Percy Newberry (1868–1949). On Newberry's advice, the original plan to survey a large area in Middle Egypt was replaced by an exhaustive study of a much smaller area that included the Middle Kingdom tombs at Beni Hasan, where the painted wall scenes would be copied and recorded. This work commenced in 1890, and was published in 1893 and 1894. It was important because it exemplified the principles laid down by Griffith, which were comprehensive publication of all monuments at a site and reference to all available earlier recording or documentation. The survey continued its early work at many other locations, including Deir el-Bersha, Deir el-Gebrawi, Tell el-Amarna and Meir.

The Archaeological Survey was also significant because of the quality of the artists who were engaged on its projects. Howard Carter (1874–1939), the British Egyptologist who later discovered and excavated the tomb of Tutankhamun at Thebes (see pp. 145–6), first went out to Egypt in 1891 to join Newberry at Beni Hasan as a member of the Archaeological Survey, and he produced the drawings for the publications of Beni Hasan and Deir el-Bersha. He joined Édouard Naville as draughtsman at Deir el-Bahri, where he worked (1893–9) at Hatshepsut's temple. With other artists, he copied the scenes and inscriptions there, and his drawings are included in the six volumes of *The Temple of Deir el Bahari* (1895–1908), published as excavation memoirs by the Egypt Exploration Fund. In this work in particular, he demonstrated that he was a copyist of considerable ability.

In 1898, the British Egyptologist Norman de Garis Davies (1865–1941) first went out to Egypt to join Flinders Petrie (see Chapter X) at Denderah, and was subsequently employed as surveyor by the Archaeological Survey. He had originally trained as a Congregational minister, and his interest in Egyptology started during his ministry at Ashton-under-Lyne, where he became acquainted with Kate Bradbury, who later married Francis Llewellyn Griffith. Norman de Garis Davies was an outstanding copyist, not only because he was an excellent draughtsman, but also because he had gained far-reaching knowledge of Egyptian archaeology and an awareness of the language, which helped him to understand the art. Under the editorship and direction of Griffith, Davies spent a number of years recording tombs at Saqqara, Sheikh Said, Deir el-Gebrawi, Tell el-Amarna and Thebes. These were published in ten volumes of the *Archaeological Survey Memoirs*, for which he prepared both the plates and the text. He perhaps achieved his greatest results at Tell el-Amarna, where he copied all the non-royal tombs and the boundary stelae of the city; this material was published in six volumes (1903–8), and for this work he was awarded the Leibniz medal of the Prussian Academy of Science in 1912.

In 1907, Davies had married Nina Cummings (1881–1965), a British artist and copyist who trained at the Slade School of Art and the Royal College of Art in London. A visit to Alexandria in 1906 had started her enthusiasm for Egyptology, and following their marriage, Norman and Nina de Garis Davies went to Thebes, where they worked for over thirty years for the Theban Expedition of the Metropolitan Museum of Art, New York. Norman Davies was commissioned to record scenes in principal non-royal tombs at Thebes, and they both retained their links with the Egypt Exploration Fund, and worked on *The Theban Tomb Series* (1915–33) which was edited by Sir Alan Gardiner. Nina de Garis Davies also spent periods working at Tell el-Amarna (1925–6) and Beni Hasan (1931–2), and two volumes of her work were published as *Ancient Egyptian Paintings* in 1936.

The partnership produced some of the finest results ever achieved in copying tomb paintings. Nina Davies's work in particular set new standards in copying line and colour, while her brushwork most closely followed the work of the original artists. Her innovative techniques included the use of egg tempera rather than just watercolour, and one of her greatest skills was her ability to record the colours as accurately and closely to the original as possible. This task was undertaken long before colour photography was used to record whole monuments, and so the consistency she managed to produce in her colours was particularly valuable because it preserved accurate information about these scenes, which was not otherwise available. Her work, which followed in the tradition of Burton, Hay, Wilkinson and Carter, made a very valuable contribution to the technique of copying ancient Egyptian paintings.

Aylward Manley Blackman (1883–1956), who became Professor of Egyptology in the University of Liverpool (1948–56), succeeded Davies as surveyor for the Archaeological Survey in 1911. He had previously worked as a member of the University of Pennsylvania expedition to Buhen (1909–10), and from 1911 to 1915 he recorded the Nubian temples of Biga, Dendur and Derr, as part of the major project to preserve scenes and inscriptions in an area which was now threatened by the lake created by the construction of the first Aswan dam. In his work for the Archaeological Survey, Blackman made full-scale tracings of scenes in the Old and Middle Kingdom tombs at Meir in Middle Egypt, which had been badly damaged, although his work there was interrupted by the First World War. His material was published in the four volumes of *The Rock Tombs of Meir* (1914–24); two further volumes were added in 1953. The fourth volume (1924) also marked the final stage of the survey carried out on the monuments in Middle Egypt.

Further work commenced at Abydos in 1925–6 (see page 105), and after the Second World War (when the activities of the Survey had been suspended), a new era emerged when Ricardo Caminos and other scholars contributed studies on the graffiti and the historical and religious inscriptions found in the sandstone quarries and nearby buildings at Gebel es-Silsila. Also, through the association of the Egypt Exploration Society with Brown University, Providence, Rhode Island, Caminos was able to copy scenes and inscriptions at various sites, as part of the Nubian Rescue Campaign, undertaken to preserve evidence which was threatened by the construction of the High Dam at Aswan. This included the recording (1960–64) of the temples at Buhen, Semna and Kumma, and the rock inscriptions and shrines at Qasr Ibrim.

The Archaeological Survey has fulfilled many of its early objectives, although its original aim – to provide an all-encompassing study of the monuments of Egypt – was over-ambitious. However, by concentrating on particular sites and areas, it has preserved much information which otherwise would have been lost. Although there is still an urgent and ongoing need to record those monuments which have never been copied or published, the Survey has been successful in establishing principles which have laid the foundation for continuing work and in developing new standards and techniques for epigraphic studies.

Other epigraphic projects have concentrated on perfecting techniques which preserve, as accurately as possible, the details of scenes and texts which are found on the monuments. Two of these projects were established to record entire temples: the monuments at Medinet Habu at Thebes and the Temple of Sethos I at Abydos. In order to understand the temples of Egypt, Egyptologists have had to record their architecture, scenes and inscriptions, and then attempt to understand and interpret their history, and religious and ritual use. Unlike many of the tombs, these massive buildings were never entirely covered by sand, and therefore did not require extensive excavation; however, early travellers were often unable to identify them correctly because they were either half-buried in the sand, or had been turned into churches, or local inhabitants were using the temple interior as a place to build their own dwellings.

The task for Egyptologists has been to clear and reclaim these monuments, and to restore their architectural features wherever necessary, and then to preserve and record the wall scenes and inscriptions. Many of these temples were visited, described, and, wherever possible, identified by early travellers and the great epigraphic expeditions. Subsequently, they were cleared and partially excavated by the early archaeologists, which gave copyists and epigraphists the opportunity to record the scenes and inscriptions. Finally, translation of these inscriptions has enabled Egyptologists to identify the divine and royal ownership of each temple, to understand the history of the building, and to reconstruct the ritual and other uses of all the areas and chambers within the complex. Epigraphic studies of the temple walls, covered with scenes and inscriptions, form one of the richest sources for interpretation of the temple.

The work of the artist David Roberts (1796–1864) provides information about the appearance of many of the temples which were still partially submerged when he first visited Egypt in 1838–9. A Scottish artist who began his career painting stage sets, Roberts travelled throughout Egypt and the Holy Land, recording the monuments and scenes of contemporary life in drawings and watercolours. This material formed the basis for a series of magnificent lithographs which appeared in his two publications, the three volumes of *Egypt and Nubia* (1846–9), and *The Holy Land, Syria, Egypt and Nubia* (1842–9). The detail he captured so successfully in the lithographs gave his work a realism which was only surpassed by photographic records such as Frith's *Egypt and Palestine* (1858–63).

However, these general surveys of the temples were soon expanded to include specific studies of individual monuments. Maxence de Rochemonteix (1849–1891), a French nobleman, was one of the first to record a complete temple. On his second visit to Egypt in 1877, he began work on the Temple of Edfu, which he published in 1892. The study of Edfu, a temple dedicated to the god Horus built and decorated between 237 and 57 BC, was continued by another French scholar, Émile Chassinat (1868–1948), who was responsible for completing and publishing the project in fourteen volumes (1892–1934).

Other major epigraphic projects on temples of the Graeco-Roman Period included the study undertaken on the unique 'double' temple at Kom Ombo, dedicated to the gods Sobek and Haroeris, which was published by Georges Legrain (1865–1917) in association with de Morgan and by the Swiss archaeologist, Gustave Jéquier (1868–1946). The Temple of Esna, dedicated to the ram-headed god Khnum, has scenes and inscriptions which date to the early centuries AD; here, Serge Sauneron (1927–1976) made a detailed study of the temple and its religious rites, publishing the material in several volumes between 1959 and 1982. Finally, two other French scholars, Chassinat and François Daumas (1915–1984), published the Temple of Hathor at Denderah in a series of volumes brought out between 1934 and 1978.

These monumental publications all served to increase knowledge about individual temples and also, more generally, about the rites and festivals associated with temple worship. There are two further projects which are of particular importance, not only because they recorded major temples, but because they developed epigraphic techniques which marked significant advances in this field.

The first was the publication of parts of the Temple of Sethos I at Abydos. This temple of Dynasty 19 has many unique and original architectural and ritual features, and preserves the most complete set of wall-scenes depicting the daily temple ritual, the essential element in the function of an Egyptian temple. Here, the skilfully executed wall reliefs are unsurpassed in beauty, and much of the original colour of the paintings still survives. When the Archaeological Survey transferred its fieldwork from Tell el-Amarna to Abydos in 1925–6, in order to concentrate on recording the Osireion, the strange subterranean building at the rear of the Sethos temple, it was suggested that the Survey should also make a photographic record of the two nearby temples of Sethos I and his son, Ramesses II.

Although this project achieved good results, it soon became evident that these magnificent reliefs required a different approach which would involve the production of a series of line-drawings based on the original photographs. Amice M. Calverley (1896–1959), an artist who had been persuaded to develop her skill for archaeological drawing by Sir Leonard Woolley, joined the project in 1928. Her initial work, which included coloured reproductions of some of the finest of the painted reliefs, was highly regarded by the leaders of the Archaeological Survey. Seeking additional funding to produce a more elaborate publication which would do justice to the quality of the scenes and to Miss Calverley's work, the Egyptologists turned to John D. Rockefeller Jr, who visited Abydos with Professor James Breasted in 1928–9. He was readily persuaded to finance the publication, as a joint project between the Egypt Exploration Society and the Oriental Institute of the University of Chicago.

Miss Calverley worked at Abydos until 1950, and in 1930, Myrtle Broome (1888–1978), a British artist and former student of Flinders Petrie and Margaret Murray, went out to assist her in the work of recording the temple. The scenes and inscriptions copied during those years formed the core of a magnificent publication, in four volumes, entitled *The Temple of King Sethos I at Abydos* (1933–58). A fifth and final volume will eventually complete this study. The large format of the individual volumes, the quality of the colour plates, and the standards set by the epigraphic work resulted in a publication of the highest quality. The financial support provided by Rockefeller was crucial to its continuation and success.

The wealthy American philanthropist, John D. Rockefeller Jr (1874–1960), had become interested in Egyptology through his contact with James Henry Breasted (1865–1935), an American Egyptologist who held the first Chair of Egyptology in America, becoming professor of Egyptology and Oriental history at the University of Chicago in 1905. Between 1919 and 1924, Breasted received an annual grant from Rockefeller, with which he founded the Oriental Institute at Chicago; in 1924, he also established Chicago House at Luxor as the Institute's field-station. One of the Institute's main areas of research was to salvage and record standing monuments. From 1930, Chicago launched a major epigraphic survey of the temples of Medinet Habu. Over the next forty years, this survey experimented with techniques to develop a system for copying large areas of temple wall surfaces. Under H. H. Nelson (1878–1954), field director of the Epigraphic and Architectural Survey at Luxor from 1924 to 1947, and Uvo Hölscher (1878–1963), a German archaeologist and architect who worked at Medinet Habu for eleven years, new standards were set in place for copying and publishing temple reliefs. Their publications (*Medinet Habu* (1930–70) and other volumes) display the combined skills and expertise of Egyptologists, architects, draughtsmen and photographers, and provide the most detailed record yet produced of a major Egyptian temple complex.

Useful work has also been carried out to record the existence and location of tombs. For example, at Thebes (Luxor), Alan Gardiner and Arthur Weigall produced a listing of 409 non-royal tombs on the West Bank, in *A Topographical Catalogue of the Private Tombs of Thebes* (1913). They identified the tombs with the official number that had been allocated to them by the Antiquities Service, and subsequently, other scholars have added further tombs to this list. However, the most ambitious and important topographical study to date was started by Francis Llewellyn Griffith. The settlement he received from his first wife's father not only enabled him to pursue his own studies but also formed the basis for the endowment he left to build and maintain the Institute of Near Eastern Studies at the University of Oxford. This was built after the death of his second wife in 1937 and, as the Griffith Institute, was opened in 1939. In addition to a substantial financial endowment for maintenance, the institute also received Griffith's fine Egyptological library and papers. It was well equipped to provide the base for producing an extensive topographical bibliography.

Griffith himself had prepared bibliographies from 1829 onwards, and fully recognised the importance of recording monuments and their inscriptions in a systematic manner. In effect, this was a special development of the grand scheme of surveying and copying the standing monuments that the Archaeological Survey had tried to establish, although, in this case, the topographical bibliography would be funded from Griffith's own resources. From 1924, Rosalind Moss (1890–1990), a former student of Griffith, became editor of this work which, as *The Topographical Bibliography of Ancient Egyptian Hieroglyphic Texts, Reliefs and Paintings*, has had the onerous and ongoing task of recording (according to their location in Egypt) all the known inscribed monuments and objects still in place at the sites or held in museum collections. From the beginning, the material has been organised for publication in a series of volumes which cover the various areas of Egypt, and today the work continues at the Griffith Institute, where new or revised material is prepared and added to the *Bibliography*. At first, Rosalind Moss collaborated on this project with another of Griffith's students, Bertha Porter (1852–1941); subsequently, she worked with another British bibliographer, Ethel Burney (1891–1984), with whom she travelled to sites and museums in Egypt, the Sudan, Europe and America, to gather information for the *Bibliography*.

The importance of early records in helping modern archaeologists to rediscover 'lost' monuments is well exemplified by the work which has been carried out since the 1970s by the joint Egypt Exploration Society/Leiden Expedition at Saqqara. The main aim of this expedition was to gain new evidence about the history of the burial area associated with Memphis during the New Kingdom, particularly from the reigns of Tutankhamun to Ramesses II. At Thebes (Luxor), which remained the religious capital throughout the New Kingdom, the temples and tombs have been studied and partly documented since the days of the early travellers. However, by comparison, Memphis, which was the administrative capital in the later New Kingdom, has survived very badly; its proximity to Cairo ensured that the buildings of Memphis were extensively raided and dismantled for use in the construction of the later Arab capital. In recent years, the Egypt Exploration Society has initiated a detailed study of the Memphis area, with the aim of producing the first comprehensive plan of a large ancient Egyptian city. This has involved selective excavation of the site itself, as well as initial work at Saqqara, where the tombs of the government officials, priests, craftsmen and palace employees of this period are located.

The Saqqara Expedition decided to locate, excavate and record the tomb of one individual, Maya, the overseer of the King's Treasury in the reign of Tutankhamun, who was probably in charge of the building programme which accompanied the reinstatement of traditional religion after the death of the heretic pharaoh, Akhenaten. From documentary evidence and inscriptions, it was clear that Saqqara was an important necropolis at this period, but the exact location of these tombs had been lost. However, the records of pioneer Egyptologists and the existence of unprovenanced but inscribed blocks and statues in museum collections provided the impetus for the search.

As we have seen, expeditions in the nineteenth century recorded some monuments which have subsequently disappeared, either destroyed by natural or human agents, or simply covered up by sand. During his expedition to record the standing monuments of Egypt and Nubia in the 1840s, Lepsius visited the vicinity of the causeway of the Unas pyramid at Saqqara, and mentioned parts of several New Kingdom tombs; he also recorded the presence of wall reliefs in the courtyard of the tomb of Maya. His surveyor then marked the position of these tombs on a map of the area which provided the only indication of the location of Maya's tomb. However, some blocks from the tomb had also entered museum collections, and three statues of Maya and his wife Meryt were acquired by the Leiden Museum in the 1820s.

In this area of the desert, windblown sand has undoubtedly obscured many ancient buildings. Even Lepsius only glimpsed tombs which were mostly buried under the sand, and he was unable to determine the overall nature of the area. Originally, there would have been streets of tombs (now covered by sand), rather than the isolated monuments he saw. Using Lepsius's map, the surveyor of the modern expedition was able to identify the situation of Maya's tomb within a limited triangle, but due to a slight inaccuracy in the old map, the archaeologists missed this tomb. However, instead, they uncovered the long-lost tomb of Horemheb, commander of Tutankhamun's army. This was a very important find because, although the tomb was never used for Horemheb's burial (he later became king and was buried in the Valley of the Kings at Thebes), much of the superstructure of the Saqqara tomb was preserved, and its extremely fine relief scenes provide information about many aspects of life and religion at this period.

The expedition correctly concluded that Horemheb's tomb was the nucleus of a group of officials' tombs of the later New Kingdom, and subsequently, over several seasons, they had considerable success in discovering and excavating several of these monuments, including the tomb of Maya which had been the original focus of the expedition. The tomb of Tia, sister of Ramesses II, and her husband Tia, discovered in 1982, was an unexpected find, since it might have been expected that so close a relative to the king would have been buried at Thebes. Again, there was earlier documentary evidence about this tomb: the capstone had been published in 1737–9 in a collection of plates produced by Alexander Gordon, a Scottish traveller and writer, who brought the stone from Alexandria in 1722. The stone was last seen in the garden of Sir James Tylney Long in Essex.

The excavations have continued at Saqqara, and the expedition has taken the approach that all excavation should be accompanied by meticulous copying of the monuments and their scenes and inscriptions; thus, as the tombs are uncovered, the evidence is recorded in this way. This project has also demonstrated that the notes and records of earlier workers in the field, and museum collections, with their wealth of inscribed blocks, statues, stelae, funerary objects and papyri, can provide vital clues about the location and ownership of tombs which still await discovery.

In epigraphic studies generally, techniques used in earlier times, such as taking squeezes or making plaster casts of the wall reliefs and inscriptions, have been replaced by other, less intrusive and potentially destructive methods. The use of colour photography to record complete monuments has not been widely employed, because colour photography is not an entirely reliable method. There are problems regarding the long-term preservation of these records, and in particular, difficulties can be encountered in ensuring that the colours remain accurate in the future. It is the line drawings and coloured copies produced by the most skilful draughtsmen and artists in this field that have produced some of the most accurate and detailed records of the monuments, scenes and inscriptions. In some cases, a combination of techniques has produced excellent results as, for example, when the Oriental Institute of Chicago developed a method first proposed and introduced by Howard Carter. This involved photographing the large relief scenes on the monuments, and producing large prints on which the scenes and inscriptions were then inked in with permanent ink. The print was subsequently immersed in iodine solution, with the result that the photograph disappeared but the line drawing remained intact. Today, the enormous task of recording the monuments continues alongside the excavation of the archaeological sites, and remains a vitally important aspect of Egyptological studies.

CHAPTER X

EXCAVATING THE SITES

—— ·◆· ——

The decipherment of hieroglyphs was perhaps the most important advance in the history of Egyptology, but an almost equally significant development was the gradual evolution of archaeology from the pursuit of hidden treasure into a scientific discipline. Even in antiquity, robbers had ransacked tombs, and there is an account by the fifteenth-century AD Arab writer, Ibn Khaldoun, that treasure-seeking was so widespread that it was classified and taxed as an industry. Once Mohammed Ali had opened up Egypt to foreign influences in the early nineteenth century, and Champollion's decipherment of hieroglyphs had made Europeans aware of Egypt's rich heritage, there was a great intensification of treasure-hunting. Collectors sought a wide range of antiquities including small objects such as scarabs, amulets and papyri as well as coffins, mummies and large inscribed blocks cut from the walls of tombs and temples. These antiquities were required for museums and private collections, and dealers and collectors employed excavators to undertake treasure hunts which would provide them with spectacular pieces. In addition, wealthy travellers and tourists to Egypt sought out curios to take home as souvenirs.

This phase of Egyptology was played out against a background of rivalry and jealousy among European nationals who vied with each other to acquire substantial collections for their own countries. Diplomats and their agents were frequently involved in these activities, and national pride and the desire to possess the finest treasures were the driving force behind this earliest phase of excavation. Particular objects were often removed abroad because of their financial value rather than because of any scientific significance, and although displays of Egyptian objects in foreign museums probably increased an awareness of Egyptian civilisation among the general public, those pieces that entered private collections were not infrequently disregarded and disposed of, once the owner had tired of them. Furthermore, in seeking out these pieces at the sites, the excavators often paid little attention to the objects' context and to other, less spectacular finds in the area, so that much of the historical and archaeological value of a site and its contents was destroyed.

It was sometimes argued that these collectors were actually saving the heritage of ancient Egypt by removing the material from the country since, it was claimed, the Egyptians had no interest in their pharaonic past, and continuous local quarrying of stone from the monuments was destroying the tombs and temples. In addition, it was said, since Egypt had no national museum to house the antiquities, their safety could only be guaranteed by removing them to museums abroad.

Fashionable interest in Egyptology had been growing since the seventeenth century, when scholars had been sent to Egypt on behalf of wealthy patrons in Europe to acquire antiquities. The diplomatic staff at the embassies and consulates, who often acted as local agents, made significant collections of objects, and laid the foundations of what would become some of the finest national collections in Europe, particularly in Italy, France and Britain.

From this arrangement, it was a natural development for foreigners to seek permission from the Turkish rulers of Egypt to allow them to establish and organise their own excavations. However, when Mohammed Ali became the effective ruler of Egypt, he was persuaded by Champollion to issue an ordinance in 1835 which tried to stem the worst excesses of the antiquities trade. It was the first serious attempt to prohibit the export of antiquities, and recognised the need to establish a national museum in Cairo where the newly excavated objects could be housed. It also forbade the destruction of ancient monuments, and confirmed that the government was responsible for conserving national antiquities. However, it had only a limited success in controlling the export of the treasures, as there were many attempts to circumvent the restrictions it imposed. In one case, when, in 1843, the famous King List was cut from a wall in the Temple of Karnak and then exported to France, this was achieved by simply ignoring the need to acquire a *firman* (permission), because this would have forbidden the export. Even Mohammed Ali himself was guilty of making gifts of monuments and antiquities to foreign visitors and advisors whom he wished to please, in order to gain the support of their countries. One of his most generous gifts were the two obelisks which originally stood at the entrance to the Temple of Luxor; these were donated to France, as a memorial to Napoleon's soldiers, although eventually only one was removed and set up in the Place de la Concorde in Paris in 1836.

However, despite the destruction which was occurring in Egypt at this time, some of the greatest European collections were being established. The men associated with the acquisition of antiquities were often strong personalities who frequently found themselves in conflict with each other; some of them eventually played important roles in establishing the major Egyptian collections in European museums.

The Italian excavator and collector Giuseppe Passalacqua (1797–1865) was born at Trieste, and originally went to Egypt as a horse-dealer, but when this business failed to prosper, he became an excavator and collector of antiquities. He worked at Thebes (1822–5), where he excavated the tombs of priests and priestesses of Amun in the causeway area of Hatshepsut's temple at Deir el-Bahri. He managed to build up a significant collection from Thebes and other sites, and this was exhibited in Paris in 1826. He offered it to the French government for 400,000 francs, but when they rejected it, most of the objects were acquired for the museum collection in Berlin by Frederick Wilhelm IV of Prussia, who paid only 100,000 francs for the collection. Passalacqua took up the post of Conservator of the Egyptian collections in Berlin in 1828, and remained there until his death; during this time, he undertook the major task of organising the objects he had excavated. His work greatly assisted the ambitions of the Prussian ruler who had wanted to acquire a collection which would rival those already established by other European powers.

Three men who played a major role in forming the Egyptian collections in France, Italy and Britain were the diplomats Bernardino Drovetti and Henry Salt, assisted by the colourful excavator and entrepreneur, Giovanni Battista Belzoni. Drovetti (1775–1852) was an Italian diplomat and politician who had been trained as a lawyer and also pursued a career as a soldier in Napoleon's army in Italy. In a diplomatic career in Egypt that began in 1802, he rose to become French consul-general between 1811 and 1814. A visit to southern Egypt in 1811 inspired his interest in antiquities, and he eventually acquired three renowned collections, although the methods he employed to do so have been criticised by later archaeologists. He used local agents to excavate sites and to purchase antiquities from local excavators. One of his greatest acquisitions was the Turin Canon of Kings which, although badly handled and damaged in transit to Italy, where it entered the Turin Museum, nevertheless played an important part in establishing the chronology of Egypt.

Drovetti, who had taken French citizenship earlier in his life, offered his first collection to the king of France but it was rejected; subsequently purchased for 400,000 lire by the king of Sardinia, it became a major part of the collection in the Turin Museum. King Charles X commanded that Drovetti's second collection should be bought for France; it was acquired for 250,000 francs, and became part of the Louvre collection. Finally, Karl Lepsius, the renowned German Egyptologist, ensured that the Berlin Museum acquired the third collection for 30,000 francs in 1836. Drovetti, who ended his days in a mental asylum in Turin, was a complex and difficult character. He sometimes used unscrupulous methods, but this was in keeping with the times, and he demonstrated great skill in bringing together pieces that formed the basis of three world-class collections.

Drovetti's activities drew him into contact and conflict with Henry Salt (1780–1827), who was engaged in acquiring material for the British Museum, and also in establishing his own collection. Salt had trained as a portrait-painter, but when he was appointed British consul-general in Egypt in 1815, he began to excavate and acquire antiquities through several agents, following the well-established pattern of the European collectors.

One of his agents, Giovanni Battista Caviglia (1770–1845), was an Italian sailor, employed to excavate and investigate the Pyramids and Sphinx at

Giza, where he made new discoveries. Another agent, Giovanni d'Athanasi (1798–1854), the son of a Greek merchant who had settled in Cairo, became Henry Salt's servant, and excavated for him at Thebes (1817–27).

Since Mohammed Ali wished to please both England and France, he granted *firman* to excavate both to Salt and to Drovetti, and there was frequently direct conflict between their workforces, who used violence and bribery to gain their ends. The power struggle between Salt and Drovetti dominated this whole era, and they were able to virtually monopolise the antiquities trade.

One of Salt's most successful agents was Giovanni Battista Belzoni (1778–1823), an Italian excavator and explorer. Born in Padua, the son of a poor barber, Belzoni left his home to go to Rome when he was only 16; eventually, he travelled to England where his stature (he was 6 feet 7 inches in height) doubtless helped him to gain employment as a weight-lifter at Sadler's Wells Theatre. Later, during a stay in Malta, when travelling around Europe, he encountered an agent of the ruler of Egypt, Mohammed Ali, who invited him to take his skills in hydraulic engineering to Egypt. Belzoni had probably originally studied hydraulics in Rome, and he had designed hydraulic displays for public entertainment when he was in England. It was his plan now to build irrigation equipment in Egypt, and when he arrived there in 1815, Mohammed Ali invited him to construct a water-wheel and paid him a monthly allowance.

However, although he spent nearly a year designing the machine, it did not receive the approval and support of Mohammed Ali's advisors. Seeking alternative employment, Belzoni was recommended to Salt (who had just taken up his post as British consul-general) to help him with the task of acquiring antiquities. The Swiss traveller, Johann Ludwig Burckhardt (1784–1817), had become acquainted with Belzoni in 1815, and he advised Salt to use Belzoni's talents to remove the upper part of a great statue of Ramesses II from Thebes; this would eventually be transported to the British Museum.

Acting as Salt's agent, Belzoni travelled to Thebes in 1816, with the necessary *firman*, and was able to inspect the colossal granite statue with a view to its removal. The upper part of the body above the waist remained intact and had once formed part of an imposing statue that had stood in the funerary temple complex of Ramesses II (the Ramesseum). This piece was the inspiration for Shelley's famous sonnet on King Ozymandias (derived from one of the names of Ramesses II, User-maat-re). In order to move the statue, Belzoni used a wooden platform, rollers and seventeen men to transfer it to the riverbank. This procedure took seventeen days, and Belzoni had to employ bribes and force to encourage the men in their endeavours. It was then necessary to leave the statue at the Nile's edge until the inundation allowed the colossus to be floated downstream. Despite the attempts of Drovetti's agents to prevent Belzoni completing this task, he eventually managed to transport the statue to Cairo, and it finally arrived at the British Museum, presented by Salt and Burckhardt, in 1817. Belzoni was also able to move the remains of the enormous granite sarcophagus and lid of Ramesses III from Thebes; the sarcophagus eventually became part of the collection in the Louvre, while the lid now forms the centre-piece of the Egyptian galleries at the Fitzwilliam Museum in Cambridge.

During the period when negotiations over the Ramesses statue were in progress, Belzoni had travelled south to Aswan and Nubia; a highlight of this tour was his visit to the temples of Abu Simbel, which he had heard about from Burckhardt, the first European to see these monuments. The temples were largely covered by sand, but Belzoni was able to glimpse the four colossal statues cut out of the rock, which form the temple's facade, and in his description, his excitement at seeing this monument and at speculating about the possibility of excavating it is very evident. He took on forty men as labourers but could not make much progress in his first season. However, returning later, he and a colleague, Henry Beechey (whom Salt had sent to supervise Belzoni's work), were able to make drawings of the scenes and inscriptions on the walls, once the temple had been successfully cleared.

Back in Luxor, Belzoni undertook excavations in the Temple of Mut at Karnak, where he uncovered over twenty statues of the goddess Sekhmet. On the West Bank, he made several dramatic discoveries, including six royal tombs. In the tomb of King Ay, he and Beechey copied the wall reliefs and inscriptions, but his greatest find was the deep rock-cut tomb of King Sethos I in the Valley of the Kings. This contained a fine alabaster sarcoph-agus which was intended for the British Museum. However, when this and a large collection of other Egyptian antiquities were shipped to England in 1818, the museum's trustees decided that the collection was overvalued, and eventually offered only £2,000, which did not meet the costs of excavation and transport; they also rejected the sarcophagus of Sethos I. This was now purchased for £2,000 by Sir John Soane for his own museum in London, where it still remains as a spectacular centrepiece.

Belzoni lived in Sethos' tomb for some time, taking wax impressions of the wall scenes and inscriptions. He used these as the basis for two full-scale reproductions of chambers from the tomb, and a large model of the tomb which, together with antiquities including statues, mummies and papyri from other locations, went on display in 1819 in a large exhibition held in the Egyptian Hall in Piccadilly, London. While working in the tomb, he had taken notes of the original colours still visible on the scenes, and the repro-ductions gave the visitors a real insight into the beauty of the wall scenes. The 'unrolling' of a mummy was carried out in front of a medical audience, to mark the opening of this very popular exhibition which closed in 1822.

Belzoni received acclaim as a traveller as the result of this exhibition, and the publication of his work, entitled *Narrative of the Operations and*

VUE DU SPHINX ET DE LA GRANDE PYRAMIDE, PRISE DU SUD-EST.

Figure 16 A view from the south-east of the Great Pyramid and Sphinx at Giza. Most of the Sphinx is covered by sand. From *Description de l'Égypte* (1809–29), V: pl. 11.

Recent Discoveries within the Pyramids, Temples, Tombs and Excavations, in Egypt in Nubia (1820), generated great public interest in Egyptology. However, he remains a controversial figure with regard to his archaeological methods and techniques. His description of his search for funerary papyri in the Qurna tombs indicated how much damage he inflicted on the mummies buried there – 'Every step I took, I crushed a mummy in some part or other.' On one occasion, he describes how he

> sought a resting place, found one, and continued to sit; but when my weight bore on the body of an Egyptian, it crushed like a band-box. I naturally had recourse to my hands to sustain my weight, but they found no better support so that I sunk altogether among the broken mummies with a crash of bones, rags and wooden cases, which raised such a dust as kept me motionless for a quarter of an hour, waiting till it subsided again.

In addition to his discoveries at Thebes and Abu Simbel, Belzoni also opened the Chephren pyramid at Giza in 1818, where he carried out a careful exploration. He also found Berenice, the Ptolemaic port on the Red Sea, and he visited the oases of Bahariya and the Fayoum. Belzoni was undoubtedly an aggressive treasure-seeker who was willing to use unscrupulous methods to seize antiquities for his employers and himself, and he probably destroyed far more than he saved. He was untrained and inexperienced, and his archaeological methods left much to be desired when compared with those of later excavators with a more scientific approach. His disregard for the archaeological context of his finds is perhaps one of his worst faults. However, he had flair and patience, and identified some remarkable treasures; he remains an important figure in the history of Egyptology because, although he started out in his career with the same aggressive aims and methods as his contemporaries, he gradually developed techniques that were superior to theirs, and became the most successful excavator of his time. His talent for publicity ensured that his achievements and discoveries became well known in England, and consequently gave Egyptology a higher profile.

Belzoni was successful in selling his collection in London but, despite his achievements, he was unable to obtain funding for further excavation in Egypt. He left England on an expedition to try to locate the source of the River Niger and, as he made his way to Timbuktu, he died of dysentery in Benin in 1823. Belzoni's wife, Sarah, who had accompanied him on his travels to Egypt and Nubia and participated in much of his work, now opened an exhibition in London where his models and drawings of the Tomb of Sethos I were shown, but it met with little success, and closed in 1825.

Belzoni and Salt were inextricably linked in their particular approach to archaeology. They shared the common goal of hunting out spectacular pieces to sell to European collectors, but they regarded the recording of information about the objects and their find-spots to be of secondary importance. Nevertheless, Salt's activities in Egypt helped to establish some major national collections in Europe. Unable to sell his first collection to the British Museum for an appropriate sum, he fared better with his second collection, which he had put together between 1819 and 1824. He sold this to the king of France for £10,000, while the British Museum acquired many pieces from his third collection (formed 1824–7), which was auctioned at Sotheby's in 1835 and realised £7,168.

Therefore, it was during this period that the great museums of Europe were acquiring and developing their collections. They bought from excavators and agents such as Salt, Drovetti and Belzoni, but also from men such as Passalacqua and Minutoli who are less well known today. The last, Johann Minutoli (1772–1846), a Prussian army officer, was sent by his government on a scientific expedition to Egypt in 1820–1. He excavated at Saqqara and el-Ashmunein (Hermopolis), and formed a large collection of antiquities, some of which were bought for the Berlin Museum. The great

Egyptian collections in museums in Europe could now be visited and seen by the public. They helped to increase people's growing awareness of Egyptian civilisation and they provided scholars such as Champollion with study material for their researches on hieroglyphs and other aspects of Egyptology.

By the middle of the nineteenth century, Egyptology stood at a crossroads. On the one hand, there was increased public interest in the subject, inspired by the museum collections, the decipherment of hieroglyphs, the many, well-illustrated books which were now produced, and by the increasing number of tourists who travelled to Egypt. On the other hand, the archaeological methods, which often damaged the sites and resulted in the rescue of only some selected antiquities which were dispersed to collectors in a random manner, were haphazard and frequently destroyed more information than they saved. It was the life and career of a French archaeologist, Auguste Mariette (1821–1881), which now changed this situation and ensured that such treasure-seeking was finally replaced by a more scientific approach to Egyptology.

Mariette, the son of a town hall official, was born at Boulogne in France. He pursued several careers, but he became a teacher in a local college in Boulogne, and then Professor of French in 1843. As a relative of Nestor l'Hôte, who had accompanied Champollion as a draughtsman on his expedition to Egypt, Mariette had been asked to go through l'Hôte's papers, which the family received in 1842. It is believed that Mariette's interest in Egyptology dates from this event.

Mariette now began to study the Egyptian alphabet and to learn Coptic. In 1847 he produced his first article – a catalogue of the Egyptian antiquities in the museum at Boulogne. Moving to Paris, he was appointed as an assistant in the Egyptian Department at the Louvre, where he devoted his time to copying all the inscriptions then held in the collection, a work which eventually provided the foundation for a general inventory of the Egyptian monuments.

In 1850, on the recommendation of Charles Lenormant of the Collège de France, he was sent to Egypt to obtain Coptic, Ethiopic and Syriac manuscripts. While undertaking these duties, however, Mariette became interested in the pharaonic monuments which he now had the opportunity to visit, and in October of the same year, while he was searching the necropolis at Saqqara, he noticed the head of a sphinx protruding from the sand. He had seen similar sphinxes in gardens in Alexandria, Cairo and Giza, and he realised that the Saqqara site must be the location from which the householders were obtaining these ornaments.

In the vicinity of the sphinx's head at Saqqara, he found a libation tablet with a dedication to the god Serapis. He recalled the description given by the Classical geographer Strabo of an avenue of sphinxes leading to the Serapeum where the sacred Apis-bulls were buried. Realising that he was

Figure 17 This drawing shows the main gallery of the Serapeum at Saqqara, where the Apis-bulls were buried in large sarcophogi. The Serapeum was discovered in 1850 by Auguste Mariette. From Gaston Maspero's *Histoire ancienne des peuples de l'Orient Classique* (1899).

standing over the site of this avenue, Mariette gathered together a group of thirty workmen and began to excavate. He had no official permission, and only the funds to purchase the manuscripts, but he was convinced that he was correct in his identification of the site, and was also sure that, when his funds were exhausted, he could persuade the French government to support a large excavation at this prestigious site.

He duly uncovered the avenue of sphinxes, consisting of 141 statues, and although the associated temple had disappeared, he found the galleries and vaults where the Apis-bulls had been buried in the New Kingdom and later dynasties. In one undisturbed tomb, there was an intact burial of a bull, with the mummified remains of the animal encased in a large granite sarcophagus. The burial had taken place in the reign of Ramesses II (*c.* 1290 BC), and no one had entered the chamber in the intervening years; in the sand, Mariette found the footprint of a workman who had attended the burial.

In addition to the Apis galleries, Mariette found other important material at Saqqara. His sensational discoveries enabled him to raise funds from the Louvre to excavate for a further period (1850–4) at Saqqara. The finds established Mariette's career as an Egyptologist, and he was appointed Assistant Conservator in the Egyptian Department at the Louvre (1855–61). During his lifetime, he went on to uncover almost 7,000 principal monuments, and devised a plan to reproduce and publish them in transcription. The volumes of notes that he made are now kept at the Louvre; only a small proportion was ever published, but in his *Choix de monuments* (1856), Mariette included plates of selected objects from the Serapeum, which should perhaps be regarded as his greatest discovery.

Mariette's significance, however, rests on his achievements other than excavation, although his success as an archaeologist was considerable. He is most notably remembered and honoured as the man who created the first national Antiquities Service, who established in Cairo the first national museum in the Near East, and who generally raised awareness about the urgent need to stop the destruction and exportation of antiquities from Egypt. He also emphasised the need for proper care and conservation of the monuments.

The ordinance introduced by Mohammed Ali in 1835 had brought some improvement to the general situation. By prohibiting the export of antiquities, it discouraged collectors from cutting large sections from the walls of tombs or temples, as the restrictions of the ordinance would make it difficult to smuggle them out of Egypt. It also had an effect on the conduct of the excavators who, until then, had concentrated on treasure-seeking. Now, because there was every chance that an agent would not be allowed to retain the objects he had found, and remove them from the country, different motives began to influence the methods of excavation. Nevertheless, the ordinance was difficult to enforce, and other measures were required.

Some people continued to be critical of the export of antiquities, and particularly of the part played by diplomats in this trade. It became evident that new procedures were required to ensure that the excavations were organised on a more scientific basis, by keeping records of the work, retaining finds if they had an archaeological or historical significance rather than just a value as collectors' items, and by ensuring that the monuments and antiquities were properly conserved. In order to protect Egypt's heritage, it was also essential that a national museum should be established in Cairo.

This was not a new idea. In 1821, the traveller Edward de Montule had suggested that a great museum should be set up in Cairo or Alexandria. This would defeat the excuses given by some European collectors that Egypt could not house and safeguard its own treasures. As part of the proposal in 1835 to establish a national Antiquities Service, the government had started a collection of antiquities which were originally housed in a small museum in Ezbekia Gardens in Cairo. Later, the material was moved to another building in the Citadel of Saladin in the same city. However,

Mohammed Ali's successors adopted different attitudes towards the fate of the country's antiquities, and a later ruler, Abbas Pasha, took the opportunity to give the whole of this collection to the Austrian Archduke Maximilian on his visit to Egypt in 1855.

Mariette, however, successfully persuaded Said Pasha, who became ruler after Abbas Pasha's assassination in 1854, to support his scheme for saving the antiquities. Mariette obtained the good offices of Ferdinand de Lesseps (1805–1894), the creator of the Suez Canal, who carried considerable influence with Said Pasha, and it was agreed that an organisation should be established which would maintain control of the Egyptian standing monuments. In 1858, Said Pasha appointed Mariette as the first Director of Egyptian Monuments, and when a new museum to house the pharaonic antiquities was established at Boulaq in Cairo, Mariette was again appointed as its head. At Boulaq, a small Nile port a few miles north-east of Cairo, the accommodation for the new museum consisted of a deserted mosque, some sheds, and an old house, and posed many problems. However, Mariette used his many talents to good effect: he made pedestals for the statues, cases for the amulets, and painted the walls of the house, where he set up home. He even introduced an ambitious programme to record the antiquities, photographing the larger objects inside the building, and taking the smaller ones outside into the sunlight.

Unfortunately, despite his valiant efforts, the first museum was doomed. A disastrous flood in 1858 washed away many of the objects which Mariette had amassed from his excavations, and others were stolen. The remaining collections were moved in 1890 to an old palace at Giza that had belonged to Ismail Pasha. Eventually, in 1902, the fine purpose-built Cairo Museum was created. Designed in the neo-classical style by the French architect Marcel Dourgnon, this had exhibition galleries arranged on two floors. It was a fitting tribute to Mariette's foresight and determination, and held the world's largest collection of Egyptian material, numbering some 120,000 objects. Even after Said Pasha had agreed to support the idea of a museum, however, Mariette still had to rely on the ruler's whim to provide continuing funding. Fortunately the international status of the growing collections ensured the ruler's support, but sadly, Mariette did not live to see his dream realised, as he died before the new museum was built. He was given a state funeral and buried in a sarcophagus in the vicinity of the Boulaq museum. Once the new museum building was completed, the sarcophagus was moved to the forecourt there, and the burial place was marked by a bronze statue of Mariette by Xavier Barthe, unveiled in 1904.

As Director of the world's first national Antiquities Service, Mariette began an extensive programme of excavation throughout Egypt, making many important discoveries at sites including Saqqara, Giza, Thebes, Abydos, Tuna, Esna, Sais, Mendes in the eastern Delta, Bubastis (Tell Basta) and Elephantine. These excavations provided an important historical collection for the new museum. He also authorised the clearance of sand and rubbish and even modern dwellings from some of the temple sites. This allowed the buildings to be seen for the first time in their complete form and provided the opportunity for the wall-scenes and inscriptions to be copied and studied.

Altogether, Mariette excavated at thirty-five locations throughout Egypt over a period of thirty years. Among his many important discoveries were the burial and jewellery of Queen Ahhotpe at Thebes and the monuments and statues at Tanis. At Mendes and Bubastis, he employed over 7,000 workmen, and the size and extent of his excavations led later archaeologists to criticise his methods and lack of supervision. Mariette was also condemned for his distrust of other excavators and his alleged attempts to prevent them from digging in Egypt.

However, like Belzoni, he has to be evaluated in terms of his peers and of the external circumstances over which he had little control. He had to retain the interest of the Khedive in order to continue the Service, since he was unable to obtain a permanent grant from the government for his department, and was forced to rely on the ruler for any funding he required. Since the Khedive wanted spectacular finds, Mariette sometimes had to resort to extreme measures. His lack of adequate recording of finds and the occasional use of dynamite as an archaeological method are to be deplored, but they have to be set against his wisdom in establishing workshops at various sites where the newly excavated objects could be treated and conserved immediately. He can perhaps be justifiably criticised for his lack of adequate publication of his results, and for his desire to make 'major discoveries', sometimes at the expense of less dramatic but more significant objects. However, when he is compared with his contemporaries and with immediate predecessors such as Drovetti and Belzoni, Mariette's achievements were considerable. His career exemplified a period of struggle and transition: his foundation of a permanent museum and antiquities service ensured that some check could now be exercised on the export of antiquities, and by raising public awareness of the need to clean and preserve the monuments, he pioneered the idea that these should be saved for posterity. He firmly promoted the concept that it was Egypt's right and responsibility to retain and protect its own heritage so that this could be experienced by everyone as an important and unique contribution to the history of civilisation.

Mariette's actions marked the end of the worst excesses of pillaging antiquities. Although his own archaeological methods were incomplete and imperfect, the fact that he excavated so many sites helped to prevent them from being destroyed by the archaeological methods of less scrupulous operators.

His political and diplomatic skills were essential characteristics which helped him to achieve his aims: Said Pasha was undoubtedly persuaded to support the establishment of a national museum because he could see its value in terms of international kudos. One of Mariette's famous discoveries, the jewellery of Queen Ahhotpe, played its own part in this diplomacy. In 1859, the workmen employed by Mariette at Thebes had discovered a tomb containing a gilded sarcophagus, which Mariette instructed should be sent to Cairo. However, in his absence, the local governor of Qena went to Thebes and declared that he was taking possession of the treasure in the name of the government. He then opened the coffin and took the jewellery off the mummy; subsequently, he sent the coffin to Cairo as a gift for the Khedive, but kept the jewellery for his own harem.

When Mariette became aware of this, he followed the governor and boarded his boat, and after an exchange of blows, forced him to hand over the treasure. Mariette then went to Cairo to report his actions to the ruler and presented him with some pieces of the jewellery for one of his wives. The ruler, greatly impressed with Mariette's actions, ordered that the rest of the treasure should be reserved for the museum which he had decided to establish at Boulaq.

However, the ruler's support was mercurial, as Mariette discovered when he was sent in 1867 to Paris to supervise the installation at the International Exhibition of a major display to reconstruct the life of ancient Egypt. Examples of the finest Egyptian craftsmanship were shown, including as a centrepiece the jewellery of Queen Ahhotpe, and this now caught the eye of the Empress Eugénie, who asked the Khedive if she might receive it as a gift. When the Khedive told her to ask Mariette, he refused, and incurred immediate displeasure. Said Pasha was always anxious to retain French good will, and Mariette now found himself in disgrace, facing further problems in obtaining funding for his work. However, when French influence declined in 1870, Mariette was once again restored to favour with the Khedive. This was confirmed when, in 1871, the first performance of the three-act opera *Aïda* took place in Cairo. This work had been composed by Verdi to celebrate the opening of the Suez Canal on 17 November 1869, and as a leading authority on ancient Egypt, Mariette was invited to assist in writing the libretto.

Mariette's successor, Gaston Maspero (1846–1916), represents the beginning of the modern era of Egyptology. Whereas Mariette had concentrated on preserving Egypt's heritage, the later part of the nineteenth century now saw the development of new archaeological methods and techniques. There was great public interest in excavation, fostered by the establishment of societies which undertook scientific excavation and the publication of their results. The broad outlines of most of the historical periods had now been established, but the new concept and purpose of archaeology was not merely to discover antiquities, but to use the evidence to interpret the lives of the ancient Egyptians.

In his book *A Century of Excavation in the Land of the Pharaohs* (1923), James Baikie says of the archaeologist:

His purpose, and his business, if he has any real understanding of the
end for which Providence created him . . . , is not the mere gathering
of facts, but the reconstruction by means of these of the life of the
past, for the interest, the help, and the guidance of the present . . .
Unless he keeps this in view as his real object, he is misconceiving
his whole purpose, and substituting means for ends (p. 37).

Baikie continues to develop his idea that the prime concern of the archaeologist, and indeed his main contribution, is to enable the modern world
to understand and appreciate the lives of ancient people. The daily existence
of ordinary people is as important as the achievements of the rulers in
helping us to understand any society, and Baikie quotes R. A. S. Macalister's
statement that 'Archaeological research consists principally in the discovery
and the classification of the common things of daily life, houses, personal
ornaments, domestic utensils, tools, weapons and the like' (p. 39).

Maspero himself promoted this view of archaeology. In addition to
numerous academic works, he published historical accounts for a general
readership. These included his *Histoire ancienne des peuples de l'Orient
Classique* (1875); *The Dawn of Civilisation – Egypt and Chaldea* (1896);
The Struggle of the Nations – Egypt, Syria and Assyria (1896); *The Passing
of the Empires* (1900) and *Les Contes populaires de l'Égypte ancienne* (1882).
In the introduction to the last, he comments: 'The lofty personages whose
mummies repose in our museums had a reputation for gravity so thoroughly
established, that nobody suspected them of having ever diverted themselves
with such futilities in those days when they were only mummies-in-
expectation.'

Therefore, there was now a marked change in the perceived purpose of
archaeology. It was no longer sufficient to uncover colossal statues, great
monuments, and treasure which related particularly to the rulers' achievements. Archaeologists were now required to interpret the evidence in order
to explain how people had lived, and consequently they needed knowledge
of art and architecture, language, religion, and of the various skills and techniques, such as stone-working, mummification, and agriculture, which the
ancient Egyptians had pursued.

Earlier excavators had not appreciated the need for a scientific approach
to archaeology; instead, they had looked for monuments and inscriptions
that would confirm or correct the history and chronology of Egypt. Because
of this approach, many small and seemingly insignificant objects had been
discarded with the result that material of archaeological importance was
often lost.

The new objectives changed the focus of archaeology; they influenced
the choice of sites to be excavated, and dictated the type of material that
was preserved and studied. As Baikie so appropriately commented: 'Perhaps
the change may be expressed most simply by saying that while the explorer

of two generations back looked for colossi, his present-day successor looks for crockery' (p. 43).

Spectacular royal discoveries such as the tomb of Tutankhamun obviously still occurred, but the search for treasure was no longer paramount, and even when such finds were made, painstaking methods of excavation and conservation of the objects were generally given priority over hasty removal of the treasure.

Maspero's career can therefore be regarded as a key event in this process of 'humanisation' of archaeology. His appointment occurred against a political background in Egypt where the French, although losing their political advantage, were nevertheless determined to retain their influence over the arts and archaeology. A military revolt in Egypt in 1881 caused concern in France and Britain, who were anxious that any political instability should not affect their holdings in the Suez Canal and their industrial investments in the country. Britain sent a fleet and expeditionary force to Egypt in 1882, to ensure that order was restored. Although an Egyptian ruler (the Khedive) remained in nominal control, British power was now considerably enhanced as the result of the installation of a British agent in the person of a consul-general. Although this man had no formal authority over the Khedive, his influence was great, and for many years British officials, appointed to positions in the departments of defence, foreign affairs, finance, public works, and the police force, dominated many aspects of life in Egypt. The French were therefore particularly determined to ensure that one of their own scholars succeeded Mariette.

Gaston Maspero, a French Egyptologist of Italian origin who was born in Paris, had became interested in hieroglyphs at an early age. When he was 21, he met Mariette, who gave him two hieroglyphic texts to study which he translated within a couple of weeks. He became Professor of Egyptian philology and archaeology at the Collège de France in 1874, and first led an archaeological mission to Egypt in 1880 to record scenes and inscriptions in tombs, particularly in the Valley of the Kings.

In 1881, he succeeded Mariette as Director of the museum at Boulaq where he continued Mariette's work, organising and cataloguing the collections and re-arranging the displays. One of Maspero's greatest and lasting achievements was to edit fifty volumes of the *Catalogue* of objects in the Cairo Museum. His meticulous and systematic methods laid a firm foundation for the rapidly expanding development of this collection.

Like his predecessor, Maspero was also Director of the Antiquities Service. He continued to build on Mariette's initial efforts in this post, and he continued Mariette's scheme to open up the smaller pyramids, authorising Heinrich Brugsch (see page 82) to copy the texts in the pyramids of Pepy I and Merenre at Saqqara which Brugsch had discovered. Maspero opened three further pyramids, where he copied and translated the inscriptions, publishing them as the first edition of the famous funerary spells known as

LA CHAMBRE FUNÉRAIRE DE LA PYRAMIDE ET LE SARCOPHAGE D'OUNAS¹.

Figure 18 The archaeologist Gaston Maspero in the burial chamber of King Unas' pyramid at Saqqara. When the pyramid was opened in 1881, the earliest examples of the Pyramid Texts were found inscribed on the walls. From Gaston Maspero, *Les Origines Égypte-Chaldée* (1895), drawing by Boudier based on a photograph by Émile Brugsch-Bey taken in 1881.

the Pyramid Texts. He also set in place a system to clear the rubbish and debris from the Temple of Karnak, and to take steps to preserve this great monument, thus continuing Mariette's own emphasis on conservation.

Maspero was rather more relaxed in his attitude towards foreign excavators than Mariette had been, and although he retained the same general principles that Mariette had set down, he interpreted some of the restrictions more leniently, so that a system was set in place to allow museums in Europe and America to acquire some antiquities. He showed great foresight in employing the American archaeologist G. A. Reisner to undertake the Archaeological Survey of Nubia (1907–9), and was able to gain the help of the British consul-general, Lord Cromer, in developing the Antiquities Service. It now became possible to inaugurate five inspectorates to oversee excavation in various areas of the country.

Maspero published more works (around 1,200 titles) than any other Egyptological writer, varying from scholarly works to popular accounts. One of his most famous endeavours was the rescue of the cache of royal mummies of the New Kingdom, which he had removed from Deir el-Bahri to the Cairo Museum in 1881. His account of this discovery (which will be discussed in Chapter XI) was published with E. Brugsch in *La Trouvaille de Deir-el-Bahari* (1881).

The careers of several other French Egyptologists were of significance in the development of the subject at this time. Eugène Grébaut (1846–1915) succeeded Maspero as Director of the Antiquities Service in 1886, but he was temperamentally unsuited to the task of liaising with the Egyptians and with other Egyptologists, and he resigned in 1892. In his early career (he had studied under Maspero and others) he had shown considerable promise, and had succeeded Lefébure as Director of the French Archaeological Mission in Cairo from 1883 to 1886.

Eugène Lefébure (1838–1908), a lecturer in Egyptology at Lyon, became Director of the French Archaeological Mission in Cairo in 1881. Although ill-health prevented him from making a full contribution to fieldwork, his most important achievement was the publication of the tombs of Ramesses IV and Sethos I in the Valley of the Kings. Another French scholar, Victor Loret (1859–1946), interested in Egyptology since childhood, was another of Maspero's pupils who accompanied him to Cairo in 1881 as one of the first members of the French Institute of Archaeology. His work for the Institute (of which he became Director in 1886) included a joint venture with Lefébure on copying and publishing texts from tombs at Thebes. In 1897, he became Director-General of the Antiquities Service, but he too lacked the necessary diplomatic skills and resigned in 1899. However, he achieved some archaeological success in this post, continuing the programme of work in the Valley of the Kings, where he discovered the second cache of royal mummies in the tomb of Amenhotep II. He also founded the *Annales du Service,* which became a prestigious journal and major publication of the service.

Georges Daressy (1864–1938), who was Assistant Keeper at the Boulaq museum in 1887, was responsible for displaying the collections when they moved to the Giza palace in 1891, and subsequently to the new Cairo Museum in 1902. Daressy also worked as an archaeologist for Maspero, helping with the programme of temple restoration at Karnak, Luxor,

Figure 19 An early photograph showing the clearance and restoration undertaken in the hypostyle hall area of the Temple of Karnak, Thebes.

Abydos and Medinet Habu, and together with Grébaut, he removed the cache of Dynasty 21 mummies from Thebes in 1891.

The programme of temple restoration initiated by the Antiquities Service was greatly assisted by the work of Georges Legrain (1865–1917). He was not only a renowned copyist but also initiated a vast restoration and rebuilding programme at the Temple of Karnak, where he cleared the hypostyle hall and surrounding area, and carried out works to make the buildings safe. He established a methodology for this work which has been emulated by later restorers, and in the course of this building programme, in 1903, he discovered a famous cachette of some 17,000 statues and figures.

Other leading figures of the period included Émile Chassinat (1868–1948), who first went to Egypt in 1895 to work for the French Institute of Archaeology. As Director (1898–1911), he expanded the scale of excavations and extended the Institute's role to start a major programme of publication. Other successes included his work, undertaken on behalf of Rochemonteix (see p. 104), on the Temple of Edfu; and, as a member of the Cairo Catalogue Commission, his studies on the coffins of the high-priests of Amun that had been excavated at Deir el-Bahri.

Another scholar who contributed to the Cairo Museum and to the Antiquities Service was Gustave Lefèbvre (1879–1957). He had joined the Antiquities Service at Maspero's invitation, and became Inspector for Middle Egypt (1905–14); he also held the posts of Assistant Keeper (1919) and Keeper (1926–8) at the Cairo Museum. He produced an important publication of the tomb of the high-priest Petosiris (1923–4) at Tuna el-Gebel; this has been cleared to reveal wall-scenes that represent a unique combination of Egyptian and Greek art styles. His study (1929) of the high-priests of Amun at Karnak was another major contribution.

Mariette and Maspero established the lines along which Egyptology would develop over the next 150 years. The foundation of the Egyptian Museum in Cairo and of the Antiquities Service ensured that Egyptians now retained the most important antiquities in their own country. They also now began to develop an interest in their own heritage, although it was only after the Egyptian revolution of 1952 that Egyptians replaced Europeans as directors and administrators of these two institutions.

The next step was to develop the scientific methodologies and techniques which began to emerge in the second half of the nineteenth century. The person who first stated the aims of scientific archaeology was a Scottish antiquarian, Alexander Henry Rhind (1833–1863). He had trained as a lawyer, but poor health encouraged him to travel in southern Europe and Egypt, where he excavated tombs at Thebes (1855–6 and 1856–7). The antiquities he acquired in Egypt were eventually bequeathed to the National Museum of Antiquities in Scotland. While he was excavating an undisturbed burial at Thebes, he began to develop a new system of excavation. As a key feature, he pioneered the practice of recording the exact location of each object as it was found, a method which contrasted vividly with the 'gunpowder' techniques being used by contemporary excavators.

However, in the words of James Baikie (op. cit.),

> if the name of any one man must be associated with modern excavation as that of the chief begetter of its principles and methods, it must be the name of Professor Sir W. M. Flinders Petrie. It was he,

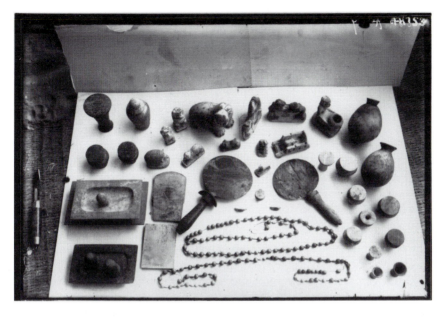

Figure 20 This early photograph, taken at Abydos in 1907, shows a selection of small funerary objects which were now being retained in the course of excavation, for further study. This was an entirely different approach to archaeology from the treasure-seeking of the previous centuries.

as one of the most brilliant exponents of his methods has recently stated, who first called the attention of modern excavators to the importance of 'unconsidered trifles', as means for the construction of the past (p. 46).

Baikie continues:

Above all, it was he who first taught us that for purposes of certainty in the establishment of the succession of different periods, the 'broken earthenware' of a people may be of far greater value than its most gigantic monuments. And it has been men trained in the principles which he established who have during the last generation been doing the work which has made the past of the Classical East a living thing to the world today (p. 47).

Petrie was the pioneer who introduced an innovative set of scientific principles for excavating new sites, and he also used these techniques to rework sites which previously had been inadequately excavated by others. He was the first to put into effect the aims of scientific archaeology which Rhind had outlined in 1862, and he developed a methodology which would ultimately have a great impact on all archaeology, in Egypt and elsewhere. Petrie recognised the importance of all excavated material, however seemingly insignificant, and he retained anything from his excavations that might be of scientific interest to himself or others.

He was unreservedly critical of his predecessors' efforts. His first visit to Egypt had profoundly affected him, when he became aware of the rate and extent of destruction to which the monuments and antiquities were being subjected. He wrote:

> Nothing seems to be done with any uniform and regular plan, work is begun and left unfinished; no regard is paid to future requirements of exploration, and no civilised or labour saving devices are used. It is sickening to see the rate at which everything is being destroyed and the little regard paid to preservation (M. S. Drower, *Flinders Petrie: A Life in Archaeology* (1985), p. 43).

It was an opinion shared by his two great supporters and patrons, Amelia B. Edwards and Jesse Haworth.

Petrie was always very conscious of the responsibility of archaeologists to conserve and preserve the monuments and antiquities which they uncovered. He strongly criticised those who excavated and then left their discoveries to be plundered or destroyed by exposure, claiming that, in these instances, it was preferable to leave the site covered for future generations to investigate. His interest in the post-excavation welfare and continuing history of the objects within a museum context encouraged him to play an important part in establishing collections such as those held in the Petrie Museum at University College London and the Manchester University Museum. However, despite his interest in the conservation and display of objects, he was well aware that all excavated material would eventually deteriorate and that therefore it should be promptly published. He wrote over a thousand books, articles and reviews which provided reports of his excavations, and also proposed and developed theories that he was able to work out from the evidence provided by material he had excavated and the methodologies he had pioneered. Some have criticised the superficiality of his approach to publication, but Petrie's aim was to make his findings known as soon as possible, so that others could rapidly assess his new evidence, and this approach was certainly preferable to the delay or lack of publication of which most earlier excavators were guilty.

Amelia B. Edwards wrote that the archaeologist or explorer, 'like the poet, is "born, not made!" The wonder perhaps is that he should ever be born at all.' Her role in supporting Flinders Petrie's career and in founding the Department of Egyptology at University College London and the Egypt Exploration Fund (now Society) was crucial to this next phase of Egyptology. Amelia Edwards (1831–1893) was born in London, and followed a career as a journalist and novelist. In 1873–4, she visited Syria and Egypt. This was part of the now fashionable habit of travellers from Europe and America to spend the winter in Egypt where the warm, dry climate had many health benefits. Some went as tourists with agencies such as Thomas Cook, travelling along the Nile or visiting the major sites on an overland journey that could be accomplished in three weeks. However, others chose to sail along the Nile for three months, chartering a sailing vessel (*dahabeah*) and travelling southwards from Cairo to the Second Cataract. These were delightful journeys, sometimes undertaken by a group of friends, who could share the unfolding pleasure of watching the life of the villages along the riverbanks, making shopping expeditions into the local bazaars, or 'grubbing' for antiquities at the various archaeological sites.

Miss Edwards's journey became the subject of her best-selling book, *A Thousand Miles up the Nile* (1877), in which she shared with her readership her own joy at watching the timeless river scenes, and her awe and wonder at the sight of the monuments. However, perhaps most importantly, it was the widespread destruction and deterioration of the monuments which affected her most profoundly, and changed the course of her life, and the course of Egyptology. She became determined to instigate some action, and for the rest of her life devoted herself to the task of finding ways to promote scientific exploration and the systematic recording of the monuments in Egypt. To raise public awareness of the problem, she lectured about the subject and wrote numerous articles. However, she fully recognised the need to establish a society that could promote this work, and in 1882, with the help of Reginald Stuart Poole, a renowned orientalist, and the surgeon Sir Erasmus Wilson, Amelia Edwards founded the Egypt Exploration Fund in London. She became its first secretary, and henceforth devoted her time exclusively to Egyptology. Talks and articles in journals and newspapers helped to promote the Fund's work, and Amelia Edwards visited the United States in 1889–90, where her lectures generated further interest in the work and helped to promote an American branch of the Fund.

Amelia Edwards's other great contribution was to have equally far-reaching results. She recognised the need for a university centre for Egyptology in Britain, where new ideas could be developed and taught. Under the terms of her will, she bequeathed her library, her collection of Egyptian antiquities, and the sum of £5,000 to found the first chair of Egyptology in Britain, at University College London. It was her wish that Petrie should be appointed to this post, where he would have the opportunity to develop his new approach to archaeology.

This opportunity changed the life and prospects of William Matthew Flinders Petrie (1853–1942), and consequently had a major impact on the history of Egyptology. Petrie developed an entirely new approach: he recognised the need to examine each site with great care, preserving seemingly insignificant objects as well the finest treasures, because he correctly argued that only a detailed study of a site and all its artifacts could enable the civilisation of ancient Egypt (or any other land or people) to be correctly interpreted.

Petrie was the son of a civil engineer and surveyor, who taught him surveying and geometry. He received no formal education, but his interest in Egyptology was kindled when he was only 13, as the result of reading Charles Piazzi Smyth's book *Our Inheritance in the Great Pyramid* (1864). Petrie and his father had a great interest in ancient monuments, and surveyed Stonehenge in 1872. Their plan to visit Egypt, and undertake a detailed survey of the pyramids, was inspired by Piazzi Smyth's claims that divine knowledge was concealed within the measurements of the Great Pyramid. It was their ambition to obtain their own calculations, and in 1880, Flinders Petrie finally set out for Egypt, with packing cases full of the measuring equipment which he had prepared for his expedition.

One of the most important results of Petrie's first visit to Egypt was his recognition that the monuments were being destroyed at an alarming rate, and that in fact the disorganised archaeological methods of the contemporary excavators were contributing to the loss of antiquities. He realised that excavation without preservation was disastrous, and claimed, 'Anything would be better than leaving things to be destroyed wholesale; better spoil half in preserving the other half, than leave the whole to be smashed.' The desperate situation in Egypt persuaded Petrie that he must pursue a career there as an excavator, so that he could bring a new philosophy to archaeological method.

He was already interested in small objects, and had collected coins when he was a boy. Before he left England, he visited Samuel Birch, Keeper at the British Museum, to seek his advice about his tour to Egypt. Birch had suggested that Petrie might being back some samples of pottery, which excavators generally discarded as rubbish. Petrie followed this advice, and on his return, Birch acquired this collection. With this initial pottery collection, Petrie put in place some of the steps he was to develop later: he noted and marked on each pot or shard the exact location where it had been found, and also listed the other artifacts present in the same context. Using the pottery as the guideline, he was then able to allocate some of the other objects to specific historical periods.

With his pyramid survey complete, Petrie returned to England in 1882, but he was determined to return to Egypt and regarded his duty as 'that of a salvage man, to get all I could quickly gathered in'. The Egypt Exploration Fund (EEF) had been founded in London, with the initial aim of exploring the Delta, in the hope of discovering lost evidence of the Hebrew sojourn in Egypt. When, one season, Édouard Naville, the fund's excavator, found himself unable to pursue his fieldwork because of writing commitments, the Fund's committee invited Petrie to replace him.

Petrie excavated for the Fund from 1884 to 1886, at Tanis, Naucratis (a site which Petrie discovered himself) and at Tell Nabesha (Tell Farun) and Tell Dafana (Defenneh). However, a series of disagreements between Petrie and some members of the EEF culminated in the reappointment of Naville as excavator. Some months later, Petrie resigned from the Fund.

Since he had no private resources and no other means of continuing his excavations in Egypt, he now faced the prospect that his career in Egyptology was prematurely ended. However, Amelia Edwards, one of the founders of the EEF, had recognised the talent that Petrie possessed and supported him in his conflicts with the sub-committee. Miss Edwards had become acquainted with Jesse Haworth, a wealthy Manchester businessman. He and his wife had read Amelia Edwards's account of the Nile journey, and inspired by this, they had travelled along the Nile. They were much affected by the monuments and also by the rate of destruction they observed. Jesse Haworth, a religious man, was now prepared to finance Petrie's excavations in Egypt in the hope that this would shed new light on the Bible. Initially, Haworth (as an anonymous sponsor) was interested in obtaining a throne which may have been part of the funerary furniture of Queen Hatshepsut, but subsequently he revealed his identity and his wish that Petrie should develop his excavation methods in the cause of science. Haworth did not wish to acquire a collection for himself, but he supported Petrie's excavations for many years, and the substantial division of antiquities from these sites which were sent to Manchester eventually came to form the nucleus of the Manchester University Museum collection.

The first major sites which Petrie excavated with Haworth's support were Illahun, Kahun and Gurob. Kahun and Gurob were important as examples of settlement sites where Petrie found objects of daily use, and was able to demonstrate that such material could be as significant as royal treasure.

He soon realised the need to establish an organisation that would raise funds from the public to support his excavations (although he did excavate again for the Egypt Exploration Fund in 1896–1906). However, in 1894 he founded the fund-raising body known as the Egyptian Research Account, which later became the British School of Archaeology in Egypt. Also, the terms of his appointment as the first Edwards Professor of Egyptology at University College London (which he held from 1892 to 1933) enabled him to continue his excavations in Egypt.

Petrie pioneered the first systematic archaeological work in the Near East, and in over forty years of digging, excavated more sites than Mariette. Eventually, when he left Egypt and worked in Palestine from 1926 until 1938, he excavated Hyksos and other sites. He made more major archaeological discoveries than any other Egyptologist, and revolutionised the excavator's approach by insisting that everything that was found was worthy of consideration, and that all objects should be organised and

Figure 21 Petrie's excavation at Kahun was the earliest investigation of a pyramid workmen's town. This photograph, taken by C. T. Campion when he visited the site in 1914, shows Flinders Petrie (holding the pole), his wife Hilda, and the photographer.

studied according to typology. He also made study collections of antiquities for research and teaching purposes.

He was scathing of contemporaries such as Émile Amélineau (see page 135) and Maspero, and of his predecessors, including Mariette. In particular, he was critical of their organisation of excavations. He employed entirely different principles to direct his workforce, and whereas Mariette had initiated many excavations with the result that he had little opportunity to personally supervise his workforce, Petrie kept direct control over his men. At Quft (Koptos) north of Luxor (Thebes), he personally trained selected people in his methods so that they could eventually become foremen at other sites. Until the present day, their descendants (known as Quftis) still provide the trained overseers at many sites in Egypt. Petrie ensured that his workmen were properly housed and he gained their loyalty and prevented them from selling the objects to dealers, by paying them a fixed price for different types of objects.

Petrie dug sites all over Egypt and discovered material from most of the ancient historical periods. Among his most notable finds were the hitherto unexplored towns of Kahun and Naucratis, a city which had been built to accommodate Greek residents living in Egypt. At both sites, Petrie found foreign pottery which not only demonstrated that Egypt had commercial contact with her neighbours and had not developed in isolation, but also enabled him to establish a chronology which helped to identify dates for discoveries then being made in Greek archaeology. The foreign pottery found at the Egyptian sites was tentatively identified as Greek in origin, and inscriptional evidence at the Egyptian sites enabled the foreign pottery found there to be closely dated. This then provided a historical and chronological framework for the sites in Greece where similar pottery occurred. Thus, when Sir Arthur Evans discovered the palace of Knossos in Crete a short time later, he was able to use the parallel foreign pottery (Kamares ware) found in Egypt to provide a framework for the material revealed at Knossos.

Other major discoveries made by Petrie included the Middle Kingdom jewellery of the royal women which was found in a tomb at Illahun and, in the cemeteries of the Graeco-Roman Period at Hawara, the painted panel portraits which had been placed over the faces of the mummies. These provided a unique opportunity to study realistic portraiture in the Hellenistic style, adopted here for Egyptian funerary purposes. Also, he excavated (1891–2) Tell el-Amarna, the capital city of the heretic pharaoh Akhenaten, where discovery of the records office, with the archive of correspondence from contemporary rulers of other Near Eastern countries, threw new light on the politics and diplomacy of that period.

However, perhaps his greatest archaeological contribution was to reveal entirely new evidence about the Predynastic and Early Historical Periods. At Abydos, Petrie was able to use his new methodology to good effect, and to excavate royal and non-royal tombs of Dynasty 1. He obtained the concession to excavate the site from Maspero in 1899, following the French archaeologist Émile Amélineau (1850–1915) who had worked there from 1894 to 1898. Amélineau had sought only decorated or inscribed pieces and ordered his other finds to be broken up and discarded. Petrie now reworked the site, and mapped, recorded and photographed the remains; he also studied Amélineau's discarded pieces, and was able to reassess the significance of this earliest historical period.

Petrie also revealed for the first time the existence of an extensive period of civilisation before Dynasty 1, which is now referred to as the 'Predynastic Period'. In the mid-1890s, Petrie became involved in a dispute with the French archaeologist Jacques de Morgan (see page 137), who in many ways represented the old school of archaeology. Their excavation methods were quite different, in terms of organisation of the workforce and handling of the finds. In 1894–5, Petrie began his excavation of over two thousand graves in the cemetery near the modern town of Naqada, and at Ballas, slightly to the north. He and his co-worker Quibell uncovered pottery which was unlike any other found in Egypt; the accompanying grave goods were also distinctive, and there was no evidence of writing. Petrie wrongly decided that these graves – which did not fit in with other Egyptian evidence – belonged to a 'new race' who had conquered the area and replaced the earlier inhabitants. He tentatively placed this 'invasion' in the First Intermediate Period, and speculated that the 'new race' may have come from Libya. In fact, these graves represented the indigenous predynastic people whose descendants became the population of the historic kingdom of Egypt. However, although his hypothesis met with criticism (and was quite inaccurate), Petrie continued to promote this idea, and it was de Morgan, his despised contemporary, who in fact first recognised and claimed that these cemeteries represented the Egyptian prehistoric culture, and not a foreign invasion. The evidence eventually forced Petrie himself to accept this conclusion. At Naqada, he now assigned relative dates to the graves that he was excavating, in order to develop a system – known as sequence dating – by which the stylistic changes of Naqada grave goods could be noted, reconstructed and arranged in a chronological order. This dating system was based on the changes seen in the pottery found in the graves; these pottery types were then arranged sequentially, and other classes of grave objects such as slate palettes, flints, figurines and ivories were similarly divided into broad categories. The contents of each grave were recorded on a card, and clusters of certain types of objects were noted. Ultimately, Petrie devised a 'corpus' or list of types which could be consulted, with the aim that any excavated object of the period could then be compared with this list and, accordingly to its stylistic criteria, could be assigned to a chronological place within the scheme. Sequence dating was not a perfect system, and it was later modified, but it did enable material to be positioned chronologically even when other dating criteria were absent, and it has been used effectively by subsequent generations of Egyptologists.

Petrie's dominant personality and determination enabled him to make great progress, but at times he was inflexible and unwilling to consider the validity of other viewpoints. Nevertheless, he profoundly changed the nature of archaeology in Egypt, and influenced the attitudes and methods of his co-excavators and students.

Early in his career, Petrie's ideas and methods had contrasted markedly with contemporary excavators such as Édouard Naville (1844–1926), the Swiss Egyptologist who was the first excavator of the Egypt Exploration Fund. At the Fund's invitation, Naville had excavated at Tell el-Maskhuta in 1883, and subsequently at several other important Delta sites including Wadi Tumilat and Bubastis (Tell Basta). Later, at Deir el-Bahri, Naville and H. R. Hall worked on the Dynasty 11 temple of Mentuhotep. In contrast to Petrie's meticulous excavation of small finds, Naville was only interested in working on large monuments, but his work added an important dimension in some areas, particularly in relation to the Exodus and its route (he identified the area near Wadi Tumilat as the land of Goshen).

Another contemporary who pursued a very different approach from Petrie was Jacques de Morgan (1857–1924), Director of the Egyptian Antiquities Service from 1892 to 1897. Although Petrie was scathing about his working methods and his lack of qualifications to excavate, de Morgan made some important discoveries, including the magnificent royal jewellery of the Dynasty 12 princesses at Dahshur (1894–5) and the Dynasty 1 royal tomb of Queen Neithhotep at Naqada (1897). Perhaps, however, his major contribution was to identify the strange grave goods at Naqada as predynastic rather than the product of any 'new race' and, with Petrie, he pioneered the study of predynastic Egypt.

Many archaeologists of this period worked with Petrie and pursued the scientific principles he had established. Guy Brunton (1878–1948) was one of Petrie's students in London who subsequently excavated with him at Illahun (1912–14), when the great discovery of the Dynasty 12 royal jewellery was made. He also worked at Qau and Badari with Gertrude Caton-Thompson (see page 139), and at Der Tasa, contributing to knowledge of the Tasian and Badarian phases of predynastic culture. Reginald Engelbach (1888–1946) assisted Petrie at several sites, including Illahun and Gurob (1919–20). He was appointed Chief Keeper at the Cairo Museum in 1931, where, again perhaps reflecting Petrie's own enthusiasm for museum organisation, he initiated the museum register with its index of 100,000 numbers.

James Quibell (1867–1935) also pursued a distinguished career, assisting Petrie at Koptos (1893), and then accompanying him to Naqada and Ballas, where the crucial evidence was revealed about Egypt's predynastic period. Subsequently, he excavated the town and area of Hieraconpolis, where important early dynastic discoveries were made. As an Inspector for the Egyptian Antiquities Service, he also undertook important excavations at Saqqara and elsewhere, and made improvements to the collections during his time as Keeper at the Cairo Museum. He is generally regarded as one of the best excavators of his time, who developed and improved Petrie's own techniques.

Quibell's co-excavators at Hieraconpolis – Somers Clarke (1841–1926) and F. W. Green (1869–1949) – also made important contributions. Somers Clarke, a distinguished architect, produced a plan and section of the Hieraconpolis temple which, in terms of Egyptology, first demonstrated an understanding of stratification. His study of buildings and plans of tombs and temples also showed a great improvement on previous attempts. Green, working at Hieraconpolis, discovered the Decorated Tomb, No. 100, which contained the earliest known attempts at wall painting in Egypt. This, however, was only the most impressive of a group of graves which they excavated at Hieraconpolis but, although they made some spectacular discoveries at the site, particularly the famous Narmer Palette and carved maceheads, they disregarded much evidence. Even the exact find-spot of

Figure 22 The Narmer palette, *c.* 3100 BC, now in the Cairo Museum, was discovered in the temple deposit at Hieraconopolis. The recto (left) shows King Narmer (Menes) brandishing a macehead over the head of a captive from northern Egypt. The verso (right) shows composite animal forms in the middle register that are reminiscent of Mesopotamian art. The palette probably commemorated Narmer's conquest of the Northern Kingdom and his subsequent unification of Egypt.

the Narmer Palette was not recorded accurately, and most of the 200 graves excavated by Green, with their valuable evidence relating to the town's population, were not published.

Others who worked with Petrie included Edward Ayrton (1882–1914), who first dug with him for the EEF at Abydos (1902–4). Subsequently, he excavated the predynastic cemetery at El-Mahasna (1908–9), and assisted Naville and Hall at Deir el-Bahri (1904–5) and Theodore Davis in the Valley of the Kings (1905–8). D. Randall-MacIver (1873–1945), who worked for Petrie at Denderah and Abydos (1898–1901), subsequently curated the Egyptian collection at the University Museum of Pennsylvania, and undertook excavations in Egypt and the Sudan. A. Weigall (1880–1934), Petrie's assistant in 1901 on the EEF excavations, undertook further work with R. L. Mond and Theodore Davis in the Theban necropolis. Following Petrie's example, he initiated a programme of conserving the tombs and temples there, and set in motion a system to number the nobles' tombs. The *Topographical Catalogue of the Private Tombs of Thebes* which he and Alan Gardiner published provided a basis for further study of this area.

Another of Petrie's students who made a considerable contribution to the study of predynastic Egypt was Gertrude Caton-Thompson (1888–1985). She participated in Petrie's excavations at Abydos and Oxyrhynchus in 1921–2, and at Qau in 1923–5. She undertook pioneering work at the predynastic village of Hemamieh, which she excavated with unequalled attention to detail, and she carried out the first extensive archaeological and geological survey in the Fayoum (1924–8), and subsequently excavated in the Kharga Oasis (1930–2). Her method of combining detailed excavation techniques and extensive regional surveys placed her at the forefront of environmental archaeology.

Percy E. Newberry (1868–1949), one of the first specialists in archaeobotany, assisted Petrie in his publication of Hawara and Kahun. He subsequently directed the Archaeological Survey expedition at Beni Hasan and El-Bersha (1890–4), and undertook various excavations at Thebes. He was appointed Brunner Professor of Egyptology in the University of Liverpool (1906–19), where he contributed to the development of the Liverpool Institute of Archaeology which Garstang had founded in 1904.

J. Garstang (1876–1956) was a colourful character who was Professor of Methods and Practice of Archaeology at Liverpool from 1907 to 1941. He excavated at various sites in Egypt and Nubia, including Beni Hasan, Edfu, Abydos, Esna and Meroë. At Beni Hasan, he set up his living and working quarters in some of the tombs and entertained distinguished visitors there in some style, while his camp at Meroë enjoyed the benefit of a golf course in the desert. Archaeology was the route by which some distinguished philologists also entered Egyptology at this period. T. E. Peet (1882–1934), who held posts at Liverpool (1920–33) and Oxford (1933–4), is best known for his translations of papyri dealing with the Ramesside tomb robberies,

Figure 23 Life in Professor Garstang's excavation camp at Meroë provided some diversions. This photograph, taken in 1912, shows Garstang (left) and friends after a shooting expedition.

but he was initially trained as an Egyptologist by excavating with Garstang at Abydos, and then subsequently with Naville for the EEF Francis Llewellyn Griffith (see pp. 84–5), the foremost philologist of his generation in Britain, started his career by accompanying Petrie and Naville (1884–8) on excavations at Delta sites, including Naucratis and Tanis.

In the years towards the end of the nineteenth century, therefore, there had been some great advances in the archaeological exploration of Egypt. Establishment of dedicated societies such as the Egypt Exploration Fund, and the pioneering scientific methodology developed by Petrie and continued by his students, ensured that the subject was now a precise academic discipline. Discovery of the prehistoric and early historic periods had greatly enhanced understanding of the civilisation, and the foundations were now in place for further developments in archaeology.

In contrast to earlier periods, the twentieth century has been characterised by an increase in the number of excavations which have been undertaken by many nationalities, and by the rescue archaeology which has been necessitated because of new building programmes which have threatened the monuments. These salvage campaigns, undertaken as international projects, have produced successful and often spectacular results.

Figure 24 Excavation at Meroë in 1912 involved the use of manpower and mechanical devices to remove the debris from site 119. Garstang installed a small railway line to facilitate this work.

Whereas, in previous centuries, archaeologists often concentrated on tombs and temples, the twentieth century has increasingly emphasised the importance of settlement sites such as the royal workmen's communities at Tell el-Amarna and Deir el-Medina, although unsurpassed royal funerary treasures such as those found in the Tomb of Tutankhamun at Thebes and at Tanis have also been discovered.

In general, there has been an increased awareness in Egyptology of the need to use multidisciplinary scientific techniques in excavation, following the example of other areas of archaeology where fewer large monuments or written texts have survived, thus forcing the archaeologists to seek evidence of a different kind. However, despite this new approach, which is now followed at various sites in Egypt, no systematic survey of the whole country has yet been undertaken and completed.

One of the most successful and effective archaeologists of the early twentieth century was the American G. A. Reisner (1867–1942). Supported by the philanthropist Mrs P. A. Hearst, Reisner undertook a series of excavation campaigns which included sites across the range of prehistoric and historic periods. His main achievements were in his studies of the dynastic cemeteries at Giza and Naga-ed-Der; at Giza, he discovered the intact tomb

Figure 25 Garstang (right) stands in a corner of Tomb No. 12 at Beni Hasan. On the trestle table in front of him, there are some of the fine models he discovered in these tombs.

of Queen Hetepheres, the mother of the builder of the Great Pyramid, and also the important mastaba tombs of the Old Kingdom nobility, as well as the Valley Temple of Mycerinus. However, he also carried out pioneering studies in Nubian prehistory, where his excavation of graves and cemeteries enabled him to establish a system of relative dating which has been of continuing significance.

Reisner was Professor of Egyptology at Harvard from 1914 to 1942, and he is remembered as the archaeologist who developed Petrie's systems of detailed recording. He worked at the Berlin Museum in 1895, and was strongly influenced by the Berlin School, particularly by Adolf Erman. He carried out the first fully scientific excavations in Egypt, taking the recording of objects to new lengths. Each piece was noted in an objects register and also photographed; in addition, he kept a diary, so that subsequent researchers would be able to reconstruct all the details of his discoveries. His work at Naga-ed-Der established new standards for archaeology in Egypt and elsewhere, and he set out five basic principles that were to be the foundation for all his work. These were:

1 the need to have an organised staff of Europeans and workmen, who were fully trained in excavation and recording methods;

Figure 26 Professor and Mrs Garstang (standing and seated right) entertain friends in a tomb at Beni Hasan. The table, set with china and flowers, makes a marked contrast to the surroundings.

2   the need to excavate whole sites and cemeteries rather than individual tombs, and the unacceptability of searching for beautiful objects as museum specimens;

3   the correct method of excavating every building or cemetery, by removing and recording each layer in inverse chronological order;

4   the need to keep a complete record – notes, drawings and photographs – of every stage of the work; and

5   the need to publish, as completely and carefully as possible, the records of each tomb.

Reisner's attention to detail ensured that his publications were monumental in size, and contained a wealth of information which previously had not been made available. However, because of the amount of material he amassed, much of his work remained unpublished when he died. Dows Dunham (1890–1984), an American Egyptologist whom Reisner had trained, became one of his ablest assistants. In addition to his involvement in excavations where he worked with other archaeologists, Dows Dunham was at Giza with Reisner in 1914–15 and 1925–8, and at Gebel Barkal in 1916. He also took part in the Harvard–Boston expedition in the Sudan in 1919–23, and held posts at the Boston Museum of Fine Arts, where he eventually succeeded Reisner as curator. When he retired, Dows Dunham published Reisner's excavations, thus ensuring that Reisner's great achievements could be fully appreciated.

Another major study at Giza was undertaken by the German Egyptologist H. Junker (1877–1962), who, from 1912 to 1929, systematically cleaned and recorded many of the Old Kingdom mastaba tombs. The inscriptions and other evidence from his work provided information about the Old Kingdom officials, and from their names and titles, it has been possible to reconstruct much of the social, economic, religious and administrative details of that period. Junker pursued a carefully prepared academic career, and although he never achieved the standards reached by Petrie or Reisner, his organisational methods and general competence as a scholar ensured that his contribution to Egyptology was significant.

Junker and Newberry had been the inspiration for a young Egyptologist, Selim Hassan (1886–1961), who was the first Egyptian to be appointed as Professor of Egyptology in the University of Cairo (1928–36), and later (1936–9) became Deputy Director of the Egyptian Antiquities Service. He also worked at Giza, where he undertook excavations, clearing mastaba tombs, the Great Sphinx and its temple, investigating other areas, and excavating at the Great Pyramid and its associated mortuary temple.

However, interest in the pyramids extended beyond the Giza group. Earlier archaeologists had worked at sites such as Illahun, Hawara and Dahshur and, at the turn of the century, important studies were carried out on the pyramids of Dynasty 5. L. Borchadt (1863–1938), founder of the German Institute of Archaeology, excavated the sun-temple of King Niuserre at Abu Ghurab (1898–1901), and the pyramids of Abusir (1906). U. Hölscher (1878–1963), a German architect and archaeologist, worked with him at Abusir, and their publications and studies brought a new dimension to the history of architecture. Hölscher later led the excavations undertaken at the temple of Medinet Habu by the Oriental Institute of Chicago, where they set new standards in clearing and copying the monuments.

The early part of the twentieth century was also a time for intensive activity in the Theban necropolis. The discovery of two caches of royal mummies at Deir el-Bahri and in the Valley of the Kings in the 1870s and 1890s undoubtedly aroused renewed interest in the area. Theodore M. Davis (1837–1915), an American businessman who became interested in Egyptology, obtained a permit to excavate (1903–12) in the Valley of the Kings. Although Davis financed these expeditions, the Egyptian government now requested that all excavation should be carried out by an experienced archaeologist, and so Davis employed several workers who included the Englishmen Weigall, Ayrton and Carter. These expeditions were very successful, and revealed the royal tombs of Hatshepsut, Horemheb, Siptah and Prince Montu-her-khepshef. Carter also discovered the tomb of Tuthmosis IV. In 1907, Davis excavated Tomb 55 in the Valley of the Kings, whose occupant, originally identified as Queen Tiye, still remains a controversial figure. Another important tomb, that of Yuya and Thuya, the parents of Queen Tiye, was found, and here much of the treasure remained intact. Theodore Davis not only sponsored these excavations, he also supported the cost of the resulting publications. The remarkable objects from these burials eventually entered the collections of the Cairo Museum, the Boston Museum, and the Metropolitan Museum, New York.

However, the greatest prize in the Valley of the Kings still awaited discovery. Howard Carter (1874–1939), the British Egyptologist who had first joined the Archaeological Survey in Egypt in 1891 as an artist. He was subsequently trained as an archaeologist by Petrie, Griffith and Naville, and worked for Petrie at Tell el-Amarna and for Naville at Deir el-Bahri. Made Chief Inspector of antiquities of Upper Egypt in 1899, he was in charge of Theodore Davis's excavations in the Valley of the Kings from 1902, and he returned to the area to work for Lord Carnarvon from 1904. The fifth Earl of Carnarvon (1866–1923), a British collector who first visited Egypt in 1903, supported Carter's excavations at Thebes, and this proved to be a very successful partnership.

From 1917 to 1922, Carter's searches in the Valley of the Kings had produced few results, but in November 1922, he discovered the tomb of Tutankhamun, justifying his earlier claim to Lord Carnarvon that the area was not exhausted and that they should continue their search.

This almost undisturbed tomb, complete with the body of its original occupant and most of his funerary treasure (the tomb had been entered by robbers in antiquity), was the most spectacular archaeological discovery ever made in Egypt. However, in terms of the development and progression of Egyptology as a discipline, it is almost equally important to be able to state that Carter did not ransack the tomb to gain immediate access to the treasure, as many of his predecessors would have done. Instead, he worked with a team of experts to ensure that the contents of the tomb were carefully cleaned, packed and transported to the Cairo Museum. The whole process took ten years to complete.

Carter left diaries and detailed records of his work which are now held in Oxford. Although he produced a detailed general account of his discovery of the tomb, which conveys his personal feelings at finding the burial, ill-health and other problems prevented him from producing a full report of his discovery.

Among the members of the team who worked on the tomb were Arthur Mace (1874–1928) and Harry Burton (1879–1940). Mace, a British Egyptologist who had worked with Petrie, with Reisner at Giza and Naga-ed-Der, and for the Metropolitan Museum at Lisht, joined Carter at Thebes in 1922–4. Burton, a British Egyptologist and photographer, had worked for Theodore Davis at Thebes, and in 1914 he became photographer to the Egyptian Expedition of the Metropolitan Museum of Art, New York. It was arranged that he should work for Carnarvon and Carter (1922–33), and he produced the extensive photographic archive of the contents of Tutankhamun's tomb. Another important contribution was made by Alfred Lucas (1867–1945), who, as Chemist to the Antiquities Service (1923–32), was seconded to work for nine winters on cleaning and restoring these treasures.

Other areas of the Theban necropolis were also under investigation during this period. H. Winlock (1884–1950), an American archaeologist, undertook important excavations for the Metropolitan Museum of Art, New York, where he eventually became director (1932–9). These sites included Lisht and the Kharga Oasis, but his most notable excavations were at Thebes, where he continued the work of Naville at the Dynasty 11 temple of Mentuhotep and the Dynasty 18 temple of Hatshepsut. At Mentuhotep's temple, he discovered two intact royal burials and, interred in the royal precinct, the bodies of sixty soldiers who had died in battle and, as an honour, had been buried in their king's temple area. At Thebes, Winlock also discovered important tombs which contained many works of art, including the tomb models of the house and estate workshops of a Dynasty 11 Chancellor, Meket-Re. He also uncovered the archive of letters belonging to Hekanakhte, and through this family correspondence and his other discoveries, Winlock was able to contribute substantially to knowledge of the First and Second Intermediate Periods. Petrie, Weigall and others praised his meticulous excavation techniques, and his achievements as a historian are equally valued.

Another major feature of twentieth-century excavation in Egypt have been the salvage campaigns undertaken in Nubia as a result of the second raising of the first Aswan dam and the construction of the High Dam (Sadd el Aali). After the first Aswan dam was built at the First Cataract (1899–1902) and subsequently raised, the increased water level threatened many of the important archaeological sites in this area, some of which would be lost for ever. The Egyptian Survey Department therefore inaugurated an Archaeological Survey of Nubia, which involved a survey and general description of the whole area, to show the sequence of cultures, and also an urgent and rapid excavation of sites of special significance. This survey was undertaken by Reisner (1907–8), who developed a new methodology for dealing with a project of this magnitude. His discoveries allowed an overview of the culture to be built up, and he established the basis for future work in Nubia. Further south in the Sudan, his exploration of pyramids and sites there provided new information about the Kushite kingdom that had conquered and ruled Egypt in Dynasty 25. As well as the excavations in Nubia, another important aspect of the survey were the specialised palaeopathological studies carried out on large numbers of skeletal remains by G. Elliot Smith and F. Wood Jones.

In the 1950s, the governments of Egypt and the Sudan decided to build a new dam at Aswan. The earlier dam had formed a reservoir with a capacity

Figure 27 An early twentieth-century photograph showing the Great Temple of Ramesses II at Abu Simbel in its original location. After construction of the High Dam at Aswan, it was moved to a new location as part of a major UNESCO project to save the monuments of Nubia.

of 5 milliard cubic metres, whereas the new dam was intended to produce 150 milliard cubic metres. Because of the great rise in the population of Egypt since the early 1900s, the new dam was needed to regulate and distribute the water effectively so that the land could be more extensively irrigated to increase the food supply. Also, the hydroelectric capacity provided by the new dam would cancel the existing need to import fuel, and would supply the means of electrification required for industry. It was envisaged that the extended agricultural capacity and the savings achieved on coal and oil imports would offset the costs of constructing the dam.

With aid provided by the Soviet Union for the preliminary stage of the work, construction on the High Dam began in 1960. The dam would contain 43 million cubic metres of material, to form a barrier some 980 metres (3,215 feet) in height. Behind it, a great stretch of water would be created which would cover an area 500 km (312 miles) in length extending in parts to a width of 19–26 km (12–16 miles). Thus, the land from Aswan in Egypt to Aksha in the Sudan would be covered by water, with the resultant loss of many archaeological sites, as well as people's homes and agricultural land.

The effect on the landscape was obviously going to be profound and irreversible. When the earlier dam had been built, some land had been submerged, but the local population had been able to build their villages on higher ground. Now, however, Nubia would effectively disappear, and it was planned that the people would leave their land and make new lives, many in purpose-built villages around Kom Ombo and Esna.

There was worldwide concern about the loss of the monuments of Nubia, which were regarded as part of the universal heritage of civilisation, and an appeal was made through UNESCO for international assistance to save as many of the monuments as possible before the projected date for completing the dam in 1965. Various schemes were included in the overall project. First, there would be a thorough process of documenting the monuments, using photography, epigraphy and photogrammetry, a technique which renders the relief of buildings and statues into contour lines so that accurate reproductions could be made. Second, there would be a programme of urgent excavation to complete existing work and to undertake new projects. Aerial photography would be used to record the features of the area and enable a map of the sites to be produced. Finally, there would be an elaborate scheme to rescue the most important monuments. Some of these would be dismantled and cut into sections, and then moved to new sites where they could be reassembled. It was planned that several sites should be turned into 'oases' for some of the monuments, where they could be surrounded by natural scenery. These included the promontory near Aswan, now known as 'New Kalabsha', where the Temple of Kalabsha, the 'kiosk' of Kertassi and the Temple of Beit el-Wali were eventually reconstructed; the area near the former site of Wadi es-Sebua where the Temples of Wadi es-Sebua and Dakka were to be reassembled; the area near the former site of Amada, where the Temple of Amada would be rebuilt; and the park in Khartoum where several temples from Sudanese Nubia would be set around a stretch of water that imitated the Nile. Two major monuments, however, would have to be preserved near to their original locations, as their natural settings were so much an integral part of their original architectural design. These were the rock-cut temples at Abu Simbel and the group of buildings originally erected on the island of Philae.

The UNESCO appeal received a sympathetic response; the Director, M. René Maheu, stated that 'The rescue of Abu Simbel is a spiritual act.' Countries expressed their willingness to engage in a co-operative salvage operation, and provided architects, engineers, archaeologists and copyists. In return, Egypt offered generous rewards to participating countries: they would be allowed to keep at least half of the finds (except some unique

Figure 28 An early twentieth-century photograph of the Temple of Dendur in Nubia. As part of the Nubian rescue project, the temple was dismantled and re-erected at the Metropolitan Museum, New York.

pieces) from the excavations; they would be given concessions to excavate at sites in Egypt which hitherto had been unavailable; some archaeological material from the state collections would be offered to them; and some of the temples and monuments, which otherwise would have been submerged, would be presented as gifts and transferred to these countries.

The project was ultimately successful: not only were many monuments removed to new locations in Egypt and the Sudan, but others were transported to special museum sites in Europe and America. However, most publicity focused on two high-profile rescue missions carried out at Philae and Abu Simbel.

Philae, the ancient Egyptian Pi-lak, was an island situated at the First Cataract which, as a place of great natural beauty, came to be regarded as a pre-eminent religious centre. To the ancient Egyptians, it represented the primeval island where creation was believed to have taken place, and the cult of the main temple was dedicated to Isis, the chief mother-goddess of Egyptian mythology. When the first Aswan dam was built and then raised early in the twentieth century, the ancient monuments on Philae were submerged for nine months of every year. However, the construction of the High Dam would have resulted in the continuous although partial submersion of the monuments and, with no respite period in which to dry out, ultimately the walls would have eroded and collapsed.

When it was decided that the Philae monuments should be saved, several schemes were put forward, including the suggestion, originally proposed in 1902, that the buildings should be dismantled and reassembled on a neighbouring island. Another proposal involved creating a 'receptacle' around Philae, which would itself be contained within a larger receptacle, so that the waters of the newly created lake could be prevented from reaching the island, but this posed problems because it would be difficult to ensure that the receptacles remained watertight. Ultimately, it was decided that the monuments should be dismantled and rebuilt on the neighbouring island of Agilkia. This has ensured that they remain above the water level throughout the year, and that the temples can now be visited at any time by scholars and tourists. Also, the magnificent island setting of the original location has been preserved.

The most difficult rescue operation, however, centred around two temples built by Ramesses II at Abu Simbel. These still formed an integral part of the great sandstone cliff out of which they had been hollowed. The Great Temple, dedicated to Ptah, Amen-Re, Re-Harakhte and the deified Ramesses II, contained important scenes of Ramesses II's military campaigns. Discovered by Burckhardt in 1813, and subsequently excavated by Belzoni, the temple has colossal statues over 20 metres (65 feet) in height along its facade, and was designed to impress the ancient Nubians with the might and power of their Egyptian king and overlord. The nearby Smaller Temple, built by Ramesses II and dedicated to Hathor and to a favourite wife, Nefertari, is also impressive.

Because these monuments harmonised with their background and were such an integral part of the cliffside, it was decided that it was necessary to move them to a similar setting and so, between 1964 and 1968, they were transferred to a new site slightly further away from the river and at a higher level. This has ensured that the temples remained beyond the rising waters of Lake Nasser, that stretch of water within Egypt which has been created behind the High Dam.

Other schemes were proposed, such as the French plan to erect a huge semi-circular dam around the temples which would hold the water at bay, but this had the disadvantage that the temples could then only be viewed from above. There were also technical difficulties in trying to prevent the infiltration of water underneath the protective dam, and so the scheme was eventually abandoned, although it had received support from many archaeologists because it had the considerable advantage that it left the temples in their original locations.

A second French scheme involved building concrete tanks around the temples and then using the increased volume of water brought into the tanks to raise them up, but again cost and technical difficulties proved insuperable and the scheme was abandoned. An Italian proposal, which would have surrounded the temples with a framework of concrete and then used hundreds of jacks to raise the buildings on 'pedestals' to a site where they would be away from the floods, was also too expensive.

The scheme eventually adopted in 1963 had been devised by a Swedish company. It involved removing the mass of rock above the buildings, and releasing the temples from their cliffside locations. A coffer-dam was built to hold back the water of the lake, and the buildings were then cut up into sections and dismantled; all the large blocks were then taken first to a holding area, and eventually to the new site. In the new location, the facades and interior walls of the temples were then rebuilt some 64 metres (210 feet) above and 180 metres (590 feet) further back from their original locations. A dome-shaped structure of reinforced concrete was also built which acted as a replacement for the original cliffside from which the temples had been cut. This surrounded and held together all the reinstated sections, and it supported the rock facade.

This scheme was less complex and expensive than the others. It also had the advantage of allowing visitors to have continuing access to the temples and enabling them to see the sun enter the sanctuary of the Great Temple twice a year to illuminate the divine statues within. This had been a feature of great importance in the original temple. However, critics of the scheme claimed that the removal of the temples from their original location has destroyed the impact of the buildings. Nevertheless, when the temples were re-opened in 1968, they were regarded as appropriate symbols of the success of this UNESCO operation. Specialists from several countries had joined together to save the temples from destruction, and the whole Nubian salvage operation has been an outstanding example of international co-operation which is unprecedented in the history of archaeology.

In the second half of the twentieth century, new archaeological evidence has continued to emerge, forcing Egyptologists to change and adapt many of their ideas and conclusions. It has been essential to reassess and re-evaluate many important aspects of Egyptian civilisation.

The Delta is one area where a wealth of new discoveries has posed fresh questions. One of the most extensive sites, usually known by its Greek name of Tanis, was probably the ancient Egyptian town of Dja'net. It lies near to the modern village of San el-Hagar, and early excavations were carried out there by Mariette (late nineteenth century) and Petrie (1883–6). The most spectacular finds, however, were made by Pierre Montet, who worked there from 1921 to 1951. Montet (1883–1966), a French archaeologist who also excavated the coastal site of Byblos in Lebanon, discovered a series of intact royal tombs at Tanis which had belonged to some of the kings and princes of Dynasties 21 and 22. The tombs were well concealed, within the temple precinct; they had no superstructures and the burial chambers were underground. Because the environmental conditions of the Delta are not conducive to preserving organic material, the royal mummies did not survive here, but gold and silver coffins, jewellery and the other equipment which were found in these tombs almost equalled the funerary treasure of Tutankhamun. The discovery of such magnificent pieces in the tombs of this period, when Tanis had become the chief capital and royal residence, forced Egyptologists to reassess these dynasties. They had previously been regarded as a period of decline when the kingdom was virtually divided between the kings ruling from Tanis in the north, and the high-priests holding power at Thebes in the south. Before this discovery, no one could have imagined that the kings of Dynasty 21 would have been able to prepare such lavish burials for themselves.

The excavations at Tanis also raised other questions of historical significance. In the central area of the site, where the Temple of Amun was situated, much of the inscribed material dated to the reign of Ramesses II. Montet therefore speculated that this site was the Ramesside town of Pi-Ramesse, a major residence built and used in Ramesside times. However, it is now thought that these inscribed pieces of Ramesside date were probably brought to Tanis as dismantled building material from other, earlier sites, since none of the buildings that have been excavated at Tanis have provided a date earlier than the reigns of the kings of Dynasty 21. It is most likely that the city was actually first established in Dynasty 21.

Nevertheless, there have been several interpretations of the site by different archaeologists, and it is an excellent example of how the same evidence can be used to support very different theories. Mariette claimed that the evidence of the statuary and inscriptions at the site indicated that Tanis was both Pi-Ramesse and the earlier city of Avaris, founded by the Hyksos as their capital. Petrie supported the idea that it was Pi-Ramesse, but other scholars concluded that, because of the geographical position of the site and the textual evidence, Tanis could not be identified with either Pi-Ramesse or Avaris.

It was this controversy that first intrigued Montet and prompted him to apply for permission to excavate Tanis. There were also other, conflicting theories. Mahmoud Hamza (1890–1980), an inspector in the Antiquities Service, had excavated at Qantir, a site 22 km (15 miles) to the south of Tanis, and evidence there led him to propose that Qantir was in fact the site of Pi-Ramesse. A leading Egyptian Egyptologist, Labib Habachi (1906–1984), who excavated throughout Egypt, paid particular attention to the Delta sites of Bubastis (Tell Basta) and Qantir. He supported the identification of Qantir with Pi-Ramesse, and also suggested that the monuments at Pi-Ramesse, which bore the name of Ramesses II, had later been dismantled by the kings of Dynasties 21 and 22, and used to build their new city at Tanis, thus explaining the large number of Ramesside inscribed stones at Tanis.

The most recent conclusions are that the site of Qantir was indeed Pi-Ramesse, the Delta residence of the Ramesside kings which was mentioned as Ramses in the biblical account of the Exodus. The site of Tell el-Maskhuta, explored by Naville in 1883, was probably Pithom, the other ancient Ramesside city named in the Bible.

Over the past few years, the Austrian team directed by M. Bietak has carried out excavations at Tell el-Dab'a, a site near to Qantir on the Pelusiac branch of the Nile. Evidence from this site has provided exciting new information about the presence of foreigners in Egypt, and has indicated that there was a large influx from Asia in the Second Intermediate Period, at a date around the time when the Hyksos began to rule in Egypt. It is now considered most likely that Tell el-Dab'a, rather than Tanis or Qantir, was the site of the Hyksos capital of Avaris. At Tanis, the French mission continues to excavate and has revealed that there was some large-scale building activity in the temple area, at various times throughout the Third Intermediate Period.

Another feature of twentieth-century Egyptology is an increased awareness of the importance of the study of communities and the lives of ordinary people, in contrast to the earlier obsession with great temples and tombs. Petrie pioneered this approach with his detailed and painstaking excavation of the Dynasty 12 pyramid workmen's town of Kahun. Subsequently, two other royal necropolis workmen's towns have been uncovered, providing a wealth of information about the lives of these special royal workforces and their families.

At Deir el-Medina, the town and cemetery were built to accommodate the families of the royal workmen who were engaged in creating the New Kingdom tombs in the Valley of the Kings. The Institut Français d'Archéologie Orientale has excavated the site since 1922, and B. Bruyère (1879–1971), who became Director of Excavations for the Institute in 1928, worked at Deir el-Medina for many years, producing detailed reports of his fieldwork there. Jaroslav Černy (see page 36) worked on the extensive collection of ostraca found at the site, and altogether, the evidence from Deir el-Medina has produced unequalled information about the working conditions, legal arrangements, and religious organisation of the workmen's community. At Tell el-Amarna, careful excavation of the royal workmen's village by B. J. Kemp for the Egypt Exploration Society has added new insight about the religious practices at Tell el-Amarna, and has provided further information about the lives of the royal necropolis workers.

However, in addition to the settlement sites or towns, new excavations of the great ancient cemeteries have also revolutionised our knowledge of the funerary practices. The Egypt Exploration Society has had a long association with Saqqara, the necropolis of the capital city of Memphis.

The earliest work involved epigraphic studies, but in 1952 W. B. Emery was appointed as the Society's field director, and he began to undertake excavations in the Archaic Necropolis.

Emery (1903–1971) had previously worked for the Egyptian Antiquities Service as Director of the Archaeological Survey of Nubia (1929–35), excavating graves and houses, and also the Nubian fortress at Quban. Then, from 1935 to 1939, he became the Service's Director of Excavation at North Saqqara, when he excavated the Dynasty 1 cemetery, and, in 1935, he uncovered the famous Tomb of Hemaka. He later became Edwards Professor of Egyptology (1951–70) at University College London, and worked on the fortress at Buhen in the Sudan (1957–63), and at Qasr Ibrim, making a major contribution to the UNESCO salvage operation.

The discoveries he made at Saqqara relating to the tombs of Dynasty 1 are of great significance, because, until then, the only major studies of this period had been provided by the work of Amélineau and Petrie at Abydos. Emery's finds at Saqqara revealed new information about the art, architecture and technology of this most significant period. One theory he proposed was that the great mastaba tombs which he was excavating at Saqqara were in fact the burial places of Egypt's earliest rulers. He regarded the tombs at Abydos, which Petrie had claimed were the earliest royal burial places, as cenotaphs.

Following the war, in 1952 Emery resumed his excavations in the Archaic Necropolis at Saqqara and, as field director of the Egypt Exploration Society, he now gained new evidence about the architecture of the earliest dynastic tombs. The Suez crisis in 1956 and the desperate need to salvage the monuments of Nubia led to a temporary cessation of the work at Saqqara, but Emery returned there in 1964, as Director of the Egypt Exploration Society's excavations, to search for the tomb of Imhotep, the man who was the vizier (chief minister) of King Djoser and architect of the Step Pyramid at Saqqara.

Emery believed that Imhotep's tomb was located in the Archaic Necropolis in North Saqqara, and when, in 1956, he discovered a mud-brick tomb there, datable to that period, he was convinced that he had found Imhotep's burial place, or possibly his cenotaph. However, subsequent work carried out there between 1964 and Emery's death in 1971 revealed that this was not Imhotep's tomb but a vast complex which contained the burials of sacred animals, including ibises, baboons, falcons and cows (mothers of the Apis-bulls), who were worshipped at Saqqara. These cults were a feature of Saqqara, and the Serapeum, first excavated by Mariette, had been the centre of the cult of the Apis-bull, the most important of these animal cults. Excavations undertaken by Emery revealed not only the sacred animals' burial places but also the chapels, shrines and associated administrative buildings, which provided a wealth of information about the animal cults and the religious practices which were prevalent in the Late Period and the

Ptolemaic era. Bronze temple furniture and cult implements, and mummified animals found at the site have since formed the basis of several important studies, while the discovery of huge quantities of objects and papyri has
provided unparalleled information about Memphis at this date. Of particular note is the Archive of Hor, who was a scribe who lived in the reign of
Ptolemy IV (181–145 BC). Hor wrote or dictated documents which comprised a whole archive. Some of these have been discovered and translated,
and are of considerable historical significance. Emery's work at Saqqara contributed greatly to our understanding of both the earliest and latest periods
of pharaonic history, and subsequently it has been continued by the Egypt
Exploration Society. One aspect of this work, carried out on the Saqqara
plateau, has been undertaken by a joint EES–Leiden team, initiated and
directed by G. T. Martin. This has set out to rediscover tombs initially visited
by Lepsius's epigraphic expedition in the 1840s, and has revealed some spectacular tombs of the late Dynasty 18 and Dynasty 19, including that of
Horemheb. These tombs and their wall reliefs have provided much information about the art, architecture, funerary customs and history of that
period. In particular, their finds emphasise that Memphis and Saqqara were
of great importance even at this period when the state and religious capital
was at Thebes.

However, despite archaeological advances, some major questions still
remain unanswered. A particularly interesting example is the biblical
account of Joseph, the subsequent sojourn of the Children of Israel in
Egypt, and the Exodus. According to the Bible, Joseph, the son of Jacob,
was sold into slavery by his jealous half-brothers and sent down to Egypt.
Ultimately, he gained great wealth and power there and even became the
vizier. He brought his family – the tribe of Israel – into Egypt, and they
remained there for some four hundred and thirty years, until a later pharaoh
forced them to labour on the building sites, making bricks for the cities of
Ramses and Pithom. Moses, the child of Hebrew slaves living in Egypt
who was rescued from the bulrushes of the Nile by an Egyptian princess
and brought up in the royal palace, ultimately led the Hebrews out of
Egypt. He probably took them out from the Delta area, where they would
have lived near to the cities they were building for the pharaoh. The king's
attempts to recapture them by force were doomed to failure when the windblown waters (perhaps of the 'Sea of Reeds') parted briefly and they were
able to escape. They passed on into Sinai where Moses received the Ten
Commandments, and finally reached their destination in the Holy Land.

Despite attempts to discover any contemporary literary or archaeological evidence in Egypt which might throw further light on this account, no
evidence has yet been found. This is perhaps unsurprising because the
Egyptians would not have wished to record this successful uprising of their
workforce, and in the scheme of their empire as a whole, it was probably
not of great significance. However, scholars and others have nevertheless

tried to determine the date of the Exodus, and to identify the pharaoh who was involved in this event. The early historian Josephus identified the Exodus with the expulsion of the Hyksos by the Theban rulers (*c.* 1580 BC), but most modern scholars accept a date in Dynasty 19 (*c.* 1200 BC). However, there has been a suggestion that Joseph could have entered Egypt among the groups of Semitic-speaking peoples who took up residence there from the Old Kingdom (*c.* 2340 BC) down to the Hyksos period (*c.* 1650 BC). The identification of the expulsion of the Hyksos with the Exodus seems unlikely, not least because, whereas the Hyksos were driven out by the Egyptians, the Hebrews wanted to leave. Also, there have been other interpretations, including an attempt to identify Joseph with Yuya, the father-in-law of Amenhotep III; at one time, scholars believed that Yuya was of foreign origin. Also, it has been suggested that the Exodus could have taken place at the end of the Amarna Period, following Akhenaten's period of religious experimentation.

However, the working conditions of the Hebrews which are described in the Bible appear to indicate the late New Kingdom, by which time the Hebrews probably formed part of a group of itinerant workers (the Apiru) who had lived in the eastern Delta for many years and were now forced to work on the many building projects that the Ramesside pharaohs initiated. It has been suggested that the biblical account in fact refers to the Hebrews' involvement in brickmaking for two particular cities that were being built in Dynasty 19.

Originally, Merneptah was identified as the most likely pharaoh of the Exodus, but in 1896, archaeologists discovered a stela (now known as the Israel Stela), which Merneptah had usurped from an earlier king, Amenhotep III. He had it inscribed with a text which is a major source for Egypt's Libyan War of that period, but more importantly, it provides the only extant reference to Israel in an Egyptian inscription. According to this, Israel is already established as a geographical entity and homeland by the middle of Merneptah's reign which, if he was the king of the Exodus, would be impossible. Therefore, his predecessor, Ramesses II, is more likely to have played this role. So far, the archaeology has provided no further evidence about these important biblical events, although public interest in the subject certainly helped to gain financial support for the excavations carried out in the Delta during the nineteenth century. It is possible that renewed interest in these sites may yet produce some evidence on this matter.

CHAPTER XI

THE CONTRIBUTION OF BIOMEDICAL STUDIES

—— •◆• ——

Today, Egyptian mummies are regarded as a valuable historical and scientific resource, which can studied to provided information about disease, diet, living conditions and funerary customs. However, Europeans first encountered 'mummy' as a medicinal ingredient which, in the sixteenth and seventeenth centuries, was widely used in apothecaries' shops throughout Europe. 'Mummy' was bought to treat a whole range of illnesses and symptoms, and it even enjoyed royal approval: King Francis I of France reputedly treated his ailments with a mixture of mummy and pulverised rhubarb that he always carried with him.

According to the writings of Abd' el-Latif, the twelfth-century Arab physician who travelled to Egypt, the word 'mummy' was derived from a Persian term *mumia* which meant pitch or bitumen. This substance originated from the 'Mummy Mountain' in Persia; this flowed down from the mountain top and mixed with the water that carried it, thus forming a liquid that was claimed to have medicinal properties.

Probably even before 1100 AD, mummy had became a desirable medicinal treatment, and as its fame grew, demand exceeded supply; in addition to the material that could be obtained from the Mummy Mountain, other sources now had to be sought. Because the preserved bodies of the ancient Egyptians frequently had a blackened appearance, this led to the incorrect assumption that originally, they had been soaked in bitumen, and would thus provide an alternative supply of *mumia*. Abd' el-Latif commented that 'The mummy found in the hollow corpses in Egypt differs but immaterially from the nature of mineral mummy; and where any difficulty arises in procuring, the latter may be substituted in its stead.' Thus, when the bodies of the ancient Egyptians became valuable as an alternative source of this medicinal ingredient, the word *mumia* was applied also to them, and they became known as 'mummies', a term which is still in use today for human remains where the skin is preserved.

There was soon a flourishing trade in mummy tissue, and foreigners began to trade from Alexandria, shipping out complete mummies or packages of tissue fragments. Their methods of obtaining the tissue were unscrupulous. At first, they ransacked the tombs and broke up the mummies that they found there; when the Egyptian authorities attempted to curtail this export trade, the merchants then resorted to other means. However, even with the additional supply of the medicinal ingredient

Figure 29 A group of mummies and coffins uncovered in the ground at Abydos, 1908. Such objects were frequently transported to museums in Europe and America, where substantial Egyptian collections had been established.

supplied by the ancient remains, the demand could not be met, and by the sixteenth century, the ancient tissue was augmented by tissue taken from the bodies of the recently dead who were often executed criminals. These bodies were treated with bitumen and laid out in the sun, so that their tissues became mummified, and could then be sold as the authentic medicinal ingredient. By the eighteenth century, the undesirability of such practices was acknowledged by the authorities, and laws came into force to prevent the export of mummies from Egypt for this purpose. The traders were imprisoned, and a tax was levied, but although the worst aspects of the trade were reduced, there was a continuing demand for *mumia*, and it was still used in Europe as a medicinal ingredient as late as the nineteenth century.

One of the earliest travellers to describe his personal export of mummies was Prince Radziwill (1549–1616), a Polish nobleman who stayed in Egypt in 1583 in the course of his pilgrimage to the Holy Land. In Alexandria, he purchased two mummies which he carried on board ship when he sailed to Crete, but when a storm blew up, his companions laid the blame on the mummies, and he was forced to throw them overboard. An early study of mummification was produced by Thomas Greenhill (1681–1740), a distinguished physician and surgeon, who published *Nekrokedeia; or, The Art of Embalming* in 1705. This explained some aspects of mummification and used line drawings to illustrate various stages of the procedure.

By the eighteenth century, in Europe and America, there was a growing interest in mummies as objects of anatomical and scientific curiosity. Brought back as souvenirs by wealthy travellers to Egypt, some of these were subsequently unwrapped or 'unrolled' in front of assembled audiences. Many of these 'unrollings' were frivolous entertainments for the owner's invited guests, and much evidence of scientific and academic value was carelessly discarded. However, some of these procedures were carried out by serious researchers who sought information about ancient funerary customs and the mummification process itself, and they have left detailed accounts of their work which still have value today for researchers in this field.

Thomas Joseph Pettigrew (1791–1865) was a pioneer in the study of mummies. The son of a naval surgeon, he practised as a surgeon in Savile Row in London. In 1818 he met Belzoni, who aroused his interest in Egyptology, and he began the study of hieroglyphs. However, his medical background gave him a special facility for investigating mummies, and he published a *History of Egyptian Mummies and an Account of the Worship and Embalming of the Sacred Animals* (1842), in which he refers to his acquaintance with Belzoni, who had invited him to be present at the unwrapping of three mummies.

In fact, Pettigrew unrolled and gave demonstrations on many mummies. He purchased some of these to form part of his own collection of Egyptian antiquities, and others were presented to him by friends and colleagues. Benjamin Henderson (1788–1881), a British surgeon, bought two mummies at Thebes in 1820, and these were later sold in 1831, one to the Royal College of Surgeons in London, which was unrolled by Pettigrew, and the other to John Davidson (1797–1836), a physician whose interest in Egyptology was fostered by Pettigrew. Davidson unwrapped this and another mummy at the Royal Institution, London, in 1833 and published an account of his work in *An Address on Embalming Generally* (1833). Pettigrew also acquired and examined another mummy which had once

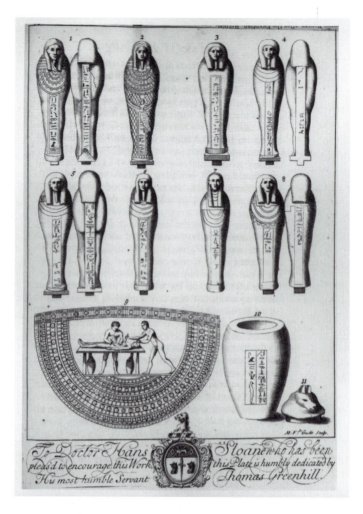

Figure 30 Some early studies included scientific accounts of mummification. This plate, dedicated to the physician and naturalist Hans Sloane, shows various mummy wrappings, the process of eviscerating the mummy, and a Canopic jar. From Thomas Greenhill's *Nekrokedeia; or, The Art of Embalming* (1705).

been in the possession of the British traveller and writer, Charles Perry, who mentions it in his book *View of the Levant* (1743).

Pettigrew performed his autopsies at various London venues, before titled, medical, literary and scientific audiences but, unlike the procedures at some unrollings, his work was meticulous. In his book, he described the procedure he followed when he unwrapped mummies, demonstrating that he adopted a multidisciplinary approach, calling on the services of experts in various fields who could, for example, provide authoritative accounts on the textile fibres of the bandages and identify the insects found in the mummies. His book also discussed the development and significance of mummification, and was later described by Elliot Smith and Warren Dawson as 'a monument of exact observation'.

At about the same time, another medical practitioner pursued similar interests. Augustus Bozzi Granville (1783–1872) was of Italian origin and spent part of his early life as a political prisoner. He eventually left Italy and travelled in the East, before moving to London and assuming the name of Granville. An interest in Egyptology led him to investigate an Egyptian mummy of the Persian Period (when the Persians conquered Egypt and made it part of their Empire), and he published the results of his findings in *An Essay on Egyptian Mummies, with Observations on the Art of Embalming* (1825), noting that the mummy showed evidence of ovarian disease.

Some researchers worked independently, such as John Warren (1778–1856), the first Professor of Anatomy and Surgery at Harvard, who in 1821 unrolled a Ptolemaic mummy which had been donated to the hospital museum, and H. W. Diamond (1809–1886), a British physician and a pioneer of scientific photography, who purchased and published an account of a mummy in 1843. This mummy was eventually given to the Royal College of Surgeons in London where, along with other mummies in the collection, it was destroyed in the Second World War.

However, the multidisciplinary approach which Pettigrew fostered was also successfully pursued by another team. These were the members of the Leeds Philosophical and Literary Society, which was founded in 1818 to enable the local scientific, manufacturing and commercial community to discuss and promote the sciences and literature. In 1824, Henry Salt, the British consul-general in Egypt, had presented a mummy from Thebes to the Society, whose honorary officers had already acquired a considerable knowledge of Egyptology and hieroglyphs.

They assembled a research team, led by William Osburn (1793–1875), who was a founder member of the Society and its secretary. The others included John Atkinson (1787–1828), Thomas Pridgin Teale (1801–1867) and Richard Hey, who were surgeons; Edward S. George (1801–1830), who had considerable experience in organic chemistry because his father owned a dyeworks; and Henry Denny (1803–1871), who was the Society's sub-curator and a talented draughtsman.

In order to pursue their studies further, the team persuaded John Blayds (1754–1827), a wealthy Leeds banker, to purchase for the Society's museum a second mummy which could be scientifically investigated by the team. This mummy was that of a priest named Natsef-Amun who had lived *c.* 1000 BC. It had been excavated at Thebes by the Italian archaeologist Giuseppe Passalacqua, and he subsequently sent it to his native town of

Trieste. This and another mummy were then transferred to London where, in 1823, mummy of Natsef-Amun was purchased by William Bullock, a showman and dealer in antiquities. Finally, it was sold to John Blayds.

The mummy of Natsef-Amun was subjected to one of the earliest recorded scientific investigations of an Egyptian mummy. The team adopted a multidisciplinary approach, and a detailed record was kept of all stages of the procedure. The results were promptly published in Osburn's *An Account of an Egyptian Mummy Presented to the Museum of the Leeds Philosophical and Literary Society* (1828), and he read an account of the work to the society's members in February 1828.

Osburn described how the mummy was unwrapped and autopsied, and provided details of its condition and associated wrappings and arti-facts. The team undertook a chemical examination of some of the substances associated with the mummy, noting that every part of the body had been covered with a 'thick layer of spicery'. This mixture also filled the chest and abdominal cavities, while powdered vegetable substance was found in the mouth, and spices and lumps of resin had been put in the cranial cavity. The chemical analysis indicated that myrrh, cassia, gelatine, tannin, resin and natron had been used in the mummification process.

An anatomical study was also carried out, which provided information about the owner's physical condition and the mummification techniques that had been used. Evidence of removal of the viscera and subsequent treatment with natron before they were returned to the body cavities, extraction of the brain through the right nostril, and the use of expensive packing materials indicated that this mummy dated to the late Dynasty 20/early Dynasty 21 period.

The body was originally wrapped in layers of linen bandages, between which were inserted a floral necklet and a leather brace. It was enclosed in two fine anthropoid coffins which were decorated with scenes and inscriptions. The Leeds team studied and translated the hieroglyphs which provided them with the owner's name and information about his profession as a priest in the Temple of Karnak.

The mummy and its coffins were fine examples of the funerary prepa-rations and techniques of mummification which flourished in the late New Kingdom, and the Leeds investigation was a pioneering study which is now regarded as a model for its time. Further radiological and dental examinations were undertaken in 1931 and 1964, and in the 1980s the Manchester Egyptian Mummy Research Project was given the unique opportunity to undertake a new scientific study of the mummy, using a range of modern scientific techniques and performing a new autopsy which employed virtually non-destructive methods of excavation. As well as adding knowledge about disease, diet and funerary customs, this exercise enabled a comparison to be made between the methodologies used in 1828 and 1989.

One of the most significant archaeological discoveries which has furthered the study of mummification and palaeopathology was the recovery of the two great caches of royal mummies in the late nineteenth century. During Dynasty 21, when Egypt was effectively divided between the legitimate kings ruling from Tanis in the north and a line of powerful high-priests of Amun controlling the south from Thebes, the high-priests of Amun undertook the rescue and reburial of some of the mummies of the kings and queens of the New Kingdom (Dynasties 17 to 20). Their original tombs had suffered desecration at the hands of the tomb robbers, and it is generally assumed that the priests removed and reburied the mummies and their remaining funerary goods in the hope of giving them another chance of eternity. The Tomb Robbery Papyri make it clear that the royal tombs had been plundered, and other documentation provides details of how the tombs were robbed, how the treasure was stolen, and how the coffins were set on fire.

Rescue of the mummies was carried out by the officials in charge of the Theban necropolis. Once the bodies had been rewrapped at Medinet Habu, the great administrative centre on the West Bank, or in some of the tombs, the mummies were moved to new burial places. During this process, careless handling probably prevented correct identification of the individual mummies, as they sometimes became separated from their original coffins and inscribed items of funerary equipment. The priests subsequently identified the mummies by putting their names on the dockets written on their wrappings and coffins, but modern studies have indicated that these were not always correct. A more recent interpretation (Reeves, 1992) of the high-priests' motives for reburying the royal mummies is that this was undertaken not merely to protect the dead but because it provided the high-priests with much-needed kudos and with a new income in the form of any of the associated treasure that the tomb-robbers had left behind, which could be used to help the struggling economy.

Until 1871, the modern world was unaware of these reburials. One cache of mummies had been reburied in the unfinished tomb (No. 320) belonging to Queen Inha'pi, which lay to the south of Deir el-Bahri. This was discovered in 1871 by Ahmed Abd er-Rasul from the West Bank village of Qurna, who was a dealer in antiquities. This find immediately supplied his family with a source of antiquities, and as papyri and other inscribed items began to come on to the market, Maspero, the Director of the Antiquities Service, realised that they must be emanating from an illicit excavation. As the result of official enquiries at Luxor, suspicion fell on the er-Rasul family and, as a result of a family quarrel, police began to make enquiries. Another brother, Mohammed, who confessed and obtained immunity from punishment, took the archaeologist Émile Brugsch, who was acting on behalf of the Antiquities Service, to visit the cache in 1881. Brugsch later commented: 'Collecting my senses, I made the best examination of them I could by the light of my torch, and at once saw that they contained the mummies of royal personages of both sexes' (quoted in Baikie, *A Century of Excavation in the Land of the Pharaohs* (1923), p. 159). Maspero then ordered that the mummies and their funerary goods should be moved immediately to the Cairo Museum. Three hundred workers cleared the tomb in six days, and the mummies were transported northwards by river. As the steamers sailed northwards from Luxor to Quft, and the royal mummies left Thebes for ever, the riverbanks were lined with men firing rifles and women wailing and tearing their hair, in the traditional manner of mourning the dead.

Some years after the first burial of mummies in the cache at Deir el-Bahri, the ancient necropolis officials added to their number the remains of Ramesses I, Sethos I and Ramesses II, and the bodies of some high-priests. Once all these mummies had been moved from Luxor to the Cairo Museum, there was a concentrated effort to unwrap them that lasted from May until June 1886. The mummy of Ramesses II was unwrapped in front of an audience that included the Khedive himself, and Maspero commented on the mummy of Sethos I – perhaps the finest example to survive – that 'It was a masterpiece of the art of the embalmer, and the expression of the face was that of one who had only a few hours previously breathed his last' (quoted in Baikie, op. cit., p. 163).

A second cache of royal mummies had been buried in the tomb of Amenophis II in the Valley of the Kings. This contained nine royal mummies, including those of Amenhotep II, Tuthmosis IV, Amenhotep III, Siptah, Ramesses IV, Ramesses V, Ramesses VI and Merneptah. The tomb was discovered by Victor Loret (1859–1946) in 1898, while he was Director-General of the Antiquities Service. He found the burial of Amenhotep II in the main chamber (the others were in side chambers), which was a significant event because this was the first time that the mummy of a pharaoh had been found in his rightful tomb, still complete with the bandages and funerary wealth, although the burial treasure had been plundered. The mummy was actually left in place there, with an armed guard, until the tomb was rifled in 1901. Finally, this second cache was also moved to the Cairo Museum.

A third major discovery of mummies was made in 1891 when the where-abouts of another cache was again revealed to the Antiquities Service by one of the er-Rasul brothers. The family had already discovered and exploited this tomb for some years. Situated to the north of the temple at Deir el-Bahri, the tomb had extensive galleries where Georges Daressy (appointed by the Antiquities Service to excavate the burial) found about 105 coffins and mummies, and the associated funerary goods, which had once belonged to the Theban priests of Dynasty 21.

The two groups of royal mummies formed the basis for studies on mummification techniques in the New Kingdom, and for anatomical and other studies on disease. Grafton Elliot Smith (1871–1937) was an

Australian anatomist and anthropologist who became Professor of Anatomy in the Cairo School of Medicine (1900–9), and then Professor at Manchester (1909–19) and at University College London (1919–36). During his time in Egypt, he examined human remains from a number of sites. His three great interests were cerebral morphology, anthropology and human palaeontology. Some of his theories were controversial and not generally accepted, particularly those regarding the belief that all civilisation had developed from ancient Egypt, but his scientific examination of thousands of human remains discovered in the Archaeological Survey of Nubia, and of the royal mummies in the Cairo Museum, was of outstanding value.

His interest in this field was first kindled when he examined some predynastic Egyptian brains discovered by Reisner in Nubia, and from 1903 he undertook a detailed study of a large number of mummies which dated from the Old Kingdom through to the Graeco-Roman Period. His systematic examination of the royal mummies and the evidence he had acquired from other investigations enabled him to make the first comprehensive and scientific contribution to the study of mummification, and to set out the main steps in the mummification procedure. This research formed the basis for several important publications, particularly the section he contributed to the Cairo Museum Catalogue, *The Royal Mummies* (1912); his report with F. Wood Jones entitled *Archaeological Survey of Nubia, 1907–8, (2): Report on the Human Remains* (1910); and, with W. R. Dawson, his account of mummification, *Egyptian Mummies* (1924).

Other studies have been carried out more recently on the royal mummies in the Cairo Museum, particularly the radiological surveys undertaken by J. E. Harris and K. Weeks (1973) and Harris and E. Wente (1980), which have provided further information about mummification techniques such as arm position, presence of artifacts, and brain removal, as well as about age at death, aspects of genealogy of the royal family, and their dental conditions. However, the work undertaken by Harris and Wente to visualise the craniofacial skeleton of the mummies, in an attempt to identify the individual members and family relationships of the royal mummies of the New Kingdom, has encountered some problems. From this craniofacial evidence, it would appear that some of the original identifications of the mummies, based on the dockets which the priests attached to them when they were rewrapped in Dynasty 21, are wrong, and that the bodies may have been wrongly named by the priests.

One study, in which this methodology has been applied to a group of royal mummies belonging to the end of Dynasty 18, has produced some particularly interesting results. This project has been undertaken on a number of bodies which were discovered in different circumstances. In addition to the mummies found in the two royal caches, this family group included the mummy of Tutankhamun and the badly deteriorated body from Tomb 55 in the Valley of the Kings.

The only royal mummy of Dynasty 18 whose identification is certain is that of Tutankhamun, because his wrapped body was found intact in its own tomb. This mummy, therefore, has been a starting-point for several studies on the genealogy of the late Dynasty 18 and the age at death of individual rulers. The mummy was first examined in 1923 by D. Derry (1874–1961), Professor of Anatomy at the Government School of Medicine in Cairo from 1919, and who, in 1909, joined the Archaeological Survey of Nubia as an anthropologist. He undertook many anatomical studies of ancient remains, but this was his most notable examination. His results were reported in F. F. Leek's *The Human Remains from the Tomb of Tutankhamun* (1972). Derry also examined the mummy discovered in Tomb 55 in the Valley of the Kings which Arthur Weigall, working for the Theodore Davis expedition, had found in 1907. The rightful ownership of this tomb and its contents, including a gold coffin and the mummy, has been the subject of a continuing controversy. In the initial examination, it was declared that the mummy was that of a woman, and it was assumed to be that of Queen Tiye, wife of Amenhotep III; accordingly, the discovery was published in 1910 as *The Tomb of Queen Tiyi*. However, when Elliot Smith subsequently re-examined the body, he claimed that it was that of a young man aged about 25, and that the skull was distorted in a manner that suggested that its owner had suffered from hydrocephalus. This led to the speculation that it was the body of the heretic pharaoh, Akhenaten, who is shown with a distended head in the art of the period. It was argued that he had been brought from Tell el-Amarna to Thebes for a secret burial. However, when Derry subsequently examined the body, he suggested that the age at death was twenty-three and he found no evidence of hydrocephalus. Since some inscriptional evidence indicates that Akhenaten could have reigned as king for at least seventeen years, this mummy, according to these calculations, could not have been his.

In the 1960s, a team re-examined some of these mummies, and, in particular, those found in the tomb of Tutankhamun and in Tomb 55. The team was led by a British anatomist, R. G. Harrison (1921–1983), Professor of Anatomy at the University of Liverpool (1950–83). In addition to the anatomical investigations carried out on the bodies, which were based on X-rays taken with portable equipment, there were also serological and other studies. The team concluded that the body found in Tomb 55 was that of a man in his early twenties who, from a comparison of the X-rays and blood-groups, was believed to have been a close relative (probably a brother or half-brother) of Tutankhamun. It was also considered probable that both these men were sons of Amenhotep III. Furthermore, it was suggested that the mummy in Tomb 55 could have belonged to the person who is named in contemporary inscriptions as 'Smenkhkare'. Since this name replaces that of Akhenaten's wife, Nefertiti, it has been argued that this individual appears to have usurped the queen's place at some point in the reign, and become

Akhenaten's co-regent. However, a more recent theory suggests that the occurrence of the name 'Smenkhkare' does not in fact indicate the presence of a new co-ruler, but that it was simply a new name taken by Nefertiti herself, perhaps to mark some crucial stage in the reign. If this suggestion is accepted, then it would leave the identification of the body in Tomb 55 open to speculation; possibly it belonged to another prince of the royal family whose existence as yet remains unconfirmed by other evidence.

In their studies mentioned above, Wente and Harris have indicated that Tutankhamun died somewhere between the ages of 23 and 27. Doubts have also been cast on the identification of several royal mummies of Dynasty 18, including those of Tuthmosis IV and Amenhotep III, and the body in Tomb 55 which Harrison tentatively concluded was related to Tutankhamun. Harris and Wente suggest that the mummies identified as Tuthmosis IV (Amenhotep III's father), Tutankhamun and the body from Tomb 55 have similar morphologies and are probably closely related, but that the mummy labelled 'Amenhotep III' is very different from them. They concluded that the body in Tomb 55 is male and closely related to Tutankhamun, but there is no firm evidence from these studies that it was that of either Akhenaten or Smenkhkare. In this period of history, where inscriptional and archaeological evidence is confusing and sometimes seems to support contradictory theories, so far, biological investigations have not managed to provide convincing answers about familial relationships. Only further archaeological discoveries, and eventually other biological and genetic investigations of the existing mummies and of any human remains that may be uncovered in the future, will perhaps supply some of the missing answers.

However, although modern biological investigations of ancient remains cannot confirm or refute all historical theories, they have been very successful in providing information about other areas, such as diet and disease. A high-profile multidisciplinary study of another royal mummy, Ramesses II, has supplied a wealth of information about many aspects of the king's life. The mummy was taken from Cairo to Paris in 1976, so that a method could be devised to preserve the mummy, using irradiation techniques. However, during the period spent in France, the mummy was also examined at the Museum of Anthropology (Museé de l'Homme) using a range of non-destructive techniques such as radiology (including xerography and chromodensitography). In addition, there were studies on the dentition of the mummy, and on the floral and faunal remains, but investigations which would have required removal of tissue samples (for histology, serology, DNA identification) were not permitted.

In general, the study of the technique of mummification and of disease found in mummies has been greatly enhanced in the twentieth century, due in part to the large numbers of human and animal mummies that have become available through excavation, and also because of the establishment

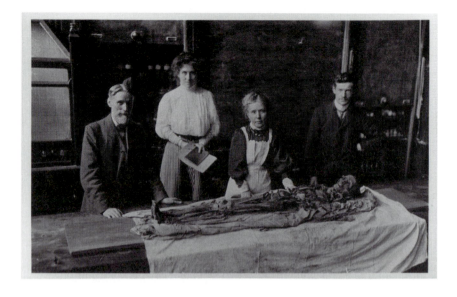

Figures 31 and 32 Dr Margaret Murray and her interdisciplinary team unwrapped and autopsied the mummies of the Two Brothers (from Rifeh, *c.* 1900 BC) in the Chemical Theatre of the University of Manchester in 1908. Here the team undertakes its investigation of one of the mummies in front of an invited audience.

of multidisciplinary projects which use a range of scientific techniques to examine the mummies. Investigations have moved on from the spectacle of unrolling mummies, with little or no scientific purpose, to projects which involve many disciplines and recognise the importance of team-work and methodology. Of particular importance has been the development of virtually non-destructive methods of investigation, such as the use of endoscopy; these now ensure that wrapped mummies can be investigated with minimally invasive techniques and confirm that there is no longer any scientific justification for unwrapping and autopsying a mummy.

A pioneer in the multidisciplinary approach was Dr Margaret Murray who, in 1908, revived interest in mummified remains. The frivolous pursuit of unrolling mummies had long since been abandoned, but Margaret Murray contributed to the new attitude that prevailed at the start of the twentieth century. She and her team of scientists unwrapped and autopsied the mummies of two brothers at the University of Manchester, and combined medical, scientific and archaeological studies to investigate the bodies and the tomb goods of the brothers, excavated at Rifeh in Middle Egypt. A few years earlier, in 1901, Grafton Elliot Smith had carried out a study on a series of ancient Egyptian bodies found in Upper Egypt, examining the mummification procedures and recording their bone measurements. With the assistance of two specialists (W. R. Dawson and F. Wood Jones), Elliot Smith also examined and autopsied some six thousand mummies that were rescued as part of the project to survey the archaeological heritage of Nubia. Without his intervention, these mummies would have been lost, as the result of alterations carried out on the first dam built at Aswan, in the period from 1900. With this survey and his aforementioned studies on the royal mummies, Elliot Smith acquired sufficient material to compile a history of the development of techniques used in mummification.

This study remained the definitive work on mummification techniques until Alfred Lucas, a British scientist who became Chemist to the Egyptian Antiquities Service (1923–32), undertook further detailed investigations and experiments. His book entitled *Ancient Egyptian Materials and Industries* (1926, 4th rev. edn 1962) was based on his personal analyses of substances and materials used by the ancient Egyptians. His studies were fundamental in illuminating the process of mummification used by the ancient Egyptians, and in his experiments, he was the first to demonstrate that the account given in the Classical writer Herodotus was accurate. One of the problems he addressed was the manner in which natron was used as a dehydrating agent. His experiments on carcasses of pigeons and chickens, and subsequent work undertaken in this area by A. T. Sandison and R. Garner, demonstrate that dry natron rather than the immersion of the body in a natron solution was the method of dehydration used to mummify ancient Egyptian corpses.

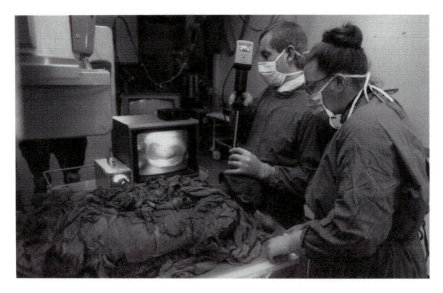

Figure 33 Today, multidisciplinary projects use a range of techniques to investigate disease in mummies. Here, members of the Manchester Mummy Research Project team insert an endoscope into the mouth of a mummy to obtain a biopsy sample.

Other details about the mummification procedure have been provided by Garner's experiments on laboratory mice and rats. He has helped to establish the validity of the methods described by Herodotus, and has been able to show that factors which may have affected the results achieved in antiquity could have included the effect of high levels of impurities in the natron samples, the use of fresh or recycled natron, and the optimum period of time required for mummification.

There has also been research on the effect of insect attack on a mummy. Insects use the mummy as a source of food, and through electron microscopy, it has been possible to identify not only parasite worms that occupied the living body as a host, but also the remains of insects that infested the body at death, during mummification, or even in the museum. The dissection microscope or SEM (scanning electron microscopy) have been employed by scientists to identify the insect remains uncovered during autopsies of mummies.

Modern studies have also revealed additional evidence about the mummification process itself. Radiology can provide information about the presence of resin and natron, and can indicate if amulets (sacred jewellery) have been placed between the layers of bandages. Sometimes, it is possible to observe if any embalmers' restorations (false limbs, eyes, subcutaneous packing, etc.) are present, and if the abdominal and thoracic cavities are filled with linen packages or with the mummified viscera that have been replaced there. Tomography and endoscopy have also enabled researchers to look for evidence of brain removal, and the routes by which this was achieved. Endoscopy now allows tissue samples to be removed with minimal destruction, and these can then be studied microscopically for further evidence about the various mummification techniques. In research undertaken on mummies from Egyptian and other cultures, it has been shown in comparative tests that tissue from ancient Egypt, which has been artificially preserved by means of natron, retains more information for microscopic studies than samples taken from mummies from other geographical areas. Research on mummy bandages and on the substances applied to them during mummification (which are isolated and characterised by means of thin layer and gas liquid chromatography) has demonstrated that the Egyptians used various qualities of linen for the wrappings, and that the bandages were impregnated with a mixture of different substances such as resin, galbanum and beeswax. Finally, studies on the plants and plant remains used in mummification have indicated that they may have been employed to kill insects and lessen the odour of putrefaction, but that they made little impact on the effectiveness of the mummification process.

Scientific techniques therefore enable us to learn more about the mummification process but, perhaps even more importantly, they can provide evidence about disease, diet and living conditions, as well as familial relationships and population movements. Egyptian mummies are a rich source for such studies because, unlike many other cultures, the body tissues as well as the skeletons are preserved. Also, because the modern population of the Nile Valley is largely unchanged from ancient times, this presents a unique opportunity to study the evolution and patterns of disease over a 5,000-year period, by comparing evidence from the mummies with data from contemporary medical surveys. In the twentieth century, the study of mummies has come to play an important role in understanding Egyptian civilisation because, unlike the art representations or the literature, the facts obtained from the physical remains have not been distorted. The idealised world of elegance, beauty, youth and health that is often represented in the statuary, wall-paintings and texts, is not reflected in the human remains which clearly indicate that all social groups and all ages suffered from a variety of debilitating diseases.

In recent decades, studies on mummies have changed and developed both in terms of the range of investigative and diagnostic techniques that have become available, and in the way in which the work is pursued. Unwrapping and autopsying mummies, even accompanied by a subsequent scientific study, have been replaced by virtually non-destructive investigative procedures. Also, intensive research programmes on individual mummies (which, until recently, have been the only studies undertaken) will probably ultimately be replaced by wider studies on disease patterns.

Over the years, the focus of the techniques employed to examine mummies has also changed. At first, radiology provided an excellent and non-destructive means of studying disease in the skeletons of the mummies. However, endoscopy now gives increased access to soft tissues inside the body, and allows workers to acquire additional material that can be examined microscopically, or by new and even more sophisticated diagnostic techniques such as DNA identification and immunological methods. In order to understand the contribution offered by this range of techniques, and the problems and limitations associated with them, it is worth briefly considering their application to Egyptology.

Radiography offers a totally non-destructive method of examination, and therefore it was the first medical technique applied to Egyptian mummies. Radiological investigations provide evidence first about the archaeological interest of the mummies and how they relate to their cultural background; and second, about the diseases or injuries from which the person suffered, and also the cause of death.

The first radiographs of mummified remains (a child and a cat) were produced by W. König in Frankfurt in 1896. An Englishman, Thurstan Holland, X-rayed a mummified bird in the same year. Flinders Petrie was the first Egyptologist to use radiography for human remains in 1898, and when, in 1903, the tomb of Tuthmosis IV was discovered and found to contain the king's body, the mummy was removed to Cairo the following year, and X-rayed by Elliot Smith and Howard Carter. This was part of a detailed investigation of the mummy which had been unwrapped in public prior to a private study being undertaken by Elliot Smith. It was a significant development because it was the first occasion that radiography had been used to examine a royal mummy.

In 1931, R. L. Moodie carried out one of the earliest comprehensive radiographic surveys of the Egyptian and Peruvian mummies in the Chicago Field Museum. Then, in the 1960s, a British radiologist, P. H. K. Gray (1913–1984), undertook a series of radiological studies in Britain and Europe on 193 mummies held in collections at several museums, including the British Museum and the Horniman Museum in London, museums in Liverpool, Oxford, Cambridge and Munich, the Rijksmuseum in Leiden, and the Louvre in Paris. His systematic approach to these studies, followed by prompt publication of the results, highlighted the contribution that radiology could make to Egyptology. Since the 1960s, there have also been radiological studies undertaken on the royal mummies in the Cairo Museum (see page 165), and in the 1960s and 1970s Harrison radiographed the mummies of Tutankhamun and Smenkhkare.

However, until the 1970s, mummies were usually radiographed either at the archaeological site or in the museum gallery, with the limitation imposed by using mobile compact equipment which produced results that could not be compared with studies of modern patients. From 1973, as part of the

Manchester Egyptian Mummy Research Project, a methodology was established where, for the first time, the radiography conditions were standardised. The mummies were removed from the Manchester Museum to the University's Department of Diagnostic Radiology, where, under near-ideal conditions, a procedure could be set in place for X-raying the mummies which involved the use of orbiting, fluoroscopic and tomographic equipment. Computed axial tomography (CAT), an X-ray transmission technique developed in Britain in the 1970s, was later added to the procedure. The use of such sophisticated equipment under controlled conditions is now the customary method of radiographing mummies, and radiological studies are an important aspect of any multidisciplinary study.

However, despite its many advantages as a non-destructive technique, X-ray examination has its problems and limitations. It provides a unique opportunity to evaluate skeletal maturity and development, based on the ossification of bone in each individual, but the North American and European radiological standards that have been applied to the Egyptian mummies to define bone age have been misleading, particularly in adults aged over 20 years.

Dental studies have also been carried out on individual mummies and as part of multidisciplinary studies. Dry skulls and mummified heads have been available to researchers, and have provided information about the teeth and the supporting soft tissue. The dry skulls have formed the basis for studying Egyptian dentitions, since information gained from these can then be used to interpret the radiographs of mummified and wrapped heads where the hard facial tissue, and funerary masks and artifacts placed over the face, can obscure the details.

There have been a number of important dental studies such as those carried out by the University of Michigan expeditions sent to Egypt since 1965 to examine the dentitions of Old Kingdom (*c.* 2800 BC) nobles at Giza, New Kingdom (*c.* 1250 BC) priests and nobles at Luxor, and the royal mummies (*c.* 1550–1070 BC) in the Cairo Museum. Other research has investigated oral health and disease in modern Egypt, especially Nubia, and used this as comparative material for work on ancient examples. Again, there have been specialised studies on diet and age determination. For example, F. F. Leek (1903–1985), a British dentist who examined the mummy of Tutankhamun as part of Harrison's team, undertook many examinations of dry skulls and mummies for his work on the dental history of ancient Egypt. In studies on the diet of the ancient Egyptians, he was able to demonstrate that the flour used for making the bread contained so many impurities (including sand and fragments of the querns), that this caused attrition of the cusps of the teeth, a condition which is frequently seen in ancient Egyptian dentitions.

Palaeopathology – the study of disease in ancient populations – includes anthropology, archaeology, palaeontology and palaeohistology. It sets out to trace the appearance, development and disappearance of diseases, and to demonstrate the effect of some diseases on ancient populations. The earliest studies in this field were undertaken in the nineteenth century, but it was Marc Armand Ruffer (1859–1917), Professor of Bacteriology at Cairo's Government School of Medicine, who pioneered the investigation of disease in Egyptian mummies and skeletons, and laid the foundations for the study of palaeohistology.

The two branches of pathology (the scientific study of disease processes) which have produced the most evidence about disease in Egyptian mummies are morbid anatomy and histopathology. Morbid anatomy involves the autopsy and naked eye study of mummies, and was available to early researchers in this field. S. G. Morton (1799–1851), an American physician and anthropologist, undertook early studies on Egyptian crania and the races of ancient Egypt, and aforementioned anatomical studies were undertaken by Margaret Murray, and by Elliot Smith and Wood Jones. In more recent times, autopsies have been carried out on mummies to enable teams of researchers to obtain tissue and other samples for further studies. These have included the autopsies of four mummies (PUM I-IV) in the collection of the Pennsylvania University Museum, and one (ROM I) in the Royal Ontario Museum, and of one mummy (1770) as part of the Manchester Mummy Research Project's investigation. However, these autopsies are destructive, and in the 1980s, the Manchester team pioneered the use of endoscopy as a virtually non-destructive method of investigation. This involves inserting rigid endoscopes through one of the natural orifices of the body or through a small incision in the chest or abdomen, and then using a small retrieval forceps attached to the endoscope to take biopsy samples of the tissue.

The next step involves the histological examination of these samples. Histology (the study of the microscopic structure of the tissues) is the second branch of pathology which has added greatly to knowledge of disease in Egyptian mummies. Most ancient populations have left only the evidence of their skeletal remains, which can provide information about diseases that affect the bone. However, in Egyptian and other cultures where the body tissues have been intentionally or unintentionally preserved, there is the opportunity to study the diseases that have left their traces in the tissues.

The technique – palaeohistology – which was developed so that mummified tissue could be examined, was first used by D. M. Fouquet (1850–1914), a French physician who was invited by Maspero to examine the royal mummies. However, it was the British pathologist Ruffer who really developed the technique of rehydrating mummified tissue and then staining and sectioning it so that, when examined microscopically, it revealed not only the state of preservation of the tissue but also any presence of disease. Ruffer was able to identify such diseases as *Ascaris* infestation and schistosomiasis, and to publish a series of articles about his work which were collected after his death and edited by R. L. Moodie under the title of *Studies in the Palaeopathology of Egypt* (1921). Since then, important work has been undertaken to develop the rehydration and staining techniques applied to mummified tissue. There have also been major studies on the identification of various diseases, by workers who include A. T. Sandison, E. Tapp for the Manchester Mummy Project, and T. A. Reyman, R. A. Barraco and A. Cockburn for the PUM/ROM investigation.

Immunohistochemistry and electron microscopy have added new dimensions to this work. Immunohistochemistry provides a great improvement in the means of identifying cell constituents, and electron microscopy allows the histologist to visualise a much greater resolution of the detailed structures of the cells in the sample or specimen. In this field, one of the earliest researchers was the Austrian J. N. Czermak (1828–1873), who carried out anatomical and microscopical studies on mummies in 1852. Now, transmission electron microscopy (TEM), analytical electron microscopy (AEM), and scanning electron microscopy (SEM) are all used to examine Egyptian mummies. In tissue samples, these techniques have made it possible to identify the remains of various parasites, and also silica particles embedded in lung tissue which indicate the presence of the disease sand pneumoconiosis. Additionally, AEM has been used to determine the presence of heavy metals in mummified tissue, and SEM has been employed to examine the structure and diseases of ancient hair samples, and to identify insects associated with the mummies.

In addition to seeking for evidence of disease, techniques have also been developed to attempt to establish familial relationships, trace population movements, and even identify the modern descendants of ancient peoples. Palaeoserology (the study of blood-groups in ancient human remains) has had a limited success in this area. In the studies carried out since the 1930s, it has been possible to demonstrate that the serologic micromethod (SMM) and the inhibition agglutination test (IAT) could be applied to the study of mummified tissue. Blood-group substances (ABO) exist in tissues as well as in blood, so analysis of tissue samples taken from mummies can be expected to supply the blood groups. However, contamination of the samples or their deterioration over the passage of time can give false or unreliable results. One notable study in palaeoserology was undertaken by Harrison's team (see page 166), to attempt to prove kinship between the bodies found in Tutankhamun's tomb and in Tomb 55 in the Valley of the Kings. However, since the 1970s palaeoserology has largely been supplanted by DNA analysis, as a means of determining familial relationships.

In 1975, S. Pääbo, a Swedish scientist, pioneered the techniques that have subsequently been used to identify DNA in mummies. This procedure requires only a small sample of tissue or bone, which can be taken from any area of the body, since the total genetic information of any individual is carried in almost every cell. This has opened up possibilities for important future studies, relating not only to familial relationships and population origins and migrations, but also to the identification of bacterial, fungal and parasite DNA which may reveal new information about infectious diseases in ancient individuals and populations. The laborious DNA cloning techniques and sequence reading strategies to analyse specimens, which were used in the earliest experiments, have now been replaced by more routine techniques and analyses. An important advance is the polymerase chain reaction (PCR) (also known as 'gene amplification') which is now used for DNA studies on ancient preserved tissues. There is every probability that, despite the problems posed by contamination and other factors in obtaining DNA from ancient specimens, this area of study will play an important role in the future.

Finally, new work is being undertaken on epidemiological studies. In 1995, it was decided to establish a joint project between the Manchester Egyptian Mummy Research Project, the Medical Service Corporation International, United States and the Schistosomiasic Research Project at the Egyptian Reference Diagnostic Centre (VACSERA) in Cairo. This project has set out to construct an epidemiologic profile of one disease, schistosomiasis, in Egypt, between the twenty-sixth century BC and the seventh century AD, and then compare this data with modern epidemiologic information made available through VACSERA, a joint venture between the government of Egypt and universities in Egypt and the United States.

Today, schistosomiasis affects 200–300 million people worldwide, and up to 20 per cent of the population of Egypt suffers from the disease. The causative agent, the parasitic trematode schistosoma, was first described in depth by Theodor Bilharz in 1852, but the disease also existed in ancient Egypt. The ancient medical papyri include symptoms which some Egyptologists regard as a classic description of infection with *schistosoma haematobium*. Also, studies on the mummies have revealed pathological evidence of the disease, indicating that it has survived continuously in Egypt for at least 5,000 years.

At the University of Manchester, the current project has established the world's first international ancient Egyptian mummy tissue bank, as a major resource for studies on this and other diseases. Tissue samples are being obtained by virtually non-destructive means from mummies held in collections worldwide. These samples will be examined for evidence of schistosomiasis, using a range of diagnostic methods. Previously, radiology, histology and the enzyme-linked immunosorbent assay (ELISA) have been employed by other researchers to identify schistosomiasis in mummies, but now, for the first time, the Manchester team have added immunocytochemistry as a diagnostic tool. Positive immunostaining upon ancient Egyptian liver and bladder tissue has been achieved, suggesting that schistosoma antigens may still be present after thousands of years. Studies on the DNA and the evolution of the parasite that causes the disease are also planned, to examine how this pathogen has developed its survival strategies so successfully, in order to evade man's immune system. It is envisaged that this epidemiological study, the first that has ever attempted to compare evidence from ancient and modern times over such a long timespan, will provide a pattern for future studies on other diseases. The fact that Egypt has the availability of preserved human remains and a population that has changed little over the centuries enables it to provide unique conditions for this type of research. It is hoped that such projects may eventually contribute generally to current knowledge of the history of disease.

In general, biomedical investigations can add immeasurably to our knowledge of ancient Egypt. However, it is clear that the conclusions reached by palaeopathologists, based on their examination of the bodies, and Egyptologists, working from the historical evidence, are not always in agreement, and it is essential that any interpretation of the scientific evidence is proposed with the utmost care. As new scientific techniques become available, the value of their application to mummified remains must be assessed and, if they can make a valid contribution, they should be added to the range of diagnostic methods which modern researchers can now employ in their work.

CONCLUSION

—— •◆• ——

This book has attempted to show how the interpretation of Egyptology has evolved and developed through the collective efforts of several generations of Egyptologists. Sometimes, their researches have radically changed existing opinions about a person or historical period (such as the Amarna Period and Akhenaten), or have identified hitherto unrecognised areas of history (such as Petrie's 'discovery' of the Predynastic era).

The early accounts of Classical writers and of later medieval and Renaissance travellers have been re-examined and reassessed in the light of Egyptian texts and archaeological evidence and, although some of their claims and descriptions have been fanciful, in many instances they have provided accurate information and details of monuments or sites which have subsequently been damaged or destroyed. Once Egyptian hieroglyphs had been deciphered, it was then possible to read the ancient texts, identify the ownership of many of the monuments, and establish a basic historical framework and chronology.

The ability to read the ancient Egyptians' own records and comments on their lives and society has undoubtedly provided historians with a much greater understanding of the civilisation, although it is important to recognise that the literary evidence has its own limitations as a reliable source. In addition to the ancient texts, the study of the standing monuments and the development and application of scientific techniques both in archaeology and in biomedical and palaeopathological research have provided important methods which help us to understand ancient Egypt. However, we cannot assume that we shall ever be able fully to comprehend the complexities of this ancient society, and we must be aware that, over a period of time, the interpretation of much of the evidence has changed and will continue to be revised by future historians.

In assessing the current state of the subject and determining how it may develop in the future, it is important to consider how the new generations of Egyptologists are being trained. As an academic discipline taught in universities, Egyptology is still mainly regarded as a humanities-based subject which concentrates on the historical perspective and on language and literature studies. Traditionally, the course makes serious demands on student's time and ability, since it encompasses the formidable scope of Egypt's long history, and the difficulties associated with learning a complex ancient language. Therefore, there is usually little time to explore other aspects of archaeology, particularly the use of scientific techniques.

Whereas other branches of archaeology have often fostered and developed this new technology out of necessity, because they have had neither the quality and quantity of archaeological remains nor the availability of literary sources to help them, it is only in relatively recent times that Egyptology has recognised the need to use a multidisciplinary approach. Opportunities for students to take part in excavations in Egypt or elsewhere can help to provide them with some archaeological training, and at graduate level, training and instruction in a variety of biomedical and scientific techniques have been introduced to help to prepare the Egyptologist in the field or the museum curator in charge of an Egyptian collection for this new approach to the subject. In the twenty-first century, such skills will become increasingly necessary in this profession.

In the field, there will undoubtedly continue to be an emphasis on the need to develop and expand the use of many disciplines in the excavation of a site, so that epigraphic and philological skills can be complemented by specialist studies on a variety of objects including pottery, botanical specimens and human remains. However, some techniques which have had a major impact in other areas of archaeology may not make such a contribution to Egyptology. For example, since we have fairly precisely documented historical periods and dates for Egyptology, the need to use carbon-dating techniques has not been as critical as in other branches of archaeology. Indeed, in Egyptology, historical and inscriptional evidence often provides a much closer context for an object or a site than a radiocarbon date.

However, in terms of palaeopathology and biomedical studies, the scope and excellent state of preservation of the human remains offer almost unparalleled opportunities to study the pattern and effect of disease on an ancient society. There will undoubtedly be major advances in this area, with the development of new diagnostic techniques and the establishment of comparative studies on the populations of ancient and modern Egypt. Ultimately, when evidence derived from biomedical studies can be set alongside the archaeological and literary sources, we shall undoubtedly gain information which will enhance our understanding of ancient Egyptian society.

In general, discoveries still occur that constantly require us to reassess our knowledge of Egyptian civilisation. Important fieldwork will continue to be directed towards cemeteries and funerary monuments. For example, at the excavations at Dahshur and Lisht, D. Arnold and a team from the Metropolitan Museum, New York, are currently gaining new information from their exploration of the Middle Kingdom pyramids and burial complexes, and new discoveries are being revealed about the Old Kingdom funerary sites at Giza and Abusir.

Another tomb project which has recently attracted widespread scholarly and public attention is the discovery of Tomb KV5 in the Valley of the Kings at Thebes, where K. R. Weeks, Director of the KV5 Project, has uncovered the tomb of some of the sons of Ramesses II who died when they were still young. First noted by early travellers such as Burton and Lepsius, the tomb was 'rediscovered' in 1987 by Weeks's Theban Mapping Project, which had been established in 1978 to prepare a survey of the entire Theban necropolis. Geophysical surveys revealed its existence after knowledge of its exact location had been lost for many years. Continuing work on the tomb and on the mummified remains that have been discovered there should eventually reveal important new evidence about this period.

However, in addition to the tombs, there is now an increased interest in excavating settlement sites, and this will gradually help to adjust the balance of the evidence gathered over the past two centuries. The current survey of Memphis seeks to investigate the earliest history of this once-great city, and at Tell el-Amarna, continuing excavation is revealing new information about Akhenaten's capital. Both projects are being undertaken by the Egypt Exploration Society, which is also carrying out a Delta survey, the first archaeological study of the area where Sais, the capital during Dynasty 26, was once situated. This survey is one aspect of an increased interest in the archaeology of the Delta sites which have been less extensively worked than those in Upper Egypt, and new evidence about this region will undoubtedly help to adjust perceptions of the part played by the Delta in Egypt's history.

In the Western Desert, the oases have also received attention this century, and current excavations there continue to reveal new information. In 1937, Ahmed Fakhry (1905–1973), Professor of the History of Ancient Egypt at Cairo University from 1952 to 1965, was the first archaeologist to make a detailed study of the sites in the desert oases. Currently, there are French excavations near Dush in the Kharga Oasis, an Italian–Egyptian mission is working in the Farafra Oasis, and the Dahkhla Oasis Project has undertaken a series of excavations over the past few years. These have included detailed studies of the agriculture, diet and health in these communities, and exemplify the modern, multidisciplinary approach to archaeology which has now been adopted in Egyptology.

Generally, however, there still needs to be a more co-ordinated approach to excavation throughout Egypt, and even in areas such as the Valley of the Kings and the Theban necropolis, where exploration has been undertaken for centuries, there is an urgent need to produce comprehensive and detailed surveys and studies of the tombs and their contents. The use of computers to gather and store information both at archaeological sites and in museum collections will continue to make a major contribution to the work of Egyptologists.

One new and exciting area of exploration in Egyptology is the field of underwater archaeology. At Alexandria, near the Qait Bey Fort, emergency underwater excavations were undertaken in 1994 and 1995 because of the threat posed by the proposed construction of a concrete breakwater to protect the fort against storms. J.-Y. Empereur, director of the project, was invited by the Egyptian Antiquities Organisation to document the site and to lift the most important of the blocks that had been discovered by the divers, so that they could be restored and displayed. Now, a team of French and Egyptian divers has started to locate and identify the remains of thousands of blocks of Greek and pharaonic buildings, as well as statues of royal and divine figures.

The site, originally pinpointed by an Egyptian diver, Kamal Abu el Sadah, in the 1960s, was subsequently made the subject of a UNESCO study in 1968, and preliminary studies were carried out by Honor Frost in 1975. The latest exploration has revealed many blocks and sculptures of pharaonic date which were probably moved to Alexandria from other sites at the behest of the Ptolemaic rulers; the topographic survey has also found granite blocks which may once have formed part of the Pharos lighthouse, one of the ancient Seven Wonders of the World. This project draws on expertise and techniques which would not have been available to earlier generations of archaeologists and there is considerable scope for future studies in this area. However, such a project raises questions about how these remains should be conserved and ultimately displayed to the public.

Despite the advances made throughout the past few decades, the monuments of Egypt still face a precarious future. Natural and environmental factors and the pressures caused by tourists at the most popular sites take their toll, and the need to conserve the monuments and antiquities once they are excavated, and to protect them, either in situ or as part of museum collections, from the effects of pollution and environmental change, is now one of Egyptology's top priorities.

There have been high-profile rescue projects such as the UNESCO salvage operation in Nubia, and more recently, the international scheme to restore and re-open the tomb of Queen Nefertari in the Valley of the Queens. There has also been a major, international initiative to arrest the deterioration of the Great Sphinx and to preserve the surrounding monuments on the Giza plateau.

Conservation of sites and monuments is now a requirement imposed by the Egyptian government on all site excavators, reflecting Mariette's opinion that preservation of the monuments should be one of the archaeologist's highest priorities, and Egyptologists are generally aware of the continuing need to monitor the effects of environmental factors, such as the raised water levels, on the monuments and wall-scenes. Each new excavation is accompanied by a programme of conservation for the buildings and the finds, and throughout the next century, there will be an urgent need for constant vigilance to ensure that the sites and monuments survive. Once the objects enter museums, environmental conditions in the public galleries and in the reserve stores are also of the utmost importance to the well-being of this material, and it is fully recognised that scientific, multi-disciplinary excavation and post-excavation techniques must be applied to all aspects of Egyptian archaeology.

Egyptology still continues to attract widespread interest among almost all age groups in many countries around the world. Museum displays and research collections, the wide range of general as well as scholarly publications that are produced each year, and the flourishing memberships of learned and amateur societies devoted to the subject – these all provide an opportunity to pursue a general interest in the subject. With increased leisure and travel facilities, it is likely that, following the pattern of the past few hundred years, an enthusiastic amateur appreciation of Egyptology will continue to develop and grow in the next century. Even the tradition of using strange theories to explain some of the Egyptian monuments still survives, and pyramidology and associated interpretations still have their adherents.

However, in terms of Egyptology as an academic discipline, new evidence is still being sought to redefine current opinions; this may eventually illuminate problems in the less well-documented periods of history or resolve some of the continuing controversies surrounding the Amarna Period. However, the quest for new evidence is now balanced, as never before, by an awareness that the monuments and artifacts are a limited and irreplaceable resource which must always be vigorously protected and preserved.

When Herodotus first brought Egypt to the attention of his readership, he wrote: 'There is no country that possesses so many wonders, nor any that has such a number of works that defy description.' However scholars choose to interpret the evidence in the future, it seems certain that, as it has done for 2,500 years, ancient Egyptian civilisation will continue to intrigue and exert its fascination over all who take up this study.

SUGGESTED READING

———— •◆• ————

Arnold, D., *The Temple of Mentuhotep at Deir el Bahari* (New York, 1979).

Arnold, D., *The Royal Women of Amarna: Images of Beauty from Ancient Egypt* (New York, 1996).

Baines, J. and J. Malek, *Atlas of Ancient Egypt* (Oxford, 1980).

Bierbrier, M. L., *Who Was Who in Egyptology*, 3rd rev. edn (London, 1986).

Bietak, M., *Avaris. The Capital of the Hyksos: Recent Excavations at Tell el-Dab'a* (London, 1986).

Breasted, C., *Pioneer to the Past: The Story of James Henry Breasted, Archaeologist* (New York, 1943).

Carter, H., and A. C. Mace, *The Tomb of Tut.ankh.Amen* (London, 1923–33).

Černy, J. *A Community of Workmen at Thebes in the Ramesside Period* (Cairo, 1973).

Cockburn, A. and E., *Mummies, Disease and Ancient Cultures* (Cambridge, 1980).

David A. R. (ed.), *The Manchester Museum Mummy Project* (Manchester, 1979).

David, R., *The Pyramid-Builders of Ancient Egypt*, 2nd edn (London, 1996).

Donadoni, S., *The Egyptians* (Chicago, 1996).

Drower, M. S., *Flinders Petrie: A Life in Archaeology* (London, 1985).

Edwards, I. E. S., *The Pyramids of Egypt* (Harmondsworth, 1985).

Emery, W. B., *Great Tombs of the First Dynasty*, 2 vols (Cairo and London 1949–58).

Emery, W. B., *Archaic Egypt* (Harmondsworth, 1962).

Fagan, B. M., *The Rape of the Nile* (London, 1975).

Flynn, S. J. A., *Sir John Gardner Wilkinson: Traveller and Egyptologist 1797–1875* (Oxford, 1997).

Fouchet, M. P., *Rescued Treasures of Egypt* (London, 1965).

Frankfort, H., *Ancient Egyptian Religion* (New York, 1948).

Frayling, C., *The Face of Tutankhamun* (New York, 1992).

Gardiner, Sir Alan, *Egypt of the Pharaohs* (Oxford, 1961).

Gardiner, Sir Alan, *My Working Years* (Oxford, 1964).

Harris, J. E. and E. F. Wente, *An X-ray Atlas of the Royal Mummies* (Chicago and London, 1980).

Hayes, W. C., *Most Ancient Egypt* (Chicago, 1964).

Herold, J. C., *Bonaparte in Egypt* (New York, 1962).

Hoffman, M. A., *Egypt Before the Pharaohs* (London, 1980).

Hornung, E., *The Valley of the Kings* (New York, 1990).

Iversen, E. *The Myth of Egypt and its Hieroglyphs in European Tradition* (Copenhagen, 1961).

James, T. G. H., *Excavating in Egypt: The Egypt Exploration Society 1882–1982* (London, 1982).

James, T. G. H., *Howard Carter: The Path to Tutankhamun* (London, 1992).

Jenkins, N., *The Boat Beneath the Pyramids* (London, 1980).

Jordan, P., *Riddles of the Sphinx* (Stroud, 1998).

Lauer, J. P., *Saqqara: The Royal Cemetery of Memphis* (London, 1976).

Lehner, M., *The Complete Pyramids* (London, 1997).

Lichtheim, M., *Ancient Egyptian Literature*, 3 vols (California, 1975–80).

Manniche, L., *City of the Dead: Thebes in Egypt* (London, 1987).

Martin, G. T., *The Hidden Tombs of Memphis: New Discoveries from the Time of Tutankhamun and Ramesses the Great* (London, 1991).

Mayes, S., *The Great Belzoni* (London, 1959).

Nunn, J. F., *Ancient Egyptian Medicine* (London, 1996).

Petrie, W. M. F., *Seventy Years in Archaeology* (London, 1931).

Reeves, C. N. (ed.), *After Tutankhamun: Research and Excavation in the Royal Necropolis at Thebes* (London, 1992).

Reeves, C. N. and J. H. Taylor, *Howard Carter before Tutankhamun* (London, 1992).

Reeves, C. N. and R. H. Wilkinson, *The Complete Valley of the Kings: Tombs and Treasures of Egypt's Greatest Pharaohs* (London, 1996).

Reisner, G. A. *The Development of the Egyptian Tomb down to the Accession of Cheops* (Cambridge, Mass., 1935).

Reisner, G. A. and W. S. Smith, *A History of the Giza Necropolis*, 2 vols (Cambridge, Mass., 1942–55).

Rice, M., *Egypt's Making* (London, 1990).

Robins, G., *Proportion and Style in Ancient Egyptian Art* (London, 1994).

Schäfer, H., *Principles of Egyptian Art*, ed. E. Brunner-Traut. Trans. and ed. J. Baines (Leipzig, 1919; repr. Oxford, 1974, 1980).

Smith, G. E. and W. R. Dawson, *Egyptian Mummies*, 2nd edn (London, 1991).

Smith, W. S., *The Art and Architecture of Ancient Egypt* (Harmondsworth, 1981).

Tillett, S., *Egypt Itself: The Career of Robert Hay* (London, 1984).

Verner, M., *Forgotten Pharaohs. Lost Pyramids: Abusir* (Prague, 1994).

Wilson, J. A., *Signs and Wonders upon Pharaoh* (Chicago, 1964).

Wortham, J. D., *British Egyptology* (Newton Abbot, 1971).

INDEX

———— •◆• ————